THE NEW SCIENCE OF THE
ENCHANTED UNIVERSE

The New Science of the Enchanted Universe

AN ANTHROPOLOGY OF MOST OF HUMANITY

MARSHALL SAHLINS

WITH THE ASSISTANCE OF
FREDERICK B. HENRY JR.

PRINCETON UNIVERSITY PRESS
PRINCETON & OXFORD

Requests for permission to reproduce material from this work should be sent to permissions@press.princeton.edu

Published by Princeton University Press
41 William Street, Princeton, New Jersey 08540
99 Banbury Road, Oxford OX2 6JX

press.princeton.edu

All Rights Reserved
First paperback printing, 2023
Paper ISBN 9780691215938
Cloth ISBN 9780691215921
ISBN (e-book) 9780691238166

British Library Cataloging-in-Publication Data is available

Editorial: Fred Appel and James Collier
Production Editorial: Natalie Baan
Jacket/Cover Design: Lauren Smith
Production: Erin Suydam
Publicity: Kate Hensley and Kathryn Stevens
Copyeditor: Dana Henricks

Jacket/Cover image: Rock art from Panel del Raudal, Serranía de la Lindosa, Colombian Amazon. Courtesy of José Iriarte.

This book has been composed in Arno

CONTENTS

PROLOGUE

THE GODS HAD TO BE removed from the canoe of the ranking Tikopia chief (Ariki Kafika) so that it could be repaired. The chief wanted one of these divinities, his sister's dead son, to remain present, so an attendant medium became possessed by him. Noting this was a common occurrence and of no particular interest to the bystanders, the New Zealand–born anthropologist Raymond Firth remarks that "it is difficult in fact to find what may be called a purely technical or economic activity" (1950, 120). Indeed, when a borer was discovered in the hull, the expert craftsman immediately summoned the gods of the canoe. "Look you hither on the canoe that I am handling here." A borer "can be coped with not only by physical means but also by the power [*mana*] of the gods" (121). For the *mana* part, a famous adze of divine origin had to be borrowed from another chief, an instrument especially useful in canoe work because it embodied a certain god in his manifestation as a gray reef eel known for its sharp teeth and its ferocity. On striking with the adze, the craftsman would invoke the eel-god, and then, it is said, "the decay and the borer disappear. He eats them on the instant, they vanish, and the insect dies" (122). So, it happened in this instance: the repairs were accomplished, and in the end the gods of the canoe were restored to the vessel.

There, they would be needed for the semiannual Work of the Gods, which included the reconsecration of the chiefs' canoes, and their use in the maintenance of the fish supply, by the offering of the first catch of each fleet to the major clan gods. Not that the crews themselves were responsible for their catch. The recurrent invocations of the gods to grant an abundance of fish—some explicitly addressing the deities to provide their own first-fish tributes—were realized in the critical participation of the principal canoe deity in the fishing itself. Stationed off the vessel on the starboard (non-outrigger) side, the god, equipped with an adze or staff, goes out to "strike down the fish he desires, and bring it to the canoe" (Firth 1967, 74). It will not be the only time that in fishing, as in other subsistence activities, the people appear as the ancillary means of sustaining the gods who have caught the fish that will be offered to them. Since here as elsewhere, the spirit-powers that be are responsible for providing the food or other offerings of the sacrifices accorded them, the self-dealing rather confirms the British social anthropologist Edmund Leach's (1976) argument that since the god could have as well killed the sacrificial offering himself, what is essentially given him by the sacrificer is deference and obedience.

ACKNOWLEDGMENTS

I DON'T REMEMBER why the great Hungarian economic historian Karl Polanyi took me aside for a teachable moment. I was one of the few graduate students in anthropology who were permitted to audit the great Trade and Markets seminar at Columbia University in the early 1950s. Polanyi told me a story that strangely stuck with me all these years, and even more strangely, took on its physical incarnation. Polanyi wanted to tell me that the mind was like a man with a crippled hand trying to take something off a table. He tries one way or another until he finds a way that is suitable to his own disconformity. The mind, Polanyi said, was like that. It finds a way to grapple with the empirical material. Of course, I always believed what he said about the mind, but when I lost partial use of my hands, I was doubly attached to the anecdote. It was a strange malady that left me unable to continue my writing and research.

I was writing a book of three parts, the overall goal of which was to revolutionize an obsolete anthropology. One could characterize much of twentieth-century anthropology as a salvage operation. Certainly in the midcentury, as students, we were told we had an obligation to preserve traditional culture as it was before it was transformed by the Euro-American juggernaut. One could say that anthropology then was the study of a disappearing object, and my three-part book was an effort to preserve the object while offering a critique of anthropologists (and others) who inscribed it. Part one set the ethnographical stage and the ontological stakes; part two was to be a study of Enchanted Economics; and the last part covered Cosmic Politics.

I had almost finished the first part of the book—a kind of preface to the study of culture, about the way anthropology should be conducted and has been, I think, sadly misconducted—when Polanyi's teachable moment became a physical reality. To the rescue came my eminent historian son, Peter Sahlins, who saw in my already-completed chapters an integral book, and who patiently worked with me to make it so. This is what you have before you, a prolegomena to a new science of the enchanted universe.

You could justifiably think of the book as the owl of Minerva taking flight at dusk. It is also something of my swan song. At least that's two birds with one stone.

Marshall Sahlins
Chicago, February 14, 2021

Marshall Sahlins died on April 5, 2021, at his home in Chicago before completing his acknowledgments. He had finished most of the book thanks to the collective efforts of his family—the Herculean labors of his grandson, Guthrie Siegman; the care and love of his daughters, Julie and Elaine; and the immeasurable contributions of his wife of seventy years, Barbara, who helped him to build a life that made this last book, and all his work, possible. Marshall's debt to Fred Henry, his former graduate student, is paid on the title page. Fred worked to edit and correct endless drafts; hunted for elusive quotations and bibliographic references; responded to the various bits of work-in-progress that Marshall shared while drafting the book; and prepared the book for production. Marshall also benefited from dialogue with friends and esteemed colleagues who will see the influence of their works on these pages: Robert Brightman, Eduardo Viveiros de Castro, Webb Keane, and Alan Strathern. Finally, thanks to the anonymous readers and the staff of Princeton University Press—especially Fred Appel, James Collier, Natalie Baan, and Dana Henricks—for agreeing to take on the project and magically transforming the manuscript into a book.

Go Blue.

Peter Sahlins
Paris, September 15, 2021

THE NEW SCIENCE OF THE
ENCHANTED UNIVERSE

Introduction

THE WORLD-HISTORICAL
CULTURAL REVOLUTION

IN THE EARLY DAYS OF the Christian evangelization of the Fiji Islands, when an admiring chief said to the English missionary, "Your ships are true, your guns are true, so your god must be true," he didn't mean what the current average social scientist would understand him to mean: that the notion of "god," as of "religion" in general, is a reflex of the real-political order, a functional ideology designed to legitimate the secular powers that be. In that case, the apparent acknowledgment of the English god's existence would be an expression, in the form of a religious imaginary, of the material force of the guns and ships. But the chief was saying something of the opposite, that the English ships and guns were material expressions of the god's power—*mana* is the Fijian term—to which the foreigners evidently had some privileged access. The Fijian for "true" (*dina*) is a predicate of *mana*, as in the common envoi of ritual speech "*mana*, it is true." What the chief said is that, as divinely endowed with *mana*, the English ships and guns were realizations of the potency of the English god.

The incident epitomizes the larger context and continuing motivation of this work: the radical transformation in cultural order that began some 2,500 years ago—in the "Axial Age," as the German psychiatrist and philosopher Karl Jaspers dubbed it in 1953—and is still unfolding on a global scale (Jaspers 1953). The distinctive civilizations that spread from their origins in Greece, the Near East, Northern India, and China between the eighth and third century BCE introduced a still-ongoing cultural revolution of world-historical proportions. The essential change was the translation of divinity from an *immanent* presence in human activity to a *transcendental* "other world" of its own reality, leaving the earth alone to humans, now free to create their own institutions by their own means and lights.

Until they are transformed by the colonial transmissions of the axial ideologies, Christianity notably, peoples (that is, most of humanity) are surrounded by a host of spiritual beings—gods, ancestors, the indwelling souls of plants and animals, and others. These lesser and greater gods effectively create human culture; they are immanent in human existence, and for better or worse determined human fate, even unto life and death. Although generally called "spirits," these beings themselves have the essential attributes of persons, a core of the same mental, temperamental, and volitional capacities. Accordingly, they are often designated in these pages as "metapersons" or "metahumans," and when alternatively referred to as "spirits," it is always explicitly or implicitly under quotation marks, given their quality as nonhuman persons. (Similarly the term "religion" is inappropriate where these metahuman beings and forces are intrinsic in and a precondition of all human activity, not a transcendent afterthought.) By this same quality, they interact with human persons to form one big society of cosmic dimensions—of which humans are a small and dependent part.

This dependent position in a universe of more powerful metahuman beings has been the condition of humanity for the greater part of its history and the majority of its societies. All the world before and around the axial civilizations was a zone of immanence. Here the myriad metahuman powers were not only present in people's experience, they were the decisive agents of human weal and woe—the sources of their success, or lack thereof, in all variety of endeavors from agriculture and hunting, to sexual reproduction and political ambition. As the early modern historian of religious encounter Alan Strathern (2019) puts the matter in an illuminating recent work on the transformation of what common social science called the passage from "immanentism" to "transcendentalism," the "basic immanentist assumption is that the capacity to achieve any worthwhile objective is dependent on the approval or intervention of supernatural forces and metapersons. These constitute the fundamental origin of the ability to produce food, survive ill health, become wealthy, give birth, and wage war" (36–37). We begin to see what is at stake, institutionally and structurally, in the immanentist/transcendentalist divide. With apologies to all the human scientists, Marxists, Durkheimians, and others implicitly grounded in the assumptions of a transcendentalist world, the immanentist cultures were subject to "determination by the religious basis"—that is, until divinity went from an immanent infrastructure to a transcendent superstructure.

It probably goes without saying, but I had better say it anyway: what is at issue is how the immanentist societies are actually organized and function in their own cultural terms, their own concepts of what there is, and not as matters "really are" in our native scheme of things. It will become all too evident that our own transcendentalist notions, insofar as they have been embedded in common ethnographic vocabularies, have disfigured the immanentist cultures they purport to describe. Take the familiar distinction between the "spiritual" and the "material," for example: it is not pertinent in societies that know all sorts of so-called "things"—often everything there is—as animated by indwelling spirit-persons. That this difference makes a fundamental difference of cultural order is the point of the book. What passes for an "economics" or a "politics" embedded in an enchanted universe is radically different from the concepts and stratagems that people are free to pursue when the gods are far away and not directly involved. In immanentist orders, the ritual invocation of spirit-beings and their powers is the customary prerequisite of all varieties of cultural practice. Compounded with the human techniques of livelihood, reproduction, social order, and political authority as the necessary condition of their efficacy, the cosmic host of beings and forces comprise an all-around substrate of human action. The multitude of spirit-persons is synthesized with social action like an element in a chemical compound, or a bound morpheme in a natural language. Or as Lévy-Bruhl said of certain New Guinea peoples, "nothing is undertaken without having recourse to enchantments" (1923, 308–9).

The famous Weberian characterization of modernity as the disenchantment of the world is a later echo of the transcendentalism developed in Karl Jasper's "Axial Age" and the large cottage industry of scholarly commentary that followed. The consensus remains today as sinologist Benjamin Schwartz expressed it early on: "If there is nevertheless some common underlying impulse in all these 'axial' movements, it might be called the strain toward transcendence" (1975, 3). The Dutch orientalist Henri Frankfort's reference to the "austere transcendentalism" of the ancient Hebrew God comes close to an ideal-typical description: "The absolute transcendence of God is the foundation of Hebrew religious thought." He is "ineffable, transcending every phenomenon" ([1948] 1978, 343). The spirits having left, humans now inherited an earth that had become a subjectless "nature." The effect was a veritable cultural revolution; or, as Israeli sociologist S. N. Eisenstadt says, a series of revolutions that "have to do with the emergence, conceptualization, and institutionalization of a basic tension between the transcendental and mundane orders" (1986, 1).

This sense of a recurring process fits better with the persistence of immanent elements in all such transcendental regimes. Immanence continues in many forms, from "folk beliefs" in hinterland regions, or descents of divinity from heaven to earth in saintly apparitions and miraculous interventions, to ascents of humanity from earth to heaven in shamanistic séances and prophetic aspirations. Thus transcendentalism had a hard time shrugging off its immanentist heritage, as in the *Confessions* of the fourth-century CE theologian Augustine, at the end of the Axial Age.

The good Bishop more or less unconsciously preserved an all-around animism in a world bereft of God. Notwithstanding Augustine's insistence that God made the earthly world of Nothing, he was still able to have an interesting conversation with the earth, the sea, "living creeping things," "the moving air," "the whole air with all its inhabitants," the heavens, sun, moon, and stars, all of whom he asked if they were God, and they told him they were not He. Said the creeping things, "We are not thy God, seek above us." Likewise, the heavenly bodies denied they were "the God whom thou seekest." So, says Augustine in response, "unto all the things which encompass the door of my flesh, 'Ye have told me of my God, that ye are not he; tell me something of Him.' And they cried out with a loud voice, 'He made us'" (*Confessions* 10.6). Thus in vain did Augustine search for a transcendent God in a universe populated by the immanent persons-of-things.

There are still faith healers and witches in our midst—even some, like Augustine, pure animists. Before I had completed this introductory chapter, the *New York Times*, citing a 2017 survey by the Pew Research Center, reported that "60 percent of Americans believe one or more of the following: psychics, astrology, the presence of spiritual energy in inanimate objects (like mountains or trees), or reincarnation" (Bennett 2019). Yet for all the rear-guard resistance of immanentism, the evacuation of the high gods from the earthly city has effectively put the culture under human control. Certainly, the critical sectors of economy and polity are clear of divinity (even if, as we shall see, immanentist language of enspirited metapersons is still pervasive). The modern "free market economy," for example: insofar as it is self-regulating by supply and demand, it is in principle motivated by the economizing projects of its individual human agents. As for politics, it is symptomatic of who's in charge that American presidents piously intone the ritual formula, "God bless the United States of America" only after they have told the Deity what they are going to do. Melanesian big-men, Polynesian chiefs, or Inca emperors would have to do that beforehand—the god, as empowering agent, being the condition of the political possibility.

Just so, the revolution initiated by the human takeover of the culture eventually produced a total reordering of the immanentist universe, eventually creating the differentiated and transcendent spheres of "religion," "politics," "science," and "economy." These abstract categories made their appearance over the course of the early modern period, between the Middle Ages and the Enlightenment. In what essentially could be called a "Second Axial Age," Western civilization produced a series of transcendent categories, each a differentiated formation, an autonomous domain that articulated with the others metaphorically and functionally. The category of "religion" itself, the origin of which the biblical scholar Jack Miles (2019, 28–29) identifies in the Christian conversion of Roman pagans, was critically refashioned, reborn in the confessional strife wrought by Luther and others during the Protestant Reformation. "Politics" appeared in a schism with "religion," as in Machiavelli's *The Prince* (1988 [1532]); "science" took shape, along with "nature" itself, as a differentiated set of laws that explained movement in the heavens and on earth (Newton [1687] 2016), and with the radical distinction of a knowing "subject" and an external "object" (Descartes [1641] 1996); "economy" (or "political economy") appeared in the work of Adam Smith ([1776] 1976) and later with Thomas Malthus ([1798] 2015) and David Ricardo ([1817] 2004). The expansion of Europe and the encounter with immanentist societies during the early modern period helped constitute "culture" as its own autonomous sphere. The genius of Giambattista Vico, author of *The New Science* ([1744] 1968), was to supply, in a transcendent fashion, an immanentist perspective that made it possible to write a science of "cultures" in their own terms, however incomplete.

Note that compared to the cultures of immanence, religion since the sixteenth century has migrated from the infrastructure to the superstructure, making it possible for "determination by the economic basis" to become the normal science of scholars ranging from traditional historical materialists to neoliberal economists—not to mention the rest of us. There is hardly any other indigenous Western anthropology. By indigenous anthropology, I mean the effect of the transcendental revolution on common average thought that envisions a categorical layer cake with economics as the foundation, topped by social relations that conform to it, a political system that upholds it, and finally a religious or ideological layer that reinforces and legitimates the totality. This idea of "culture" becomes the inverse of the immanentist structure, where the gods are the creators of culture as well as the source of power by which it is realized—thus putting together on their heads Karl Marx, Émile Durkheim, and Milton Friedman, among others.

Also specifically transcendental, and as much taken for granted, is a suite of familiar binary oppositions of ontological proportions: not only between the spiritual and the material (or spiritual and secular), but also between natural and supernatural, and people and spirits. In immanent regimes all significant material "things" are enspirited inasmuch as they embody animating powers with characteristics of persons. Hence the so-called supernatural is not distinguished from what we call the "natural," even as people are spirits.

Not that the axial civilization literature has been too enlightening on what the transition from immanentism to transcendentalism actually entails. Some axiologists are tempted to suppose a priori that whatever they take to be the salient characteristics of the axial civilizations, the pre- and non-axial societies must be characterized by the opposite. So, for example, since the axial religions distinctively focus on the ethical behavior and life-after-death of the individual—a kind of soteriological or salvation-driven individualism—the immanentist societies are distinctively "social," concerned with group prosperity in this world as opposed to individual salvation in the next (Taylor 2012). Even ignoring the common reports of individual competition for status, as among Melanesian big-men or Southeast Asian hill peoples, or the Amerindian vision quests that determine an adolescent's lifelong fate, there is the universal practice of individual persons invoking the metaperson powers that be for success in hunting, agriculture, lovemaking, war, curing, birthing, trading, esoteric knowledge, or whatever else life-giving may be wanted. (In any case, rice-farming Iban of Borneo "compete not only to assert their equality—to prove themselves equal to others—but they also seek, if possible, to excel and so exceed others in material wealth, power and reputation" [Sather 1996, 74].) In this connection to the "divine," it is difficult to imagine a more inappropriate label for the pre-axial condition than "mundane," which so many axial scholars favor. They have in mind apparently an opposition between heaven and earth, ignoring that this also entails one between the spiritual and secular— which would leave the "mundane" immanentist peoples bereft of the metaperson powers on whom their existence depends. For people living in an immanentist regime, where nothing is undertaken without enchantments, existence is anything but mundane.

In addition to Alan Strathern's (2019) recent work on the subject, there have been some exemplary appreciations of the immanent-to-transcendental transition, though not necessarily by historians or sociologists in the mainstream of the axial scholarship. Political scientist

Benedict Anderson for one, writing independently of the axial literature on the transformation worked by Islam on traditional Javanese cosmologies. Anderson explicitly recognizes and effectively describes the dominance of an immanentist worldview even under the important pre-Islamic Indic kingdoms of Mataram, Kedhiri, and Majapahit. "Since Javanese cosmology made no sharp division between the terrestrial and the transcendental world," he writes, "there was no extramundane referent by which to judge men's actions" (Anderson 1990, 70). Here was a system with "divinity immanent in the world" (70), a "Power" endemic in the human habitat, even as it was concentrated in human society as the source of "fertility, prosperity, stability, and glory" (32). "Manifested in every aspect of the natural world," the Power was present in "stones, trees, clouds, and fire, but [was] expressed quintessentially in the central mystery of life, the process of generation and regeneration." In this way it provided the "basic link between the 'animism' of the Javanese villages, and the highly metaphysical pantheism of the urban centers (22)."

Enter then a "modernist Islamic cosmology" that reduces the immanentist sense of a Power suffusing the universe to "a divinity sharply separated from the works of His hand. Between God and man there is an immeasurable distance. . . . Thus power is, in a sense, removed from the world, since it lies with God, Who is not of this world, but above and antecedent to it. Furthermore, since the gulf between God and man is vast and God's power is absolute, all men are seen as equally insignificant before His majesty" (Anderson 1990, 70). It is rather in the immanentist condition that humans can approach and even appropriate divinity—in acts of hubris that, as will be seen presently, construct a society in which people are not reduced to insignificance by an unreachable Deity but empowered by their differential relations to the godly beings all about them.

The beginnings of the liberation of human from divine authority is one of the themes of a remarkable article by the historian of late antiquity Peter Brown (1975) about the transcendental revolution, all the more remarkable because it was not about axial origins but the development of the High Middle Ages of Western Christendom in the eleventh and twelfth centuries.

The setting is testimony to the uneven development of transcendentalism, where a transcendent God abides over a human population on familiar terms with saints, ghosts, witches, and "nature spirits," including monks, who were not technically human in so far as they lived the life of angels. As for angels, Peter Brown exemplifies "the intimacy and adjacency of the holy" in the early Middle Ages by the requirement that priests serving at the altar, if they needed to spit, had to do so on one side or behind them, "for at the altar the angels are standing." The presence of "the non-human in the midst of a society," Brown comments, "is available to all, for all purposes" (141).

In Canterbury Cathedral in the year 1050 it was possible to use the same pool of water, on the same day, to baptize an infant as a Christian and immerse an adult to solicit a divine verdict in a judicial case. Starting from the condition wherein "if ever there was an area where the sacred penetrated into the chinks of the profane and vice versa, it was in the ordeal" (135), Brown takes the subsequent fate of the ordeal as emblematic of the displacement of divinity from the earthly city in Latin Christianity. In 1205, the Lateran Council undermined the ordeal by forbidding the use of the liturgical blessing that had sanctioned such sacrilegious acts of "tempting God." Finally, it was abandoned when it came under heavy clerical criticism as an ancient, vulgar, and lower-class custom that had only been tolerated for centuries "as a concession by the Church to the hard hearts of the Germanic barbarians" (136).

As is often told, beginning in the eleventh century, Western Europe experienced radical demographic and institutional changes, ranging from major increases in population and agricultural productivity to new forms of community, the revival of Roman law, heightened royal authority, the advent of chivalry, vernacular literature, the growth of cities, and much more. Not to neglect the new learning acquired from Arab and ancient Greek scholars: the latter, notably works of Aristotle, mainly transmitted through the former via Muslim Spain and Sicily.

The effect was a philosophical upheaval affecting a variety of institutional fields. "The methods of logical arrangement and analysis, and, still more, the habits of thought associated with the study of logic, penetrated the studies of law, politics, grammar, and rhetoric, to mention only a few of the fields which were affected" (Southern 1953, 181–82). Of special interest for the present discussion is the potential impact of Aristotle's *Categories* on an early medieval world in which the divine in various forms was still present and available to humankind. The *Categories*, the English medievalist R. W. Southern tells us, exercised an extraordinary fascination during the tenth and eleventh centuries. In principle, the nine Aristotelian categories could reconfigure the medieval ontology, inasmuch as Quantity, Quality, Relation, Position, Place, Time, State, Action, and Affection "were thought to exhaust the various ways in which any particular object can be regarded" (180). Note, however, that a fundamental category of the previous era is missing from Aristotle's scheme of what can be said about any object: personhood is missing, the indwelling soul or person that autonomously animates any such thing. The new age of the eleventh and twelfth centuries, as Brown notes, saw "the emergence of significantly new attitudes toward the universe. Though very different from any modern view, it was 'modern' in being no longer shot through with human reference. Previously, a thunderstorm had shown either the anger of God or the envy of demons, both directed at human beings" (1975, 141).

I am giving considerable space to Peter Brown's study because his analysis of the post-axial transition to transcendence brilliantly exposes key characteristics of the immanentist condition, beginning with this issue of subject and object. As he observes, in the early Middle Ages, the intermingling of the sacred and the profane, in making nonhuman personhood an inner quality of material things, blurred the borderline between the objective and the subjective at every turn. "It was a strangely subjective objectivity" (Brown 1975, 142). Rather than a relation of persons to things, the human relation to the world was largely one of person-to-person. Otherwise put, rather than a sense of objectivity, it was a condition of intersubjectivity. By comparison, the structural changes of the twelfth century dramatically altered the relations between the subjective and the objective. As Brown describes the transformation, by ridding human activities of their subjective, supernatural sources, matters such as reasoning, law, and the exploitation of nature take on "an opacity, an impersonal objectivity, and a value of their own which had been lacking in previous centuries" (144).

The point is well taken even if this was only a fundamental impulse of a transformation that remains to be completed. It speaks to a critical structural complement of the transcendental revolution: the emergence of humanized institutions once the divine is removed to an otherworldly reality. The human order becomes self-fashioning. "Political power was increasingly wielded without religious trappings. Government was what government did: rulers . . . settled down to exercise what real power they actually possessed" (135). Obviously, this was not accomplished completely by the twelfth century, but Peter Brown thus discovered the origins and impulses of a transcendentalism that remained to be completed in the early modern period and that was to revolutionize the practice of politics, including by Machiavelli, who justified the transcendentalist rupture by legitimating the autonomous sphere of the state.

Lastly, a word on anthropological methods. It should be clear enough that, though I have not always succeeded, I try to explicate the cultures at issue by their own immanentist premises—what used to be known as "the natives' point of view" and sometimes now as "reverse anthropology" (e.g., Kirsch 2006). I try to unfold the peoples' cultural practices by means of their own onto-logics. Implied is a criticism of a lot of received ethnography for a misleading conceptual apparatus composed of nearly equal parts of transcendentalist equivocation and colonialist condescension. The effect is an anthropology that disfigures both the discipline and the culture so described by maligning the people's mentality as a mistaken sense of reality. Not that our fieldworkers are badly intentioned. On the contrary, the great majority are committed to the welfare of the people they study—virtually by vocation; it comes with the intellectual territory. But a too common effect of even the best work is to reduce the meaningful relations of a culture of immanence to the status of convenient fantasies of the objective reality—of a world actually without such gods—thus making their culture a fictional representation of ours.

Take the great New Zealand anthropologist Sir Raymond Firth, for example, as described by his almost equally great compatriot Edmund Leach: "The exceptional detail of Firth's ethnographic material is a standing invitation for every reader to try to 'rethink' the particular explanations which Firth himself offers us" [1966, 21].) The corpus of Firth's work beginning in the late 1920s on the Polynesian island of Tikopia is one of the great all-time achievements of anthropology. But by its explicit comments on Tikopian illusions of the presence of the gods in humans, canoes, temples, weapons, and tools—as the embodiments (*fakatino*) or vessels (*waka*) of the god, among similar expressions—Firth's work is notable also for its repeated exposure of the islanders' culture for what it really is—by our lights. The effect is to dissolve an immanentist world in a transcendentalist ontology.

Consider the contradictions of Firth's description of an important rite having to do with net-fishing: "Then came the *symbolism* so characteristic of the Tikopia religion, the *fiction* that certain persons were for the time being deities in the flesh" (Firth 1967, 400; emphasis mine). The so-called symbolism concerned two women whose role was to carry the baskets that received the fish tributes due to two important goddesses named Pufine ma. As Firth continues: "When darkness fell the baskets were taken by two women, who went down to the beach and there personified the goddesses, receiving the tribute that was their due from the fisher-folk" (400). He then quotes a Tikopian on this characteristic "fiction": "'They have become Pufine ma there who have gone with their baskets'" (400). Similarly, of a group of women preparing a sacred oven during the semiannual renewal rites, the Work of the Gods, "it is *believed* by the Tikopia that these women, while engaged in the sacred task, are *under the protection* of the Te Atua Fafine, the Female Deity, who is the tutelary genius of women" (142; emphasis mine). But in shifting from "believed" and "under the protection" of the goddess, Firth also says, "In fact, they are actually identified with her." And in confirmation, Tikopia explain, "'They who are doing the work there, it is she'" (143). On other important ritual occasions, Firth had it from the god's mouth to his ear. As the time when, by Firth's description, the principal Tikopia chief "is believed to be the god in person," and the chief then explains to him, "'I who have sat there am him [the god]. . . . I there am the god; he has come to sit in me'" (1967, 157). All these identity-subtracting expressions—they are "believed" to be the goddesses; he is the "symbol" of the god, the "representation" of the god, "under the protection" of the god, and the like: all these are so many transcendental equivocations of simply, the god—"I who sit there am him" (cf. Hocart 1970, 74).

We need a considerable rectification of ethnographic terms. "Belief" is a prominent one. Wyatt MacGaffey (1986, 1) recalls Jean Pouillon's *bon mot*, "It is only the nonbeliever who believes that the believer believes." The ethnographic "believe" is often an ethnocentric reality-check on what the people actually *know*. The pioneering anthropologist of the Sudan Ian Cunnison so indicated many decades ago about East African Luapula people: "The important thing is this: what the Luapula peoples say now about the past is what they *know* actually happened in the past. Simply to say that they believe it happened in the past is too weak for they do not doubt it" (1959, 33; emphasis original). Anthropologists are prone to use the verb "to believe"—that the people "believe" in something—only when they don't believe it themselves. Anthropologists don't say, "The people believe curare poison kills monkeys"; but they will say, "The people believe the game father makes monkeys available for hunting." Anthropologists don't say, "The people believe that rain is needed for the crops to grow"; but they will say, "The people believe the gods make the rain" in New Guinea by urinating on them.

Another good candidate for oblivion is "myth," referring to the narratives people regard as sacred truth and standard European languages thus devalue as fiction. The Polish-born pioneer ethnographer Bronislaw Malinowski's (1948, 85) oft-repeated "mythical charter" succeeds in rendering the constitutional doctrine of the clan or tribe unbelievable. Then there is all the folking of indigenous peoples: their "folk medicine," their "folk art," their "folk biology"—the implication being that folk biology is to biology as military music is to music. Not to mention "folk music."

The condescension is untenable. For all our self-fashioning in a natural world, we share the same existential predicament as those who solve the problem by knowing the world as so many powerful others of their kind, with whom they might negotiate their fate. People are not the authors of their life and death, the forces of their propagation, growth and decline, their illness and their health, the plants and animals upon which they subsist, the weather upon which their prosperity depends. If people were such gods themselves, they would never want nor sicken, and they would never die. The common predicament is human finitude—which is what the next chapter is about.

This book should not be taken as an exercise in cultural comparison, however. It is a more or less disciplined attempt at generalization. Edmund Leach (1966) might have been the first to make that distinction between comparison and generalization, boldly devaluing the former as "butterfly collecting," by contrast to the inspired guesswork that sees a similar pattern of relationships in a few disparate social systems, thus launching a possible universal proposition. To be fair, the cross-cultural comparison Leach criticized is hardly the only one possible, for all its apparent popularity in British Social Anthropology of the 1960s, notably among colleagues at Cambridge. Equipped with a priori analytic categories of social structure—"ethnocentric," Leach calls them—such as "unilineal descent," "complementary filiation," "segmentary lineage systems," and so on, anthropologists set out to discover them in various societies. Mainly in African societies, but also in the New Guinea Highlands, where Australian anthropologist J. A. Barnes (1962) notoriously demonstrated that African forms of lineage order didn't exist. That precisely was Leach's complaint. Such comparisons could only lead to a catalog of variations, an endless typology. Whereas, Leach argues, if one pays attention to the actual elements, the relations of correspondence and opposition, and so forth, in any system of kinship and marriage, any system, a definite pattern could be determined; to wit, "there is a fundamental ideological opposition between the relations which endow the individual with membership of a 'we group' of some kind (relations of incorporation), and those other relations which link 'our group' to other groups of like kind (relations of alliance), and that, in this dichotomy, relations of incorporation are distinguished symbolically as relations of common substance, while relations of alliance are viewed as mystical influence" (Leach 1966, 21).

It is noteworthy that Leach based this finding on a mere handful of societies, different enough in culture and structure, but mainly just Trobriand Islanders, Tallensi, and Kachin, supplemented by Tikopia and Ashanti. Still, it has held up pretty well, at least for the "mystical influence" of affines, although, as will be discussed in a coming chapter, the pattern is generally more complex, both as regards substance and spiritual endowments. What is, however, wholly subscribed to throughout this book is Leach's methodology of generalization: "Generalization is inductive; it consists in perceiving possible general laws in circumstances of particular cases; it is guesswork, a gamble, you may be wrong or you may be right, but if you happen to be right you have learnt something altogether new" (1966, 5; cf. Viveiros de Castro 2015, ch. 3).

Assuming Leach's risks, this book addresses the configurations of immanence in radically different cultures that, despite all their experience of axial societies, remain today essentially cultures of immanence—which is to say most of humanity.

1

Human Finitude

A tradition has been handed down by the ancient thinkers of very early times, and bequeathed to posterity in the form of a myth, to the effect that . . . heavenly bodies are gods, and that the Divine pervades the whole of nature.

—ARISTOTLE, *METAPHYSICS* (1935, TREDENNICK TRANS.)

The Master said, "How abundantly do spiritual beings display the powers that belong to them!

"We look for them, but do not see them; we listen to, but do not hear them; yet they enter into all things, and there is nothing without them.

"They cause all the people of the kingdom to fast and purify themselves, and array themselves in their richest dresses, in order to attend at their sacrifices. Then, like overflowing water, they seem to be over the heads, and on the right and left of their worshippers.

"It is said in the Book of Poetry, 'The approaches of the spirits, you cannot surmise;—and can you treat them with indifference?'"

—CONFUCIUS, *THE DOCTRINE OF THE MEAN*
(1869, LEGGE TRANS.)

HERE'S THE PROBLEM. According to the traditional anthropological wisdom, people invoke the spirits' aid when an important enterprise is hazardous, or the outcome is uncertain. Religion is when human effort is at risk: in warfare, for instance; or in gardening, where the crop is subject to the vagaries of weather or the depredations of pests. Yet as the ethnographer Simon Harrison observes of Manambu of New Guinea, success, not failure, is what brings the spirits particularly into mind and play. Every adult man and woman knows how, when, and where to plant, but some people's gardens are much more fruitful than others'—because the totemic ancestors, who "release" the crops from their distant villages, have selectively favored them (Harrison 1990, 63). Similarly, about Achuar of the Upper Amazon, the French anthropologist Phillipe Descola relates that the gardeners who most assiduously call upon the goddess at every stage of the agricultural process are precisely those whose skills are sure and never fail (1994, 198). So the question is, when is there religion?—or perhaps, when isn't there?

The notion that people get religion where outcomes are uncertain and they can't control their fate has a considerable pre-anthropological and premodern pedigree. It was already established in Classical Antiquity. The ancient Greek historian Diodorus Siculus is often cited for it, as by the Scottish Enlightenment philosopher David Hume in his remarkable treatise on *The Natural History of Religion*: "Fortune has never ... bestowed an unmixed happiness on mankind; but with all her gifts has ever conjoined some disastrous circumstance, in order to chastise men into a reverence for the gods, whom, in a continued course of prosperity, they are apt to neglect and forget" (*Bib. hist.* 3.47 in Hume [1757] 1998, 143–44). Essentially the same topos recurs over and again in Hume's essay. Of special interest here, the essay itself is part of the transcendental revolution, in its pure Enlightenment formulation.

Hume sets out to prove that religion is fashioned by men—it is an expression of human nature under certain dire circumstances—by contrast to the current, reasoned arguments for the existence of God from intelligent design. For early men, in a barbarous and ignorant condition, no passions can be expected to work "but the ordinary affections of human life; the anxious concern for happiness, the dread of future misery, the terror of death, the thirst of revenge, the appetite for food and other necessaries. Agitated by hopes and fears of this nature, especially the latter, men scrutinize, with a trembling curiosity, the course of future causes, and examine the various and contrary events of human life. And in this disordered scene, with eyes still more disordered and astonished, they see the first obscure traces of divinity" (Hume [1757] 1998, 140). There is, however, a subdominant theme in Hume's argument, already suggested by "hopes" as well as "fears": that humans, being in control of neither, are subject to good fortune and bad alike. Presumably, then, they have some cause to be pious about their successes too. This is the argument I am making here, and it could well be set up by Hume saying: "We are placed in this world, as in a great theatre, where the true springs and causes of every event are entirely concealed from us" (140). In that case, the divine is as necessarily engaged in people's possible achievements as in their possible failures.

As a rule, however, anthropologists didn't get the clue. Based on his research in the Trobriand Islands, the influential structural-functionalist ethnographer Bronislaw Malinowski was an advocate of the notion that the spirits begin where human control ends. (He called it "magic," but since as a general rule what passes for "magic" actually involves metaperson beings and metaperson powers, I do not use the concept in these pages.) The occult powers were not simply those of the formulas uttered, the acts of the practitioner, or the objects he or she may use. The incantations of ritual experts—the so-called garden magician, often a paramount chief, or a designated close relative—that ensured the success of yam gardening specifically invoked the powers of the clan ancestor-spirits, and yam gardening was Malinowski's prime example. For all the Trobriand Islanders' appropriate knowledge and hard work, they regarded the ancestors' intervention, achieved in a series of rituals correlated with specific stages of the cultivation cycle, as absolutely indispensable for a successful harvest. What would happen if the rituals were not performed the people could not tell, for that had never happened. What they did know from experience is that, depending on rain and sunshine, bush pigs and locusts, some years the yams flourished and some years their gardens did poorly. Because of this uncertainty and this only, Malinowski argues, the people employed magic (1948, 11–12; cf. Mosko 2017).

Gardening is not unique in this respect: everything needs magic. "What has been said about gardens can be paralleled from any one of the many other activities in which work and magic run side by side without ever mixing" (Malinowksi 1948, 13). The people know all about canoe building and sailing, but in their fragile vessels "they are still at the mercy of powerful and incalculable tides, sudden gales during the monsoon season and unknown reefs. And here comes in their magic" (13)—not to mention all the "magic" that they put in the overseas voyaging of the famous *kula* trade to induce their trading friends to part with important valuables. Then again, there is warfare. For all a warrior's strength and courage, "the elements of chance and luck" remain, and hence the need for ritual spells (14). Still more, there are spells for the uncontrolled events of sickness, aging, and death. In the end, the only activity that Malinowski cites as completely within Trobriand Islanders' own capacities, therefore without the intervention of metahuman powers, is fishing in the calm waters of the lagoon—as distinct from the hazards of deep-sea fishing (14). (Yet I have my doubts, given the practices of enlisting the spirits in other Oceanic societies to make fishing nets effective and to bring shoals of fishes inshore in their season.) In any case, as Australian anthropologist Mark Mosko (2017) has recently reported, the Trobriand ancestors (*baloma*) are "the perceived agents of magical practices implicated in nearly all contexts of living humans' and spirits' imagined [*sic*] sociality—procreation, kinship, clanship, and affinal relations, mythology, cosmology, chiefly hierarchy and rank, ritual performance (e.g., religious sacrifice, mortuary exchange, *kula*, *milamala* harvest celebration, sorcery and witchcraft, taboo observance, etc.)" (11). As it turns out, the ancestors are indispensable agents in all varieties of human endeavor, risky or not. There is some kind of greater human dependency.

In Philippe Descola's experience, the conventional functionalist thesis that the spirits intervene where humans have insufficient technical control—he cites the American anthropologist Leslie White's version (1959, 272)—is doubly disconfirmed by Amazonian Achuar: first, because the risks that prompt gardeners to invoke Nunkui, the goddess of cultivation, are "imaginary"; and correlatively, because their gardens never fail. Achuar gardens, Descola notes, are exemplary of the technical sophistication achieved by certain slash-and-burn cultivators in the

Amazon. They are highly productive, require little labor, and beside the staple manioc yield a great variety of crops "perfectly adapted to soil and climate variations" (Descola 1994, 191). Gardening here is free of all contingencies. For by means of clandestine ritual songs (*anent*), which the women cultivators address to Nunkui, mother of cultivated plants, they are able to assume her person and themselves nurture the manioc plants as their own children.

So far as Achuar are concerned, the women who have the best array of ritual spells for invoking Nunkui achieve the best results (Descola 1994, 198, 208). By the same token, those who offend the goddess become vulnerable to "Nunkui's Curse," the threat that she will withdraw the food plants altogether, as she did to punish a foolish woman in primordial times (Descola 2016, 9). Among other threats are those posed by jealous women who call out evil spells on prosperous gardens, the soul power conveyed in their malignant *anent* working its effects on the souls of the plant-persons (Descola 1994, 212; 1996, 99–100). Again, contrary to traditional anthropological wisdom, it appears that the gardens are not governed by spirits because they are at risk of poor results; rather they are at risk of poor results because they are governed by spirits. And whether as a matter of success or failure, the spirits are responsible for both.

It is only necessary to add that, as with Trobriand Islanders, the invocation of metahuman powers to empower humans is hardly confined to gardening. Recall that for Achuar, there are appropriate spells (*anent*) for endeavors of every sort, thereby enlisting a variety of appropriate spirits in hunting, warfare, fishing, trading, lovemaking, curing illness, cooking food, and whatnot. Prerequisite to all sorts of human activities, this engagement of metahuman power is an all-around cultural praxis: meaning, the implication of spiritual powers is the condition of the possibility of human social activities of every kind.

Simon Harrison's (1990) account of Manambu of Northern Papua New Guinea, while similarly observing that the ancestors are responsible for the success of some cultivators relative to others, offers insight into this sort of all-around participation of metahuman powers in common cultural practices. Here yam cultivation is particularly significant politically because of the unique ritual control of yam garden fertility by one important dual-clan group. Like other cultivated and wild foods, yams, as Harrison says, are not created by gardening but come into existence when they are "released" by the totemic ancestors from their distant villages in response to the secret invocations of certain clan leaders. People do not *produce* their means of subsistence; they *receive* them from the ancestral sources (63).

Not that they lack the knowledge or the skills. To a man and woman, these technical capacities are possessed by all socialized adults. People know *how* yams are grown successfully, but their "religion," as Harrison puts it, "answers a different question: *why* the yams grew successfully, and to whom the social and political credit is owed" (63). The latter question will be a matter of further discussion in these pages, but inasmuch as credit goes to the ritually adept clan leaders rather than the cultivators, one might already conclude that the alienation of the workers from their product did not originate with capitalism. As for why yams grow, the lack of people's control over causes can apply to a lot of things, like the weather, procreation, animal behavior, human growth and decline, sickness and death, and other such existential matters. Especially when it comes to people making the causes, not just knowing them *but themselves being them*, their limitations amount to an all-around human finitude.

The relevant anthropology of human finitude goes back to the Neapolitan Enlightenment philosopher Giambattista Vico (1668–1744). Vico's works *On the Most Ancient Wisdom of the Italians* ([1711] 2010) and especially *The New Science* ([1744] 1968) are unacknowledged charters of an anthropology that knew how to take its informants' words as a distinctive ontology constituting worlds other than ours. Vico enacts a *rite de passage* in anthropology from its transcendentalist background to an immanentist ontology that is nothing like our own. Vico moves beyond his own transcendentalist milieu into an appreciation of the different ontological qualities of immanentist cultures, which he correlates with different stages of human development. Not to dismiss either the rebound or the enlightenment that the immanentist perspective sheds on the relativity of our own categories. Anthropology is a double cultural enlightenment of the other and of the self, and Vico was among the first to realize it. Like a good Hegelian dialectic, Vico transcends and incorporates his own transcendentalist origins to produce a description of ontologies quite different from his own, whether primitive or ancient. This is the epitome of anthropology.

The *Ancient Wisdom* begins with the famous aphorism: "For the Latins, *verum* (*the true*) and *factum* (*the made*) are interchangeable or, as commonly said in the Schools, they are convertible" ([1711] 2010, 17). As Vico's Latin is "Latinis verum et factum reciprocantur seu convertuntur"—often abbreviated as *verum ipsum factum*—one might otherwise say that the true and the made are reciprocals or convertibles, that each entails the other. From this comes the pervasive theme of his *New Science*: that what men make, they may know truly; what God makes only He can know. This is relevant anthropology because it specifies the circumstances of immanent spiritual agency in people's affairs: that is, as a function of their fateful dependence on forces and conditions of which they are not the creators—not the causative sources themselves.

Considering Vico's arguments from the *Ancient Wisdom*, the scope of such human limitations is necessarily very broad. For almost all the things people seek to know, indeed need to live, are neither contained within nor emanate from the mind by which they could truly know them. The limitations come from "a vice of the mind, namely, from its limited scope, by which all things are outside it and by which it does not contain that which it tries to know (and because it does not contain them, it does not produce as works the truths it strives after)" (2010, 27). This Vichian appreciation of religion as external forces of human existence that are then assumed within society as immanent divinity makes an interesting contrast to the much better-known theory of Émile Durkheim ([1915] 1965), where God is an idealized expression of the control society exercises over its members. God is a misplaced recognition of the power of society: people know that they are constrained to think and act in certain ways, that their lives are subject to some greater authority; but knowing not whence this coercion comes, they make a divinity of society. By comparison to Vico, the divine for Durkheim was an external idealization of internal force rather than an internal hypostatization of external force. Were they not talking of two different modes of religion, Vico of immanentism and Durkheim of transcendentalism?

The distribution of truth between the human and the divine is perhaps misleadingly determined on the basis of who makes what, as in the Vichian *verum-factum* formula. In regard to many things that people make, they are not responsible for what they are made of, nor then for their efficacy—that is, whether they will fulfill the purpose for which they were designed. Accordingly, in real life culture, even the most utilitarian human artifacts are made under divine aegis. The making is never undertaken without recourse to enchantments. "Canoe lashing will not hold the canoe together at sea, however firmly the creeper may be wound and fastened," writes New Zealand anthropologist Reo Fortune of Dobu Islanders' manufactures, "without the appropriate incantation being performed over its lashing; fish nets will not catch fish unless they have been treated with incantation" ([1932] 1989, 97). Across the Pacific, American anthropologist Stanley Walens draws the same conclusion from the great ethnographic corpus on the Kwakiutl people accumulated by George Hunt and Franz Boas—while confirming that the spirits are not simply engaged for fear of failure. Rituals here "do not act as mere palliations" for people's inability to perform actions successfully; they are means of forcing the spirits to act in their favor—"that is, they are as practical and mechanical as techniques of wood-carving or fishing. . . . No matter how skilled a woodcarver is, his carving will be excellent only insofar as he is helped by the spirits and their power to carve; the fisherman, no matter how carefully he has constructed his weir, is doomed to failure unless he can invoke spirit-power to make the salmon come to the place where he is fishing" (Walens 1981, 29). Indeed, there are no human mechanical actions that are not empowered by spiritual forces summoned by rituals, no "miracles" as distinguished from normal acts. To get to the ontological bedrock, "the prime agency of causality is not human action but spirit-power action" (24).

And what about gravity itself, not to neglect the other motions of things that humans did not make? Sir Isaac Newton was not the first to ponder what makes things fall to the ground. The distinguished Oglala

Lakota shaman, Finger, in a conversation with physician-cum-anthropologist James R. Walker, indicated that Lakota people had come to their own conclusion on the matter. Beginning in 1896, Walker spent the better part of twenty years as a government physician on the Pine Ridge Reservation, becoming increasingly adept as an ethnographer, though he seemed surprised and enlightened when Finger told him in 1914 that what causes stars to fall, and indeed anything to move, was Taku Skanskan, one of the four supreme Oglala deities. The Sky or the so-called Great Spirit, Taku Skanskan, Finger explained, was the god who gives life and motion to all things (Walker 1980, 37). In a monograph on the Oglala ceremonies, Walker (1917) presented a verbatim translation of his dialogue with Finger on the Lakota theology of motion:

WALKER: When the meteor fell you cried in a loud voice, *Wohpa. Wohpe-e-e-e*. Why did you do this?

FINGER: Because that is *wakan*. ["*Wakan*" is a generic term designating both spirit-being and spirit-power.]

WALKER: What is *wohpa*?

FINGER: It is what you saw. It is one of the stars falling.

WALKER: What causes the stars to fall?

FINGER: *Taku Skanskan.*

WALKER: Why does *Taku Skanskan* cause the stars to fall?

FINGER: Because He causes everything that falls to fall and he causes everything that moves to move.

WALKER: When you move what is it that causes you to move?

FINGER: *Skan.*

WALKER: If an arrow is shot from a bow what causes it to move through the air?

FINGER: *Skan.*

WALKER: What causes a stone to fall to the ground when I drop it?

FINGER: *Skan.*

WALKER: If I lift a stone from the ground what causes the movement?

FINGER: *Skan.* He gives you power to lift the stone and it is He that causes all movement of any kind.

WALKER: Has the bow anything to do with the arrow shot by it?

FINGER: *Taku Skanskan* gives the spirit to the bow and he causes it to send the arrow from it.

WALKER: What causes smoke to go upward?

FINGER: *Taku Skanskan.*

WALKER: What causes water to flow in a river?

FINGER: *Skan.*

WALKER: What causes the clouds to move over the world?

FINGER: *Skan.*

(154–55)

Not that Sir Isaac ever entirely rid himself of his immanentist legacy. Gravity for Newton was an immanent force that expressed at every moment God's will. Hybrids, hybrids, everywhere.

As the discussion continued, Walker learned that *wohpa*, the falling star with which it all began, was actually the goddess Wohpa, the celestial Beautiful Woman, also one of the Supreme Deities, and that she came from the stars, who are "ghosts," *waniya*. By *waniya* is apparently meant something like a life principle: "*Skan* takes from the stars a ghost and gives it to each babe at the time of its birth and when the babe dies the ghost returns to the stars" (154–55). So indeed, Skan gives life and motion to all things, people included.

It is almost as if Vico, speaking in *The New Science* of the original age of religion or age of gods, were commenting on such ethnography. "The first law was divine," he writes, "for men believed themselves and all their institutions to depend on the gods, since they thought everything was a god or was made or done by a god" (Vico [1744] 1968, 338). The age of gods and divine government was succeeded by an age of heroes—and finally by the present age of men—but even in the heroic governments, "the age of the gods coursed on, for there persisted still that religious way of thinking according to which it was the gods who did whatever men themselves were doing" (234). The gods do whatever men are doing; the spirits enact the actors' actions. I take this Vichian dictum to be the cardinal principle of the cultures of immanence—with warrant far beyond Lakota and other Siouan peoples.

During his work in the 1930s, the German Lutheran missionary Hermann Strauss (1910–1978) was early enough in the New Guinea Highlands to know Melpa (Mbowamb) and other Mount Hagen peoples, whose doings the spirits were doing. When he writes that "any manifestation of power in people or things is ascribed to supernatural or hidden powers" (1991, 88), he is referring broadly to the celestial gods who were the ultimate sources of these powers and the collective clan ancestors, spirits of famous big-men, recently deceased kinsmen, and others upon whom the powers devolved. For Mbowamb of Mount Hagen, Strauss says, all earthly things have their origin in the incessant workings of such powers. If people are lucky, have many children, good harvests, a respected position in the community, success in trade, "all this is the consequence of the benign influences of the hidden powers, and these are persuaded to look favorably upon them by constant sacrifices. A more obvious explanation, such as one which pointed to all sorts of favorable circumstances" will not do, as it has "no religious cogency." For no event is merely "impersonal, devoid of intention and purely 'objective.' There must always be some living, active being behind it, a volitional being which is pursuing a particular purpose" (88).

In the same passage, Strauss again offers an extensional catalog of the spiritual agency in human activity: for better or worse the hidden powers are the effective forces of "life and death, growth and fruition, activity and endeavor, planting and harvesting, trade, work and leisure, suffering and joy, injuries and illness, good and bad times, fortune and misfortune, individual and communal life, moral and legal matters—all these things have a place in their magical or mystical world-view, which sees all concrete phenomena as transmitters of the forces of life and death that are used in a positive or negative fashion by personal will" (88).

In a similar vein, discussing the apparently unmotivated misfortunes people suffer, Strauss writes, "One example should suffice to show how this uncanny activity of the spirits is expressed in the language: one cannot say, 'I fell down unconscious;' instead, one must say, 'It (he, she) hit me and made me fall to the ground.' What we regard as the subject very often becomes the object" (117). Recounting similar expressions, Strauss's missionary successors Georg Vicedom and Herbert Tischner rather exaggerate the people's haplessness in these matters when they remark that the Mount Hagen man "always sees a force in his environment working upon him and he is always the passive part" (*The Mbowamb*, 1943–48 [n.d.] vol. 2). For we do not know from their account whether some previous act, such as trespass on the spirit's domain, made the victim morally responsible for the accident. More generally, the authors immediately allow that the people can by "magic" bring other (presumably greater) forces to bear upon the capricious spirits. And consider again Strauss's observation that the spirits can be persuaded to turn events in people's favor by "constant sacrifices" (Strauss 1991, 88, 117). Notwithstanding that it is the gods who do whatever men are doing, it is also a cardinal principle of the cultures of immanence that the people can and do take appropriate ritual action to engage the spirits' agency— as indeed they must do, even if in so doing they manifest their dependency by their deference.

———

Even beyond sickness and health, birth and death, growth and decline, rain and shine, and the other generic conditions of human existence of which people are not the authors, there is for each society an extensive repertory of dependencies appropriate to its own cultural constitution, and accordingly an engagement of spiritual agency in the near-totality of human activity. There will be much more to say about people's active engagements of the metaperson powers that be—that's essentially the rest of the book—but at the risk of enough is too much, I close the present chapter with some exemplary notices from around the planet of people's necessary dependency on such spiritual agency. In the spirit of Leachian risk, I offer these widespread examples of the total dependence of immanentist culture on the metahuman powers, with the hope, as Leach says, of forming a generalization and learning something new.

For Dinka of the East African Sudan, Divinity (Nhialic) is one, a God or Power whose being and potency is distributed to a suite of lesser clan, totemic, and animistic metapersons. Accordingly, as the British anthropologist Godfrey Lienhardt relates in his revelatory account of Dinka,

Divinity is ultimately the grounds for everything in humanity and nature: the grounds of sterility, barrenness, and pointless death; but also of creativity, fertility, and prosperity. "There is no theoretical problem for the Dinka of reconciling an infinitely good Divinity with the presence of . . . evils in the world, on a logical or moral plane, because Divinity represents the grounds of what actually happens" (1961, 159). Most interestingly, for the Dinka as well as the other cultures of immanence, pregnancy is a three-party relationship, always requiring the intervention of some meta-person in addition to the man and woman persons—in this case, Divinity of the highest power and also of the clan power. These are the specifically creative, fecundating powers: "The verb 'to create' is never interchangeable with the verb 'to beget.' Divinity created (*cak*) men in the beginning, and the men he created begat or bore (*dhieth*) children." When Lienhardt asked a man to explain what happened in coitus, "he described the physical act, and added 'And that is called begetting (*dhieth*), and Divinity will then slowly create (*cak*) the child in the woman's belly.'" Dinka sing that God is the true husband of women and cattle (39).

For Mae Enga of the New Guinea Highlands, clan ancestors are especially influential in the lives of their descendants, both episodically by direct contacts and continuously by certain stone shrines from which their powers emanate. Among his acute reports of Enga culture, the ethnographer Mervyn Meggitt relates that so long as the ancestors are favorably disposed, the stone instantiations of their power will ensure "that the clan land remains fertile and crops grow, sows conceive and farrow without difficulty, women bear healthy children, men act bravely in war and shrewdly in exchange, and everyone avoids serious illness or injury. . . . But, when the ancestral ghosts are angry, they sulk and their potency withdraws into the stones. Clansmen must then persuade them with ritual offerings to become active again and to restore the normal course of life" (1965b, 115).

According to Reo Fortune's ([1932] 1989) early and instructive ethnography of Dobu, an island at the eastern tip of New Guinea, the ritual incantations the Dobuan gods gave to the ancestors of people did not only make their canoe lashings and fish nets effective. Incantations that thus transmitted divine powers were also the prerequisites of success in making gardens, soliciting valuables in the overseas *kula* trade, creating love, making wind and rain, causing and curing disease, and causing death. But these were only the most striking resorts to incantation. There were also spells for strengthening the memory, for inflicting mosquito plagues on others and to exorcize them from oneself, to make coconut and betel palms bear, to create pregnancy, and to prevent unwelcome visitors from visiting again (96).

Returning to the rich Kwakiutl corpus, Stanley Walens writes:

> every human activity and characteristic is in some way participant in the world of power; similarly, every animal, spirit, and plant being participates to some degree in the possession and exercise of supernatural power; and finally, all world events are the consequence of the exercise of supernatural power. In brief, the entire world is directly involved in the acquisition, the use, and the experience of supernatural power. . . . The entire universe is founded fundamentally on the workings of supernatural power. . . . Because all acts involve the participation of spirits to some degree, either through their direct intervention or through their gift to humans of their power, humans are never capable of completing an action on their own. Instead, they must always act in order to secure the cooperation of spirits in human endeavors. Thus, humans are the subordinates of spirits. . . . In fact, the basic relation of human to spirit is always that of subordinate to superordinate, and people are never considered to have complete control over the actions they perform. (28–29)

Or consider Meyer Fortes's famous studies of West African Tallensi:

> In Tale thought everything that happens has material causes and conditions, but they are effective only by grace of the mystical agencies which are the ultimate arbiters of nature and society. So they say that if a man wishes to prosper, he must have skill, industry, and thrift. But these are not enough; without the beneficence of Destiny [i.e., particular forebears] they will be abortive; and even this is not enough, for behind Destiny is the collective power of all the ancestors, notably that of the omnipotent lineage ancestors. (1956, 51)

Fortes adds that

> Tale cosmology is wholly dominated by the ancestor cult. Even the
> elaborate totemic institutions, the cult of the Earth and the beliefs
> about the dangerous mystical qualities of evil trees, animals and
> other natural phenomena are subordinated to it. . . . This means that
> ultimate responsibility is projected outside the living body politic.
> (60–61)

In Borneo, to cite the more recent ethnographic work of the Swedish
sociologist Kenneth Sillander (2016), the spirits known to Bentian
Dayak are the sources of vitality and potency, of fortune and fate, of
illness, misfortune, and other adversities:

> They mediate people's relationships with the natural environment,
> with other people and peoples, as well as with themselves. . . . Much
> of what happens, especially major events and challenging enterprises,
> and untoward experiences and exceptional conditions of most every
> sort, is interpreted with reference to the spirits and then frequently
> occasions rituals. (160)

Regarding the "ancestor gods" of Thonga of southern Africa, and the
divinations by which the ancestors' dispositions are described, the early
twentieth-century Swiss missionary-ethnographer Henri Junod writes
that "it is of the utmost importance to know what [the] gods think and
do, as the very existence of the village, of the clan, and the welfare of
every member of the clan depends on them" (Junod 1913, 360). Theirs
is the power of killing or of making alive, of enriching or of making poor:

> They are the masters of everything: earth, fields, trees, rain, men,
> children, even of baloyi, wizards! They have a full control over all
> these objects or persons. The gods can bless: if the trees bear plenty
> of fruit, it is because they made it grow; if the crops are plentiful, it is
> because they sent good wizards to increase them, or hindered bad
> ones who tried to spoil them. . . . But they can also curse and bring
> any amount of misfortune on their descendants. If the rain fails, it is
> owing to their anger; . . . if a crocodile bites you, the gods residing in

the pool have sent it; if your child has fever, and is delirious, they are in him, tormenting his soul. (360)

From the Fifth Thule Expedition of the 1920s, the Danish-Greenlander explorer-anthropologist Knud Rasmussen (1929) reports of the Inuit that

it was his firm belief that all the little happenings of everyday life, good or bad, were the outcome of activity on the part of mysterious powers. Human beings were powerless in the grasp of a mighty fate, and only by the most ingenious system of taboo, with propitiatory rites and sacrifices, could the balance of life be maintained. Owing to the ignorance or imprudence of men and women, life was full of contrary happenings, and the intervention of the *angákut* [shaman] was therefore a necessity. (32)

Later in the same monograph, Rasmussen observes that

from birth to death, human beings have to regulate their lives according to the powers that control human weal and woe, and whose anger can give rise to suffering and hardship, not only for the person who has offended, but for the whole village. (169)

Of Australian Aboriginals, the noted Australian anthropologist W. H. Stanner writes that living men strongly felt themselves to be lesser beings than the ancestors and dependent on them. The ancestors were enduringly present in the world they had created in the primeval time, the Dreaming, as was the mode of human life they then established—in modern Aboriginal parlance, "the law." The ancestors, Stanner writes:

stocked the land with rivers, springs, food, weapons, and other means of life, raised up hills and mountains, put spirit-children [of humans] into the waters, used the wind and songs as agencies of will, went up into the sky, provided dreams as a means of communicating with the living, and performed a host of similar marvels. (1959–63, 259–60)

Perhaps most important, they transformed themselves into totemic animals, and left life-giving principles in the legacies of the patrilineal clans.

"The nature of the marvels is the measure of men's dependence" (259–60). Just so, as the American anthropologist Fred Myers (1991) reports,

> Pintupi explain about The Dreaming that it is not a product of human subjectivity or will. It is, rather, an order to which all are subordinated: "It's not our idea. . . . It's a big Law. We have to sit down alongside of that Law like all the dead people who went before us." (53)

> . . . The Dreaming—"the Law"—provides a moral authority lying outside the individual and outside human creation. . . . Consequently, current action is not understood as the result of human alliances, creations, and choices, but is seen as imposed by an embracing cosmic order. (69)

Following the world and cultural order established by primordial ancestors, Australian Aboriginals highlight a condition of human insufficiency, namely people's lack of control over their own mode of existence, a condition more or less widely shared among the pre-modern cultures of immanence. Culture in these societies is not a human thing. People do not create it. They receive it, along with the rules that enforce it and the power to realize it, from gods or ancestors who made the culture in primordial times and preside over it in present times. *Verum ipsum factum.* This must be one of the most striking differences with transcendentalist sensibilities: the certainty that our way of life, our culture, is of our own making, subject to human invention and intention. That's what happened in the past—it's what history (as opposed to myth) is all about, people making and changing the conditions of their existence—and it's the sense of how and why the future will be different. At least that is the idea.

Compare the view from the interior of Madang Province in New Guinea, what the Garia people know about their cultural origins, as reported by Australian anthropologist Peter Lawrence (1984):

> The Garia explain the origins of their cosmic order in a set of myths which tell how deities shaped the physical environment, created human beings, and invented social and material culture. . . . Human beings came into existence towards the west of Garialand, near the

River Mobo, where a boulder was struggling to give birth to them. The snake goddess Obomwe took pity on it in its travail and herself performed the act of parturition. (32)

But as she should not have intervened, she brought death as well as life into the world. Other gods created culture. Certain Bush gods, by establishing their domains, presided over hunting and weather. "They attracted people to their domains, taught them their language (which they called Garia) and rules for kinship, marriage and land tenure, and in some cases . . . gave them descent names" (32). Artifacts, food plants, animals, and "vital customs" came from other deities. One set of gods invented the important slit-gong, pottery, hand-drum, "and so forth." Another group gave taro, spinach, yams, and other crops. Yet another provided pigs and dogs; still another, sorcery and initiation rites. Outside gods, especially from the coast, were incorporated when Garia bought rights to the dances invented by the foreign gods (145–46):

> Yet the deities did not concern themselves solely with the genesis of the sociocultural system. They also showed men how to control it. In the period of antiquity each god or goddess appeared to human beings in dreams or even lived with them, teaching them four things: his or her open name; the secular procedures necessary to manufacture, grow, raise or perform his or her artefact, food plant, animal or ceremony; his or her myth of origin; and the secret of his or her power, the esoteric spell (usually based on his or her secret name), the repetition of which would ensure success in the relevant activity. . . . Religion is important not merely as a form of explanation and validation: things are as they are because the gods made them so and hence they have to be right. Its role goes beyond this: it is regarded as an essential force in everyday affairs. Ritual gives men the ability to create beneficial relationships with deities and spirits of the dead, harness their power, and thereby actuate the proper functioning of the cosmic order. This is the virtual monopoly of the leaders or big men. (Lawrence 1984, 33)

Having created the culture, the gods remain the potent means of its realization. They are immanent in human affairs.

2

Immanence

The striking feature is . . . how *empirical* these spirits are, how they seem
to appear as very concrete, observable objects *in* the world, rather than
ways of talking *about* the world.

—BARTH 1975, 129 (EMPHASIS ORIGINAL)

THE NORWEGIAN SOCIAL anthropologist Fredrik Barth's surprise at
"how empirical the spirits are" was a concluding musing on various encounters people had with spirits during the eleven months he lived with
Baktaman in 1968. Baktaman are a small group of Mountain Ok or Min
people in central Papua New Guinea, a population of 183 in Barth's time,
that had to contend especially with illnesses inflicted by *sabkār*, dead
people. "In the course of my less than a year with the Baktaman, a number of persons suffered sporadically from having been entered by a
sabkār who was slowly eating away their flesh" (Barth 1975, 127). Barth
tells of a man who visited the land of the dead at this time. While hunting in the forest, he was carried away by a *sabkār* to the village of the
dead where he witnessed a seventh-degree initiation (the highest stage
ritual of the Baktaman men's cult) before returning home the next day.
Then there was a young woman who disappeared for four days before
miraculously reappearing from a sago palm people were harvesting. It
was concluded she had been carried off by a *sabkār*, "as is known to
occur not infrequently. . . . There was no evidence of doubt in anybody's

mind that these were indeed the concrete, literal circumstances of the case" (128). Beside the spirits of the dead, Barth speaks of two other kinds of malicious spirits in this context, apparently spirits of living people: one, strangers who at night lurk invisibly at the edge of the village and shoot men with magical arrows when they leave their house in the morning to urinate, upon which the men fall and are dead by the next night; and another, small invisible dwarfs, sometimes said to be souls of men from one's own village, who in groups of five attack men in the forest, and if not fought off inflict wounds that cause death in two or three days. The latter spirits "are often observed fleetingly in the forest, and sudden illness elicits discussions of them" (129).

Barth makes a general comment about the ethnography of such incidents to which I can largely subscribe, the functionalism apart, as it is pertinent to the discussions of spirits throughout this book. Essentially, it is what I shall call spirit-power thinking, following native North American usage. To consider the Baktaman experiences with spirits as fantasies, he writes, "would prevent us from asking the more useful question of how they serve the Baktaman as conceptual tools—what they enable a Baktaman to think, feel, and understand. . . . We should ask . . . how they make a person grasp aspects of his life situation and reality, and what consequences they have for the form which a person's reality takes" (123). This is what the people see and understand, the culture, and their *verum*.

Studying a related people, Australian anthropologist Donald Gardner (1987) cites Barth's observation on "how empirical the spirits are" and confirms it:

Among the Mianmin, too, spirits of one kind or another, are a basic feature of daily life. Events construed as involving "supernatural" beings are commonly reported and discussed. . . . But if we ask simply about beliefs in spirits, posing the question in terms of the categorical distinction between the natural and the supernatural, then we shall have carved out an artificial field for the investigation. For, it is well known, and perhaps no more than a truism, that animistic metaphysical schemes are characterized by an absence of the natural/supernatural distinction. The crucial aspect of such schemes is the all-pervasiveness of [metapersonal] agency as a principle of the functioning of the world and in explanation of events of all kinds. This . . . amounts to a statement of the basic (metaphysical) principles of those who live in what Weber called an "enchanted world." (161–62)

In an enchanted universe, the natural/supernatural distinction becomes meaningless. Many of its denizens are not only the all-pervasive, unseen agents of the events of this world, they often make themselves visible in its phenomenal forms, as all kinds of animals and notably as humans, to enter into people's daily lives in all kinds of ways. But then, humans are spirits too. Composed of a physical body activated by an invisible "soul," human persons are the same in constitution as embodied metapersons. By their own unseen powers of intellection and volition, moreover, by these attributes of their inner life, people are able to interact socially with the spirits: in dreams most commonly, where the interlocutors of human dreamers are thus as "real" as they are. By the same metaphysical powers, people—not only shamans but ordinary people—have been known to visit and live with spirit-peoples in their homelands under the water, under the earth, or in the sky. People even marry spirits and have children by them. All that and more being the ways of "how empirical the spirits are," the familiar opposition of natural and supernatural is foreign to the constitution of the enchanted universe. It is ontologically out of place. It belongs in the transcendental universe.

Rectification of the Categories

The Achuar [Upper Amazonia] do not see the supernatural as a level of reality separate from nature, for all of nature's beings have some features in common with mankind, and the laws they go by are more or less the same as those governing civil society. Humans and most plants, animals, and meteors are persons (*aents*) with a soul (*wakan*) and an individual life. (Descola 1994, 93)

[I]t is worth trying to evoke again the phenomenological realities of this world in which the living and the dead are co-participants in everyday life. A substantial proportion of the conversations that take place in a Kwaio settlement [Solomon Islands] are not between living humans but between the living and the dead. . . . This is not a world where ancestral shades are remote presences, creations of theological imagination. They are part of the daily social life of Kwaio communities. (Keesing 1982, 112–13)

Within the single world known to them (for they dwell little upon fancies of any "other world" of different constitution), the Dinka [East Africa] claim that they encounter "spirits" of various kinds, which they call generally *jok*. . . . These Powers are regarded as higher in the scale of being than men and other merely terrestrial creatures, and operate beyond the categories of space and time which limit human actions; but they are not imagined to form a separate "spirit world" of their own, and their interest for Dinka is as ultra-human forces participating in human life and often affecting men for good or ill. . . . I have not found it useful to adopt the distinction between "natural" and "supernatural" beings or events in order to describe the difference between men and Powers, for this distinction implies a conception of the course or laws of Nature quite foreign to Dinka thought. (Lienhardt 1961, 28)

To join the awakening ethnographic chorus: the distinction between "natural" and "supernatural" is not receivable in cultures where ancestors, gods, the *inua* or spirits of things, and other such metapersons are immanent presences in human lives. What perhaps needs emphasis here is where that distinction comes from, where it is ontologically appropriate. The differentiation of a "supernatural" realm from an earthly "nature" refers to the kind of world that the Christian God made of "nothing": a world devoid of other-than-human subjects, that accordingly works by its own inherent laws and forces—physical, chemical, biological, meteorological, and so on. "Nature" is part of the ongoing capture by transcendentalism in the world, what is left on earth by the translation of the Deity & Company (angels, saints, the deceased human elect) to a supernatural "other world." The cultures of immanence, enspirited cultures, know only one world in which people interact with the myriad of nonhuman subjects, from the deities to the dead. These species of meta-persons may have their own habitats, from the heavens to under the ground or the sea, but they are co-present, visibly or invisibly, with human beings in the one great cosmic polity. There is no "other world."

In a brilliant essay on the issues raised by translations of traditional African thought into Western categories, Nigerian philosopher Kwasi Wiredu (1992) explains that the notion of "supernatural" is not African precisely because it is not empirical. Wiredu speaks of Akan groups of southern Ghana more particularly, but he takes their cosmological concepts as typical of many African cultures. Here is the complement to Barth's surprise at "how empirical the spirits are" in the life of Baktaman: namely, how implausible is the notion of "supernatural" for Akan people, since unlike the empirical "spirits," what is "supernatural" is not phenomenal—indeed, unlike the spirits, it is not material. The empirical is not the transcendental. On the contrary, Wiredu points out, "not even Onyame ('God') is supposed to exist outside the world. That would be a veritable contradiction in Akan terms. To exist is to be *there* (*'wɔhɔ'*), and existence is the being there of something (*'sɜ bribi wɔ hɔ'*). To exist outside the world would mean to be *there* but not at any place, an idea lacking in coherence" (325). *Immanence is a quality of being.* Being is being there, and being there is being here. Wiredu's philosophical insight is golden, including in the Vichean sense that he reveals the essential mentality of immanentism: how it is that the dead, the ancestors, the demons, and other denizens of the enchanted universe are, for humans, present and "real."

Wiredu's general observations on Akan spirit-concepts can be understood as sequitur to the premise that being is being there. "The intellectual orientation of the Akan is empirical," he writes. And yet,

> this does not mean that the metaphysical bent is absent from their thinking. It does not mean, furthermore, that they are unused to thinking with concepts of the highest abstraction. What it means is only that they do not employ in their thinking certain kinds of abstract concepts, namely, those that cannot be defined in terms deriving from human experience. Now, quite clearly the concept of the

"supernatural" goes beyond the world of human experience. It envisages a world over and above this world. By no manner of deduction, extrapolation, or imaginative projection could one arrive at such a concept from empirical beginnings. . . . Of a piece with this also i[s] the absence of any conceptual cleavage between the spiritual and the physical. [The Kenyan Anglican theologian-philosopher] Mbiti observes, speaking of African thought generally, that within it "no line is drawn between the spiritual and the physical." (324–25)

Africans and others whose worlds are populated by "spirits" are commonly supposed to be "mystical"—that is, by Westerners operating on their own distinctions of the spiritual and the physical or the supernatural and the natural, their own transcendental suppositions. The irony is that these peoples are all-around, complete, world-constituting empiricists. Rather than "superstitious," "deluded," or otherwise taken in by wishful fantasies, their enchantments are effects of a sustained and radical empiricism. *Being is being there* is a basic epistemological premise of the enchanted universe.

As imported from our own transcendentalist ontology, the depiction of African "religion" and similar cosmologies in terms of a natural/supernatural opposition is a kind of ethnographic original sin. Yet it is only one of a series of related categorical distinctions that have for too long and too often corrupted the ethnographies of enspirited societies: including spiritual and material, nature and culture, subject and object, reality and belief. Based on the assumption of a divine other world apart from the human world—where "religion" is superstructural and "spirits" are immaterial—what these distinctions commonly ignore is the cosmic subjectivity of the immanentist cultures they purport to so describe. They ignore cultural worlds where "subjectivity, not physicality, is the common ground of existence . . . a sentient ecology positing a universe of communicating and interacting subjects," as the Swedish anthropologist Kaj Århem (2016b, 91), who also worked in Amazonia, describes a Vietnamese hill people. Or, in the words of Levy-Bruhl, they ignore that for humans in this enchanted universe, "the surrounding world is the language of spirits speaking to a spirit" (1923, 60).

The opposition of the spiritual and the material cannot be received where the "material" is "spiritual"; or properly said, where the phenomena of the human world are the manifest forms of indwelling persons. The opposition of "culture" and "nature" cannot be received where nature is cultural, inasmuch as the communication of its interacting subjects, focused on the one finality of the human fate, necessarily entails a universal conceptual scheme. The opposition of "subject" and "object" cannot be received where objects are subjects—that is, in a non-Cartesian world universally composed of *res cogitans*, as many have observed. Likewise, the "secular" is "sacred" inasmuch as it is inhabited by metaperson powers, and "belief" is "real" inasmuch as being is being there. One might say of enspirited societies that their idealism is materialism—and vice versa. But again, of the validity of all such distinctions as spiritual/material, it is wiser to keep in mind the (Ho)cartesian question: "How can we make any progress in the understanding of cultures, ancient or modern, if we persist in dividing what people join, and in joining what they keep apart?" (Hocart [1939] 1953, 23).

Visibility

The realm of nonhuman agencies [for Montagnais-Naskapi (Innu) of Labrador] which the European calls the unseen *is* to the northern aboriginal as often sensed by sight as are the familiar creatures of everyday life that surround the most pragmatic minded. The cannibal giant, the underwater people, the animal owners are to him not questionable beings, but realities, proved by personal experience of a nature as satisfactory to him as it would be to have seen a bear or seal. (Speck [1935] 1977, 242; emphasis original)

[T]he activities of the gods and spirits [of the dead] in helping mankind have no mystical quality [for Ngaing of interior Madang Province, Papua New Guinea]. They are believed to take place on the same plane of existence and are, therefore, just as real as those of human beings working together at any joint task. (Lawrence 1965, 218)

To judge from specific inquiries made among the Winnebago and Ojibwa, and from much of our data in general, reality does not depend necessarily upon sense-impressions. (Radin 1914, 352)

To keep in mind: the "spirits" are real, active co-workers in human economic projects. To consider here: for all their usual invisibility, the spirits are co-present with humans in the same reality. The spirits may be invisible to the people, but the people are visible to the spirits. Because they are normally—but not always or necessarily—invisible does not mean they are somewhere else, on some other plane of existence. Lots of things I know for a fact I have never seen, like the Sahara Desert; some I could not possibly see, like George Washington or Geronimo. It is incorrect to conclude, as ethnographers sometimes have, that the gods, ghosts, and other metapersons, because they are unseen or exist elsewhere as in the sky or distant mountains, are denizens of a reality or world beyond the human. More often, however, anthropologists report, as the linguist and anthropologist Roger Keesing (1982) has on Kwaio people of the Solomon Islands, that "this distinction between the visible and invisible implies no transcendence, no ultimate separation between the ancestral realm and the human" (73).

The Kwaio ancestors—especially the kindred spirits of dead parents, grandparents, siblings, and children—have an immediacy as members of one's group and participants in everyday life. People talk with them daily, Keesing notes, and encounter them nightly while their bodies sleep—the implication being that humans too have unseen spirit-powers. A substantial proportion of the conversations in which Kwaio engage are not between living people but between the living and the dead. Already by age three, a child learns that the social universe includes actors he or she cannot see, and soon enough that these unseen ancestral powers are the "source of success, gratification, and security, and the cause of illness, death, and misfortune" (33).

No child could escape constituting a cognitive world in which the spirits were ever-present participants in social life, on whom life and death, success or failure, depend. No child could fail to construct a world in which boundaries of sacredness and danger—male and female, living and dead, and their mapping out in space and expression in rules about substances and conduct—were clearly defined. (38)

Rules govern the universe, Keesing writes, and people must follow them in thousands of everyday ways or risk punishments from these ever-present ancestors, especially the kindred spirits who, despite the close relationship, do not hesitate to inflict illness and death on wrongdoers.

Rather than elsewhere, the spirits' invisibility is likely to put them everywhere. The Scandinavian ethnographer Kenneth Sillander deftly makes a point about the ubiquity of invisibility for Bentian, a small up-river Dayak group in Eastern Kalimantan (Borneo). Inasmuch as the spirits cannot be seen, "it can never be known for sure where they are, or what they are up to, meaning they should be treated a little as if continually present, with care taken so that they receive respect and are not offended by human behavior" (2016, 169). For all the uncertainties about the spirits—at one point, Sillander says, "they live somewhat as if in another dimension," or even a "parallel world" (2016, 170)—people know a lot about them and indeed often encounter them, not only shamans but also ordinary people.

> Deep in the woods, under water, and in the heavens, they [gods, the dead, some animals, species masters, demons] have villages and houses of their own, and human cultural institutions such as marriage, kinship, and leadership. Spirits are also talked to as if they were people, and given gifts similar to those appreciated by people. (168)

Both shamans and others may be possessed by spirits, which happens quite frequently, especially in rituals, and "anybody's soul may encounter spirits in dreams" (167). Hence the spirits' invisibility does not entail an existence apart from humans, and if they live in a "parallel world," then humans also inhabit it. For people themselves have invisible "souls," inner consciousnesses; they are symbolizing beings that, awake or asleep, can perform prodigies of extra-body adventures in space and time, where they meet and interact with spirits. People are spirits themselves.

People Are Spirits

There were no strict boundaries [for Inuit of the Arctic Circle] between different kinds of spirits and between spirits and human beings. Some spirits [such as Sedna] were of human origin. Other spirits could hardly be distinguished from human beings. . . . *The Inuit themselves were spiritual beings . . . and could interact with spirits.* . . . The conceptions of the spirits expressed a fundamental notion in Inuit religion, that the world was a spiritual world, consisting of innumerable personal forces. (Oosten 1976, 29, emphasis mine)

[For Kanak of New Caledonia], the *ko* [or "soul"] during its journeys far from the man it animates has an existence of its own; it can steal the goods of another; it can commit adultery. And if the man is then declared guilty, far from invoking an alibi of sleeping, he is frightened. "Perhaps," he says, "my *ko* did it when I was sleeping. . . . " The *ko* energizes thought. Of a man who acts for an unfathomable reason or intention, one says . . . "it was done by his *ko*." (Leenhardt 1930, 213; my translation)

[For Bentian Dayak of Borneo,] the human soul has the double function of being both animating principle and agency. It may become temporarily lost or weakened, resulting in illness or loss of vitality, and it may travel during sleep, or to spirit abodes during rituals in the case of the shamans' souls. It is a life force, whose condition—strength and fixity—explains well-being, but also a person-like being, which may experience things (such as affronts, fright or contentment). In the latter sense it is essentially spirit-like: an unseen agency endowed with consciousness. (Sillander 2016, 165)

[T]here seems to be a general consensus that certain parts of the deceased's body take on a life of their own [for Achuar of Northern Amazonia] . . . and after death assume the bodies of certain species of animals. The lungs turn into butterflies . . . the deceased's shadow, a brocket deer . . . the heart, a slate-colored grosbeak . . . and the liver, an owl. (Descola 1994, 92)

After hours of tedious questioning, the Innu (Montagnais-Naskapi) elder was finally able to give the early American ethnographer, Frank Speck, some understanding of the local concept of the "Great Man" or active soul of the individual using the branch of the Canadian National Railway recently run through the reservation. On this day in 1922, Joseph Kurtness explained that the *Mista ´peo* or Great Man is to the body of man as the chief of the cabin (locomotive engineer) is to the fire/toboggan (locomotive engine). "He knows his engine and just what he can do with it, and the engine works just as he directs it. Without him it is a dead mass; when it [the engine] is worn out or when it collapses, he [the soul, the engineer] goes into another one" ([1935] 1977, 39). Just so, the soul of an ancestor is reincarnated in the embryo of the child to become the person's guide through life, and notably "the means of overcoming the spirits of animals in the life-long search for food" (33). In the beginning of the world, animals lived in so many tribes of their own, just like the people with whom they could freely converse. Conflicts led them to take on the covering and shape of animals, but as the shaman says to them by song or his drum, "'You and I wear the same covering and have the same mind and spiritual strength'" (72).

This is what Naskapi call "spirit-power thinking," a useful concept of engagement of people's souls in a metaperson universe, and more generally for the efficacy of the spirit world. It consists of various means, from total concentration to drumming, singing, and rattling, for arousing and strengthening the Great Man. Drums themselves have their inner persons, even as the designs acquired from souls in dreams and embroidered by women on hunters' clothing have powers of attracting and subduing animals. Moreover, drumming induces dreams. Dreams are the main means by which the person's Great Man guides him or her through communication with other spirits. Hunting was essentially accomplished in dreams. It remained only to locate the prey by divination, primarily by means of lines on the scapula of dead animals, and finish it off by bow, gun, or trap.

Humans are essentially spirit-beings, even as spirits are essentially human. Although the current wave of interest in animism tends to highlight the latter, the person-qualities of spirits, it is critical for human existence that the two are ontological congeners. It is by humans' own spirit-powers that they articulate with the metahuman agents of their life and death. People have the same composition as embodied spirits, consisting of an invisible, internal, and intentional person ("soul," *inua*) animating a physical body, as said before. The anthropologist Erik Jensen's detailed account of the Iban could be duplicated the planet around: "All life has two parts, all life which is essential to the Iban, human, animal and even vegetable, has a physical and spirit side. "The physical, mortal, visible body (*tuboh*) is one part; the other is the spirit counterpart or spirit/soul, the *samengat*" (1974, 106–7). Or again, the American anthropologist Irving Hallowell demonstrates the point from the people's vantage: "Speaking as an Ojibwa, one might say: all other 'persons'—human or other than human—are structured the same as I am. . . . All other 'persons,' too, have such attributes as self-awareness and understanding. I can talk with them. Like myself, they have personal identity, autonomy, and volition" (1960, 43).

By frequent ethnographic report, the human soul is the condition of the "reality" of the dreamwork, the means of relating to the spirits there in attendance. As Hallowell wrote of Saulteaux (or Anishinaabe, westernmost of the Ojibwa nation) in the 1930s: "It is through dreams . . . that the individual becomes directly acquainted with the entities which he believes to be the active agencies of the universe about him. But he only sees them with the eyes of the 'soul,' not with the eyes of the body. To him, moreover, these spiritual entities of the cosmos represent a continuum with the ordinary world of sense perception. They are an integral part of reality and are not super-natural beings in any strict sense of the term" (1934, 399).

It needs to be stressed, for immanentist cultures, the issue is universal and existential: the human soul is *the* essential means of articulation and communication with the cosmic host of metahuman beings, and dreams are essential spaces of that necessary intersubjectivity. In dreams, typically, the bodily differences are resolved: plants, animals, species masters, and others appear as humans. Communication issues are resolved: the different species of spirits may have their own languages, but in dreams they typically speak the language of the dreamer. The dream, moreover, is democratic. As Descola puts it for Achuar, "Anyone, man, woman, or child, under certain circumstances, is capable of sending his soul beyond the narrow confines of the body in order to dialogue directly with the double of another of nature's beings, be it human, plant, animal, or supernatural spirit" (1994, 100). Not to underestimate relations to spirits in the waking state—"I can talk to them"—as indeed the encounters with spirits in dreams are incomplete without the subsequent wakeful interpretations.

The ancestors and gods, demons and *inua*, are always there: as witness the growth of crops, the spawning of the fish, the course of the sun, the movement of the caribou, the illness and death of kin. The recurrent in-bodily encounters and dealings with metahuman powers by means of humans' invisible cognitive capacities is not that different from dreamwork, and potentially much more extensive in scope. These spirits met or invoked in waking life are no more empirical and no less real than those of the dreamwork. In fact, dreams are often highly symbolic portents gifted by spirits that require considerable daytime interpretation. Like the dreams of Iban people concerning important undertakings from building a new longhouse, or starting a rice garden, to migrating to a new location. These dreams "provide the essential spirit endorsement" of the project, such as the dream of a successful fishing expedition by the longhouse community using the poisonous derris root: this signifies there will be a good rice harvest (Jensen 1974, 118). Likewise, if a person dreams he or she has successfully swum across a river after initially fearing to do so, this also "means that there will be a plentiful harvest" (117). As I said, the interpretation is not obvious. When Achuar men dream of plump, naked women eager to have sexual intercourse, it is a favorable sign for success in hunting peccary. (By Freudian lights, an American man who dreams of hunting plump animals might rather be symbolizing his desire for sexual success with a beautiful woman.) Waking or sleeping, humans are metaphysical beings, and by means of that quality, spiritual beings.

This is not original but in the present context it is critical: human metaphysical powers are doubly operative in speech. First, because the arbitrary relation between the signifier and its worldly referent establishes the spoken word as an autonomous, creative force; and second, because speech has potent pragmatic effects on interlocutors and their situation independent of any physical contact. These symbolic powers of speech are effectively on display in social anthropologist Stanley Jeyaraja Tambiah's seminal essay, "The Magical Power of Words" (1985), in which he elaborates on Malinowski's ([1935] 1978) observations about the potency of magical spells in Trobriand gardening and canoe construction. Tambiah cites Isaiah 55:11 in this context: "So shall my word be that goeth forth out of my mouth: it shall not return unto me void, but shall accomplish that which I please, and it shall prosper in the thing whereto I sent it." Tambiah's analysis of the relations between magical spells and practical techniques are relevant as an excellent example of the creative agency of words: "Language is within us; it moves us, and we generate it as active agents. Since words exist and are in a sense agents in themselves which establish connections and relations between man and man, and man and the world, and are capable of 'acting' upon them, they are one of the most realistic representations we have of the concept of force which is either not directly observable or is a metaphysical notion which we find necessary to use" (29).

This sense of the creative power of words makes an interesting connection with the Italian anthropologist Valerio Valeri's analysis (1985) of the associations between Hawaiian *mana* and the efficacy of speech. Noting a man may transmit *mana* to another by spitting in his mouth or breathing on his fontanelle, Valeri deduces that this "gives clues to what kind of 'substance' mana is: it seems be connected with speech, with which spit, breath, and mouth are obviously associated. Moreover, breath is connected with life ... thus we may deduce that mana is a sort of life in speech and life-giving power in speech" (99). The implications are large. Speech has the power of creating social relations and meaningful situations. Speech is impelled by breath. Breath is life. Ergo, speech is the symbolic, life-giving power of the creation of cultural order. In which case, humans are not only spirits, but the original spirit, the genesis of spirit.

The present work can hardly be accused of anthropocentrism. "Religion" is not here conceived as the ideal projection of real-social or real-political relations. Humans are here considered as limited beings, their own existence dependent upon and subordinate to a cosmic host of metahuman powers. But in this enchanted mode of unhappy consciousness, humans' symbolic power is the model of divine power itself. Divinity or spirit is the hypostatization of speech, of symbolic power. "In the beginning was the Word, and the Word was with God, and the Word was God" (John 1:1). Human speech is the essence of divine power.

Human souls are typically immortal, a main reason they are typically called "souls" in the anthropological literature, their array of person-qualities notwithstanding—consciousness, will, emotions, and so forth. The usual perspective, moreover, is solipsist and soteriological, concerned with the existence of the individual after death, if not exactly with the salvation of the soul. We are again misled by ethnocentric-cum-transcendentalist preconceptions. As a general rule, in immanentist regimes, the principal cultural value of the soul's immortality is its life-giving transformation into another being, into an ancestor, ghost, animal, or another human, rather than the perpetuation of the individual as such. The soul remains in this world, as the animating-power of an altered form. Following something like the Law of Spiritual Dynamics, souls are not created or destroyed, but transferred from one being to another. Ironically, the soul in immanentist societies is guaranteed the perpetual life that the soul of transcendental orders only aspires to—and may well fail to achieve.

The Arctic explorer Knud Rasmussen reports of Iglulik (1929) and Netsilik (1931), in a way similar to the Naskapi Great Man, that in addition to the inner soul that all humans have, a child also acquires through the reincarnation of a dead kinsman's soul certain individual powers—or indeed generations of individual powers, from all those whom that soul had inhabited. Reincarnated souls pass with names, the names of dead relatives bestowed on children when uttered at the moment of birth. Rasmussen explains the Netsilik practice: "To every name is attached a certain store of power that is transferred to those who bear the name. It is a kind of magic power, difficult to explain. It is as if a name had its own particular soul acting quite independently of the body's soul . . . According to some people, this means that the soul of the body, the real fountain of life, is the one that makes mankind human, while the soul of the name merely makes it generally strong, keeps it up and protects it" (1931, 219).

As the ethnographer and filmmaker of Netsilik people Asen Balikci put it some decades later, beyond the soul of the body, "name souls . . . possess a personality of their own characterized by great power and distinct ability to protect the name bearer from any misfortune. In fact they acted as guardian spirits, highly beneficial to humans" (1970, 199). Likewise Rasmussen: as people are continually being named generation after generation, these powers in some accumulate in the one who has the name, and "are with him, work inside him, keep danger away and become his guardian spirits" (1931, 220). The choice of recipient is made by the dead, motivated by a desire to join the living.

Rasmussen further says that people try to acquire as many names as possible, obviously later in life, the one example described being an older woman who took the name of a powerful spirit that cured her during a serious illness. Reciting her several name-souls or spirits, the woman said that through them she had been able to grow old, withstanding the attacks of shamans and "all the dangers that would otherwise have uprooted me from the dwelling places of man" (221). For Iglulik, in a briefer discussion, Rasmussen recounts how a series of names is recited when a woman is about to give birth, and the name that coincides with the appearance of the child becomes his or her name-soul, at which time "care must be taken that all the qualities that soul possessed are communicated to the child" (1929, 172). Take note, then, of this duplex soul formation, comprised of an inherent life-giving soul, of a kind shared by others inasmuch as it "makes mankind human," and an individuated soul or souls acquired from outside that give a person a differentiated identity while empowering him or her bodily, that is externally.

In these enspirited cultures, human spirit-powers are often double, consisting of a social soul of divine or ancestral derivation, shared by a determinate collective group, and personal souls or metapersonal qualities, as acquired individually. The social or ancestral soul is invariably the inner core of human being, and the means of people's powers of reproduction, growth, health, material and other success, at least in potential; but the extent to which these are realized in life typically depends on the outer soul or powers immanent in the body. Explicitly, I am not speaking of a Cartesian opposition between soul and body composed simply of an inner subjectivity and an outer physicality. Indeed, if the body were a mere physical "thing," it would be the only such significant entity in an otherwise animist universe. The body members and properties themselves are differentiated by values and powers—superior and inferior, masculine and feminine, intellect and emotion, and so forth—often as transmitted by one or the other parent in the process of procreation. Physicality is metaphysicality and, in that sense, spirituality.

It would be misleading, then, to think of the contrast between soul and body as antithetical on the order of a Christian struggle between spirit and flesh. That again is transcendentalist thinking, motivated by ethical and soteriological suppositions. Rather, both body and soul being spiritual, the relation between them as hypothesized here is complementary. The body's powers are the means by which living individuals realize, to a greater or lesser extent, the vital potencies of the ancestral soul. Only together do soul and body—inner and outer, collective and individual, eternal and conjunctural, potential and actual—make a complete human existence.

To speak first of the social soul, as, for instance, the missionary Hermann Strauss took notice of it among Mount Hagen peoples in the central highlands of Papua New Guinea: "This concept is not the individual soul in the sense in which we understand it," he writes, "but the individual's *share* or *participation* in the *communal* life-force and spiritual power, and every member of the group shares it some way or other. . . . The *min*, or [clan] 'soul,' is tied to its individual bearer, the self, but it comes to him as something else. It is something greater than the individual, for it is simply his participation in the power and the spiritual life of the community" (Strauss 1991, 99; emphasis original).

Mervyn Meggitt's (1965a) description of the mode of procreation among the neighboring Mae Enga people illustrates how a collective soul comes about. An Enga child is conceived by the mingling of paternal semen and menstrual blood in the mother's womb. However, "four months after conception a spirit animates the foetus and gives it an individual personality." Although it comes from the paternal side, this spirit is not transmitted through the father's semen. "Instead it is in some way implanted by the totality of ancestral ghosts of the father's clan and seems to be an emanation of their generalized potency.... The existence of the ancestral ghosts is thus as necessary for the birth of a normal child as the initial conjunction of semen and menstrual blood." In people's everyday comments on procreation, they put little emphasis on the father's sexual role; they are more concerned "with the child's acquisition of a spirit and ultimately of a social identity as a consequence of his father's clan membership. The father's agnatic affiliation legitimately relates the child both by descent and through ritual to a group of clan ancestral ghosts" (163).

Note particularly the ritual connection to the clan ancestors, here characterized as a collective and the source of a "generalized potency"; as well as the fundamental consubstantiality with the founding ancestor, making the members, as they say, children "of one penis" (Meggitt 1965a, 5–6). The inner soul thus acquires the powers of human and agricultural fertility (on ancestral clan land), of growth, health, wealth, and other essentials of existence afforded by the ancestors and ultimately the gods.

Enga people also stress that the mother's blood, the woman's contribution to the fetus, produces the child's skin and flesh: the maternal kin bestow the outward, bodily components and powers that enclose and protect the inward soul-powers bestowed by the paternal clan ancestors (Meggitt 1965a, 163). And to judge from Mount Hagen peoples again, the maternal contribution itself is spiritually endowed—if regrettably and resentfully so on the part of the mother's people. "They also find it regrettable that when they give their daughters in marriage, they are necessarily giving away some of their own life-force and power to another ... [totem-] group and thus strengthening it against their will" (Strauss 1991, 92). In the event, at birth the person is doubly enspirited.

Whatever else they are, kinship relations are spiritual endowments. And apparently, to demur from Edmund Leach's influential formula in this connection, "in any system of kinship and marriage," the spiritual endowments come from both the relationships, which give an individual membership in a "we group" of some kind (relations of incorporation) and those other relations which link "our group" to other groups of like kind (relations of alliance). Recall that in Leach's formulation, whereas the "we group" relations are those of common substance, the "relations of alliance are viewed as metaphysical influence" (1966, 21; emphasis original). It was already evident from Leach's own examples, however, that the relations at issue were more complex. As in the case of patrilineal Kachin, who like many other Southeast Asian peoples hold that the father contributes bone to his child and the mother her blood, an individual has relations of common substance both with a "we group" (bone from the father) and an allied group (blood from mother). Besides, there is that third endowment, markedly in unilineal systems, of the ancestor of the "we group" whose "metaphysical influences" on the child include the powers of life, growth, fertility, and possibly other capacities such as bravery, intelligence, and so on.

Without taking the full Leachian gamble of *any* system of kinship and marriage, I will risk the idea that the human spirit/soul is double, consisting of an inherent social soul, generically human or specifically ancestral, and an acquired individuated soul, by means of which the life potentials of the former may be realized. As a rule, the social soul is an internal quality of the person, the acquired, an external quality. Where there are determinate "we groups" and allied groups, the individual abilities are not only birth endowments of the latter but often ritual practices by which the ancestral endowments are achieved.

Just so, it is written of BaKongo in Central Africa, "'Man is considered a double being, made up of an outer and an inner entity,'" referring thus to body and soul; but the body itself is again doubled, as it were on the same oppositions of outer and inner, body and spirit. "'The outer body again consists of two parts, the shell (vuvudi) which is buried and rots in the ground as quickly as a mushroom, and the inner, invisible part (mvumbi) which is eaten by the magic of the bandoki [witch]'"

(K. E. Laman, cited by MacGaffey 1986, 135). In his own ethnography of the BaKongo of Lower Zaire, anthropologist Wyatt MacGaffey provides an unusually elaborate and instructive description of these spiritual aspects of the body, beginning with an allusion to the same duality as the Swedish missionary K. E. Laman recorded in the early twentieth century. "Human bodies," MacGaffey writes, "provide the personalities or spirits they contain with a physical locus and a metaphorical expression of an appropriate identity" (122). Otherwise put, to the same effect, "people generally think that the personality exists independently of the body that contains it and the vitality [soul] that supports it, that it is perdurable and that in the next life it adopts another body" (36).

A matrilineal people, BaKongo commonly say the person is composed of four parts, derived from four matrilineages, the mother's, father's, mother's father's, and father's father's. It appears, however, that the primary contributions are from the mother's and father's people. While the former conveys in the soul a generalized ancestral vitality, the "breath," and certain bodily qualities similarly having to do with reproduction, the latter, the paternal kin, are responsible for the bodily personality or spirit-qualities by which individuals socially realize these maternal powers in actual life. Or so I read MacGaffey: "The power of a personality, its capacity to engage effectively with others, is believed to be derived, in the case of an ordinary human being, from the father, in the form initially of semen, which turns into blood in the mother's womb" (1986, 135).

The observation is capital as an expression of a common rule of exogamous unilineal orders, matrilineal or patrilineal: that the life-giving and death-dealing ancestral powers of one's own line, the social soul of people's inner being, is complemented by the individual outer powers contributed by the in-marrying others—affinal/maternal kin in patrilineal organizations, affinal/paternal kin in matrilineal systems—who compose the bodily powers by which the person manages in life. More precisely, in Kongo and often elsewhere one's own matrilineal kin are also responsible for certain body parts and powers; but they are amorphous and disorganized, except as they are governed and achieved by the superior affinal or patrilineal bodily elements—in particular, the head. The complementary roles and powers of one's lineage and one's affinal lineage are thus played out in the body and career of the person.

MacGaffey spells out two related ways this is organized. In one, the body is divided into upper and lower parts, meeting at the navel and "linked through the values assigned to the head" (1986, 123). The upper part, including the head, is of paternal origin and accordingly the site of the masculine attributes of intelligence, perception, authority, and rigor. The lower part, of maternal origin, "is associated with organic functions, sexuality, emotion, and other 'feminine' attributes regarded (by men) as powerful, obscure, and disorderly" (123). MacGaffey comments that some Kongo psychologists agree with Freud that "'the secrets of the ancestors come from below the navel and emerge above it' as wisdom." In confirmation, the BaKongo ritual practice of shaving "to keep the top of the head clear for spirits that might want to land there" (124). Ritual treatments of the lower body include incisions on the hips to release potency, both in men and women.

By a second conception, the body is divided into three parts: the masculine and paternal head, the feminine and maternal loins, and a mediating region of the shoulders. The shoulders manifest divinatory powers, trembling in the case of possessed persons. The armpits convey blessings, as from father to son (of another lineage). Head hair has spiritual and masculine powers, axillary hair is associated with life transitions as well as blessings, and pubic hair more obviously with sex and reproduction. And so forth: from a lineage standpoint, the individual is bodily endowed with life-potential by his or her "own people," to be realized by the endowments in acumen, strength, valor, and other such spiritual qualities contributed by his or her "other people." Godfrey Lienhardt (1961) observed of neighboring Dinka during the late 1950s: "It is . . . not a simple matter to divide the Dinka believer, for analytic purposes, from what he believes in, and to describe the latter then in isolation from him as the 'object' of his belief. The Dinka themselves imply this when they speak of the Powers as being 'in men's bodies', but also 'in the sky' or other particular places. Their world is not for them an object of study, but an active subject;

hence the world (*piny*) as a whole is often invoked for aid along with other Powers" (155–56).

Aspects and dispositions of the body are not "objects" independent of the subjective forces that they embody. Not to speak loosely of apparently secular capacities as spiritual powers, then, for that is indeed the significance of the display of them, and especially the (political) implication of any differential manifestation of them by particular individuals. Human bodily or intellectual capacities are not exempt from the general rule of the immanence of metahuman powers in things. (Indeed, Greenland Inuit bodies have animating spirits at every joint.) There is no biology, neither of humans or others, where life and personhood extend far beyond anything organic.

Beside the animal and vegetable, are alive the mineral, the artifactual, and even the ineffable: winds, rivers, thunder, mountains, air, stones (well, some stones), fishing nets, ice, and curare. Of course, the human inhabitants of this enchanted universe know lots about bodies, including these other kinds of bodies, in what we would consider a naturalistic way. But their vital principle, the inner force of their health, their growth, their reproduction, and their death is not itself bodily; it is their indwelling "soul." Moreover, the soul or the person of things (the *inua*) is what humans share with the metahuman multitude who are the primary agents and arbiters of this vitality. Spirits in their own right, people are thus known to enter into direct social relations with the many nonhuman spirits, people in their own right: to marry them, raise families with them, play with them, trade with them, feast them, fight them, and more.

Community Relations of People and Spirits

Humans and metahumans engage in a variety of social intercourse, ranging from daily or nightly encounters with spirit-beings, to marriages between humans and metahumans, to festive occasions in which they join together. In the pages that follow, I draw on societies that are distinct in culture just as they are alike in their intercourse with ancestors, species-masters, gods, and other metapersons. I again take the Leachian risk of generalization—perhaps we will learn something new.

The American ethnographer C. A. Valentine (1965) writes of Lakalai of New Britain (Papua New Guinea): "In spite of distinctions in nature and conceptual boundaries, the world of man is thus also a world of spirits. Human beings are frequently in direct or indirect contact with non-human beings, and there is always the possibility that they may encounter such creatures at any time" (194). The contacts are often hostile, which helps explain the usual fragility of marriage between humans and spirits: "There are numerous tales of living men who marry spirit women of various categories, sometimes bringing them to their human communities but more often going to dwell with the spirits. Spirit-beings also capture living human women to be their wives. Only in a few mythological cases do such tales of exile work out happily. Otherwise [in non-mythological cases?] the captive becomes homesick, one of the parties to the arrangement becomes offended, or some other misunderstanding arises. Then the exile returns to his or her previous home" (168).

The formal unions of Achuar men with beautiful water spirit (Tsunki) women in Upper Amazonia are—unlike the Lakalai spirit marriages—highly compatible, if apparently perceived as adulterous (Descola 1994, 124, 282–83). Although the Tsunki water spirits are the source of shamanic powers—they lend their own dangerous familiars, the anaconda and jaguar, to shamans—they are for Achuar the model of domestic tranquility. In their own homes under rivers and lakes, they are not only human in appearance and customs, but in family etiquette and household architecture they provide the norms for Achuar conduct. (Unlike our own homebred social scientific notions of the projection of human social structures and relations onto metahumans, in the anthropology of immanentist cultures it is typically the other way around: spirits are the model for people, rather than people for spirits.) It is not unusual, Descola writes, to hear married men talking freely about their double married life, involving on one hand of a legitimate terrestrial family, and on the other an "adulterine aquatic Tsunki spirit family."

By Descola's report, these are not stories from primordial times, although something like that is a "mythical" topos among related Jivaro peoples. Rather, he heard tell from different men in different places under different circumstances roughly the same account of meeting a very beautiful Tsunki maiden who came out of the water and invited a man to make love. Finding the experience fulfilling, the Achuar man meets the girl regularly, and after a while she invites him underwater to meet her father. Her father turns out to be a majestic man, positioned on an impressive turtle seat in a fine house. He proposes that the Achuar man take his daughter as his legitimate wife. When the latter explains he already has human wives he cannot abandon, the Tsunki father suggests that he divide his time between his land and water families. "Each of the storytellers," Descola relates, "described at length the ensuing double life, naming his water children or boasting of his Tsunki wife's cooking" (1994, 283).

Often the humans who marry spirits are themselves endowed with special spiritual talents as mediums or aspiring shamans, whereupon the spirit-wives or husbands lend themselves to their spouses' social careers. This is apparently true for at least some of the spirit marriages of Kaluli people of the Papua New Guinea Southern Highlands, as described by Edward Schieffelin (2005). The metapersons in question, *ane kalu* or "gone men," include both the dead and others who were never human. Relations between humans and these spirits are generally cordial—unlike the problematic relations between people and kindred spirits in much of Melanesia. Besides dreams, Kaluli rely on mediums for their communication with these spirits. The medium is always a man who married a woman "of the invisible world" in a vision or dream. When he has had a child by her, he is able to leave his body in sleep and walk around in her realm. "At the same time, the people from the invisible world may enter his body as they would a house and converse through his mouth with people assembled for a séance" (97). All the people of the longhouse community gather excitedly for these séances. They ask how the dead are doing, if they have enough to eat, and how to cure their own sick, where their lost pigs might be, and what witches may be creeping about (96–98).

Besides mediums, there are the immanent dead who live among and converse regularly with the living, especially kindred spirits such as the Dobuan "Sir Ghost" and the ancestors of Solomon Island Kwaio. Recall that people talk to their Dobu and Kwaio forebears almost as much as to other people. Roger Keesing notes how even young children quickly construct an idea of these ancestral beings from evidence all around them, "first of all [because] adults *talk* to these beings—to dead parents, grandparents, siblings, or children" (1982, 33). Kwaio souls are double: one component goes to a land of the dead: and another, the "shadow" remains as an ancestral spirit (*adalo*) in the community. The child is taught that the shade of deceased relatives she or he meets in dreams are *adalo*, "ancestors," and from there it appears that the latter are more than a dream, that they are present and perceptible even when one is awake.

There was the time when a whole clan of Mianmin people in the Northern Papua New Guinea Highlands escaped the war party of an enemy group by sheltering inside a mountain with an allied community of the dead. Lest this sound simply "mythical," note that Donald Gardner, who reports it, assured his readers that although the event was unusual, the account is "regarded as an historical narrative by all West Mianmin" (1987, 164). Also of note, the Mianmin dead (*bakel*) have their own proper descendants, those born in the land of the dead; in this case the deceased protagonists consisted of a community of spirits inside Mount Bunie. The nearby living clans, the Ulap and the Ivik, although closely related, had a recent history of sorcery accusations, their antagonism culminating in the treacherous slaughter of the Ivik at a feast to which the Ulap had invited them. When the news came back to the Ivik group, they called for help from their affines and allies and assembled a large raiding party, intending revenge. But they were foiled when the Ulap called upon a spirit group to which they were allied through a strategic exchange of sisters in marriage between an important Ulap man and a big-man of the spirit people. When the latter heard of the danger threatening his Ulap brother-in-law, he suggested it was time they exchanged the pigs they had been raising for each other. The feast the two groups then prepared took place on the day the Ivik raiding party planned to attack. But when the Ulap big-man killed his pig in the manner instructed by his spirit brother-in-law, and the sky darkened as the latter killed his pig in return, both the spirit-pig and the spirit-people became visible to the Ulap. Having cooked their respective pigs, the spirit big-man rubbed all the Ulap with the fat from his, causing them to lose their "heaviness," that is, to become spirits themselves. The two

groups then exchanged their pigs and settled down to eat. The Ivik raiding party came upon the scene, heard the festivities, surrounded the
village, but unaccountably found it empty when they attacked. Twice
more they heard festive singing from various places on the mountain,
but the best they could do was break their axes on a stone from which
the songs were emanating. All of the West Mianmin people know this
is how the Ulap escaped destruction (Gardner 1987, 163–64).

The periodic return of primordial gods or ancestors to renew the
fertility of the country, ensure the food supply, and maintain the health
and reproduction of the population takes the communal relations of
people and spirits to another level—in terms of intensity as well as collectivity. These are typically prolonged annual ceremonies, rituals of the
New Year, set between the dry and rainy seasons, between winter and
spring, or in agricultural societies notably, between the harvest and the
replanting. Often a mandatory period of peace, it is the highpoint of the
year, marked by festivity and levity, song and dance, status inversion,
and in many places, sport.

But all is not simply amusement. Especially as accompanied by heightened sexuality, the celebrations also have ritual effects: as in attracting
the gods, amusing the gods, and evoking their regeneration of the world.
To do this work, the gods appear in various societies in various forms:
embodied in decorated or masked human surrogates; in images; in possessed mediums, priests, or chiefs; or invisibly but making their presence
known by perceptible happenings. The great displays of feasts and valuable goods accompanying the ceremonies are often said (by the people)
to "honor" the gods, the honor indeed being tributary sacrifices to
them—the effect of which would be the people's prosperity in the coming year. Besides, in consuming the food that had been offered and eaten
in essence by the gods, the people ingest some of the divine being and
power. At the end of the festivities, the gods may be perfunctorily sent
back to their places, leaving the people free to reap the fruits of their
generative passage—another testimony, this, of a certain ambivalence in
the relations of humans and the metahuman powers that be.

"Despite the ultimate seriousness in the aim of these ceremonies,
there is no uniform tone of awe on the ceremonial ground," reports

American anthropologist Nancy Munn about Walbiri of the Central Australian desert. "On the contrary, Walbiri performances are usually casual, filled with joking, sexual allusions, conversation, and banter" (Munn 1973, 185). Also mentioned for Walbiri by Mervyn Meggitt (1962, 226), one wonders if the levity is not a prescribed aspect of these fertility ceremonies (*banba*). Held in secluded areas of the bush, the *banba* renewal ceremonies involve large numbers of men divided in two intermarrying groups (moieties): one, the "masters," performing ancestral songs and dances; the other, the "workers," having ornamented the performers' bodies with highly symbolic designs. Meggitt reports that in the mid-1950s as many as four hundred to five hundred people gathered for combined circumcision and *banba* ceremonies.

In her own marvelous study, *Walbiri Iconography* (1973), based in the same period, Munn uncovers a fundamental relation between the graphic designs covering the dancers and the fertilizing powers by the ancestor: a relation that transforms the dancers into surrogates of the ancestor, and the songs and dances of the renewal ceremonies into the well-being of the country. The same term, *guruwari*, denotes both the pertinent designs and the ancestor's potency. Walbiri ancestors emerged from the ground in the primordial Dreamtime and wandered through the country creating its topographical features as well as rain, fire, wild oranges, yams, humans, kangaroos, and just about everything else—which, upon the ancestors going to ground, still embody them. Each patrilineal lodge or descent group has a number of ancestors, consisting of all whose ancient tracks intersect in their territory. By embodying especially the important ones in banda ceremonies, the members of the group maintain the fertility of the country—the wild yams, the kangaroos, and not least, the people. Here is where *guruwari* designs come into play. Munn explains: *guruwari* "is the name for graphic designs representing the ancestors (primarily designs owned by men) and may be extended more generally to any visual sign or visual embodiment of ancestors such as footprints, topographical features resulting from their imprints or metamorphoses, ceremonial paraphernalia, or design-marked sacred boards and stones left by them in the ground" (28–29).

Effectively then, *guruwari* as sign equals *guruwari* as ancestral potency. Enspirited with primordial power, the designs are themselves
instrumental. "This effective vitality of designs may bring about the
achievement of specific, objective ends such as nourishing children, attracting a lover, maintaining the fertility and supplies of species, and so
on" (55). Just so, the worker-moiety men hiding the bodies of lodge
members with ancestral designs in *banba* fertility ceremonies thus
transform them into active Dreamtime ancestors. "You mak'em father
[ancestor]. I want to eat." So a lodge member may call on a worker of
the opposite moiety to prepare the paraphernalia of the ceremonies.
And then in the performances, the ancestor "gets up" (as from sleep),
he is "pulled out" (from the country). In the event, "the ceremonial
constructions reembody the ancestor and as part of this process aid in
continuing the supply of kangaroos in the country; that is, in effect, they
reembody the kangaroos as well" (186).

The gods and the dead descend often from the heavens to the villages
of Araweté in the Middle Xingu region of the Amazon. They come for
the feasts following the taking of many larger game animals; they come
constantly in the small hours of the morning in the songs shamans intone
in the voice of the gods—by which means the deities largely rule the
people. All collective ceremonies are banquets of the gods and the dead,
as Brazilian anthropologist Eduardo Viveiros de Castro (1992) observes
in his remarkable study of Araweté. After the gods have invisibly eaten,
the people consume the substance, "the ex-food of the gods" (126). The
feasts thus have a sacrificial structure—with an immediate return to the
people in the form of the consecrated offering for their own consumption (75). The great feast of the year, the "Feast of Strong Beer," comes
after the end of the five or six months of the dry season, during which
Araweté have been living in villages, hunting and harvesting their maize
gardens. Soon they will begin clearing new gardens in preparation for
dispersing into the forest in family groups during the rainy season.

As the culmination of the annual ceremonial cycle, the "Strong Beer"
feast, however, will not only unite the village of its familial sponsor (the
"owner"), but uniquely attract other villages of the territory or "tribe,"
making it "the occasion when the group experiences its greatest physical

density" (Viveiros de Castro 1992, 93). (There will certainly be "collective efflorescence," but, *pace* Durkheim, the frenetic sociality does not sediment itself in a totem.) For many weeks before the festival, with increasing intensity as it approaches, bodies of men dance into the deep night "to make the beer heat up," that is, to effect the fermentation of the maize brew (93). Then, for some twenty days before the great inebriated dance at the height of the festival, the men are out hunting. On the eve of their return, the gods and the dead descend from the sky to the patio of the festival sponsor where they will partake of the beer. They are escorted to the scene and served one by one by a shaman, who is smoking and singing violently, having taken the position of the gods as well as their server, and manifesting an inebriated staggering and jolting (125).

The night of the festival is a dangerous time, as the gods are infuriated by the light of the fires and knock the village shamans down with their invisible lightning bolts. Dancing in warrior diadems of macaw feathers, the men in this way among others give the occasion a militant meaning, but in light of the forthcoming gardening season, the sexual aspects of the festival seem especially significant. The leader of the divine procession from the heavens is one Yičire očo, "a lascivious divinity who . . . always comes accompanied by a female soul" (126). (The gods marry deceased human women; they are in-laws of the living.) And more generally: "The beer festival . . . has a strong erotic tinge. Araweté say that the days after the festival are witness to intense sexual activity, for the drink causes hunger and sexual desire" (131). The hunger is satisfied by the smoked meat from the long hunt, and then they dance.

Dancing, feasting, and fornicating are also hallmarks of the Trobriand Islands' *milamala*, the annual festival of the return of the dead, well known and often remarked by anthropologists since first described by Bronislaw Malinowski (1948, 148–54). But the *milamala* is hardly the only time the Islanders encountered the *baloma*, the ancestral souls, for all these spirits' usual invisibility. Not only would the *baloma* visit their native villages from time to time, but living Trobriand Islanders might come upon them in their own communities on or beneath the extant isle of Tuma—only ten miles north of Kiriwina, the main island of the Trobriand archipelago. "All my informants from Omarakana [the village of the Kiriwina paramount chief] and the neighboring villages knew Tuma quite well," Malinowski reports (160), providing several examples of people physically meeting up with spirits there, among the many stories he had heard tell. Others regularly visited Tuma in dreams and trances. (In a version of the classic dissent of the Omaha skeptic, "Two Crows denies it" [Barnes 1984], at least some of Malinowski's interlocutors accused others of feigning such contacts in order to gain material advantages from their offices as seers.)

The *milamala* itself involved the mass movement of the ancestors from Tuma to their original villages, where they joined their matrilineal kin in festivities that lasted several weeks. The ceremonies coincided with the waxing of the moon following on the major yam harvest (August or September), though they might begin some days before the new moon, building to a crescendo of drumming and dancing at the full moon, to end in something of a whimper two days later, when the *baloma* were drummed back to Tuma. Although Malinowski claims the festival had no explicit connection to the growth of the gardens, he does note that if the ancestors were displeased by the meagerness of the *milamala* feasts, they would visit drought and destruction on the next year's crop—resulting in another poor *milamala*, more drought, and so on, in something of a vicious circle. In a recent comprehensive synthesis of anthropological writings on Trobriand Islanders' relations to *baloma*, however, Mark Mosko identifies the *milamala* as a New Year rite, "marked by activities expressive of fertility and sexuality . . . understood to be efficacious for productivity and generativity of gardens and women in the coming year" (2017, 195).

Sometimes known to camp on the beach during the *milamala*, but more commonly to live in the villages, the *baloma* made their presence felt by unusual spates of falling coconuts (which they were plucking), by intensified appearances in people's dreams, and if displeased with the performances or the sacrifices, by raining on the ceremonies. In any event, their ubiquity was evidenced by the taboos imposed during the period to shield them from injury: prohibitions on spilling hot fluids or cutting wood within the village, playing about with spears or sticks, or throwing missiles. For the most part, however, the *baloma* were seated on platforms built especially for them, from which they viewed and enjoyed the feasting and dancing. Or more precisely, platforms from which they consumed the spiritual substance of the feasts abundantly displayed as sacrifices set before them: two major village feasts at beginning and end, the waning and waxing of the moon, and daily meals provided there or in their relatives' houses. The foods of the major feasts were not eaten afterward by the providers but were reciprocally distributed by them to relatives or friends for their respective consumption. The sacrificed foods of ordinary meals were apparently consumed by the relatives who supplied them, as in the normal ritual practices of domestic meals. Mosko makes an observation of major significance about this ex-food of the gods. Having consumed the "shadow" of the food, the *baloma* leave a residue in the form of their saliva, which, when then consumed with the food by humans, enspirits them with divine power (*peu'ula*). Mosko recalls conversations on the matter: "Without the 'hot' . . . input of the spirits' . . . images incorporated in our meals through their depositions of *bubwalua* [saliva], the foods, however they were prepared, would have only minimal capacity or strength (*peu'ula*) for fueling human labors and existence generally. The eating of food by humans in any amounts without the benefit of the spirits' *bubwalua* is considered barely, if at all, sufficient . . . to sustain human life" (2017, 180).

Similarly, for the important goods offered to the spirits: the sweat the latter deposit on these Trobriand treasures, apparently including *kula*-trade valuables (*veguwa*), gives such riches their exchange and political value. The gods are thus doing what the people do. (Although the ideology is that the gods and people mutually feed each other, it does not appear that the former starve to death if they are neglected; at least in the short term they are the stronger for it, unleashing bad weather, even dreaded droughts, on their undutiful kin.) By the communion with the gods, the sacrifices of the *milamala*—as indeed the offerings that precede ordinary meals as well—thereby have immediate benefits for humans, as they are in this way endowed with divine powers of production and reproduction. Through the *milamala* period, as villages meet to dance and feast with each other, sexuality increases in the artistic and the actual performance, evidently with a proportionate loosening of exogamic rules. Accordingly, it is not just the fertility of the coming crops that will benefit, but the overall fertility of the people.

The *milamala* began with drumming, and the beat continued through the waxing of the moon. (In the mid-1950s, during the prolonged Christmas and New Year festivities—the "time of joy" [*gauna ni marau*]—in a large Fijian village, I had the similar experience of noisy sleepless nights as Malinowski had in the comparable *milamala* of Kiriwina. Only the young women and children, some gaily dressed, who were marching around the village were beating sheets of tin rather than drums.) At the full moon in the Trobriands, however, the beat changes to one recognizable as the send-off of the *baloma*. In Malinowski's day the exit was unceremonious as the gods were escorted to the road to Tuma by a small raggedy band, mostly of young children. The gods are gone but they are not. They are constantly brought to the assistance of people in spells (*megwa*); and recall, there are spells for practically everything. They are doing what the people do in gardening, canoe making, lovemaking, baby making, kula trading, woodcarving, curing, fishing, witching, sorcerizing. There is a realm and existence of the god, Tuma, as distinct from the existence of the living, called Boyowa—Mosko speaks of them as two different "worlds." But as the perpetual force in human affairs, the potentiating agency of human success and failure, Tuma is immanent in Boyowa. Or as Mosko sets forth in a capital passage, worthy of citing at length:

> Tuma . . . is not some place physically distant from Boyowa. Rather, in the view of Omarkanans, it is the hidden, invisible, "inner" . . . dimension of the universe, interpenetrating the visible, material, "external" . . . world of Boyowa so that the two realms coincide. This is how humans, animals, plants, physical features of the world, and so on, in their material manifestations can exist outwardly in Boyowa, yet harbor inwardly the *momova* [vitality] of Tuma. . . . The two realms are not spatially distant from each other . . . They coincide. It is through this intimate, simultaneous, coterminous mystical connection of the two realms, the visible and the invisible, that living humans of Boyowa are able to communicate and interact with ancestral and other spirits. (2017, 121)

As they say, examples could be multiplied. Indeed, many times over in the pages of the twelve-volume, third edition of Sir James George Frazer's *Golden Bough* ([1911–15] 2012). A brief notice of the *milamala* itself appears in volume six, in a section on the "Feasts of All Souls" (6: 51–84). Frazer begins with British missionary George Brown's (1910, 237) notice of the Trobriand *milamila* in his book about Pacific island cultures. As an annual festival celebrating the return of the ancestors and/or the gods, thus often coinciding with the rites of the New Year, the *milamala* in Kiriwina shares this space of All Souls with a variety of immanentist societies, a number of which Frazer does not precisely identify: Alaska "Esquimaux" of the Yukon; certain Amerindians of California and Mexico; Sumba of eastern Indonesia; "Sea Dayaks" (Iban) of Sarawak; Nagas of Assam and certain peoples of Bengal and Central India; some hill tribes of Burma; "Cambodians"; peoples of Northern Vietnam ("Tonquin") and Central Vietnam ("Annam"); "Cochin China" (Laos?); a Caucasus group; "Armenians"; Dahomey; two Abyssinian peoples; ancient Persians (Achaemenids); and numerous folk all over western Eurasia. (*The Golden Bough* is the world champion of the "among the" books, not unlike this one, except that Frazer was a transcendentalist, while the selective documentation of ethnographic examples here is driven by an account of immanentism.)

Often, as for Trobriand Islanders, the New Year rite is also a celebration of the harvest, and the ceremonies last for several days or even many weeks. Elaborate feasts and valuable gifts as well as daily provision are offered to the returning dead, who come either as invisible presences or as personated by the living, to be honored as well by dances, songs, and perhaps games, until after a period they are peremptorily, but more often ceremoniously, escorted back to their homes. Ceremoniously as in Sumba, when

> a little before daybreak the invisible guests take their departure. All the people turn out of their houses to escort them a little way. Holding in one hand the half of a coco-nut, which contains a small packet of provisions for the dead, and in the other a piece of smouldering wood, they march in procession, singing a drawling song to the accompaniment of

a gong and waving the lighted brands in time to the music. So they move through the darkness till with the last words of the song they throw away the coco-nuts and the brands in the direction of the spirit-land, leaving the ghosts to wend their way thither, while they themselves return to the village. (Frazer [1911–15] 2012, 6: 55–56)

Apparently they have left behind their blessings for the coming period, as in the many references to celebratory New Year and harvest or first-fruit rituals the world around scattered through Frazer's volumes (see especially "The Sacrifice of First-Fruits" [8: 109ff.] and "The Saturnalia and Kindred Festivals" [9: 306ff.]).

Also often testified as prelude or part of the New Year celebrations are encounters with spirits of another sort: demons or other "evil spirits," which must be driven out of society, or so that the world may be purified and renewed (see especially "The Public Expulsion of Evils" [9: 109ff.]). This exorcism of evil spirits is in many ways the opposite of reverential treatment of the visiting divinities. Whereas the gods and ancestors are invited into human society from their celestial or other homes, to be honored and feted with a view toward enlisting their beneficial powers, the pestilent demons and accumulated evils of the year are reviled and driven from society.

In Frazer's account of the Iroquois New Year, "on one day of the festival the ceremony of driving away evil spirits from the village took place." It seems that humans personated other greater animal beings to do so: "Men clothed in the skins of wild beasts, their faces covered with hideous masks, and their hands with the shell of the tortoise, went from hut to hut making frightful noises; in every hut they took fuel from the fire and scattered the embers and ashes about the floor with their hands. The general confession of sins which preceded the festival was probably a preparation for the public expulsion of evil influences" (9: 127). (*Nota bene*: the extinction of domestic fires, the scattering of the old ashes, and the ritual rekindling of new fire is a feature of traditional New Year rites in Polynesia and elsewhere.) The Iroquois drama of the expulsion of evil is part of what Frazer calls "a kind of saturnalia," a "time of general license," when people were out of their senses, breaking all kinds of social norms. As in the Roman Saturnalia, which was for Frazer the prototype of New Year festivals (of which the descendants are the European carnivals), society as constituted was effectively dissolved.

Or rather, as in the Roman Saturnalia, in conjunction with the return of the ancient god, all manner of political and economic distinctions were abolished in a lawless frenzy, with the effect of the reconstitution of the society as *communitas*, or a primordial *civitas* of equals under a lord of misrule, here the autochthonous god Saturn (cf. on European carnival, Bakhtin [1984, 6–8, ch. 3]; P. Sahlins [1994]). (I risk: in any chiefly or kingly system, as the reigning dynasty is characteristically foreign by origin, the annual return to the original god and communal society takes the form of a ritual rebellion of the underlying indigenous people. We miss you, David Graeber. [Graeber and Sahlins 2017].) The New Year rituals do not necessarily entail this return to the origins, but they often include saturnalian episodes, such as the suspensions or inversion of hierarchical ranks, laughter and pranks, drunkenness, wild and amoral behaviors, including heightened or orgiastic sexuality. Some of that, as noted, attended the Trobriand *milamala*, a festival that Mark Mosko (2017, 195–96) compared to the Hawaiian New Year rite, the Makahiki—which itself, as the joyously celebrated return of the primeval agricultural god Lono, compares well with the Roman Saturnalia.

In the Makahiki, the advent of Lono is preceded, and as it were made possible, by a *communitas* at once of sex and society. The night before the god appears, the people in general, sated on sacrificial meats (pig for men, dog for women) and drunk on kava, indulge in a variety of blasphemous doings and cursing. The social leveling is realized when commoners and nobles together enter the ocean where, as the Hawaiian Catholic Kepelino writes, "one person was attracted to another and the result was by no means good" (1932, 96; cf. Valeri 1985, 200ff.). When they finally emerge from their revels at dawn, there on the beach is the image of Lono, about to begin his renewed sovereignty of the kingdom. Circling the island in state, Lono receives the tributary offerings of the people in district after district, leaving them in his wake to continue their merriments. Coming at the winter solstice to renew the world and the society, the Makahiki is indeed similar to New Year rituals elsewhere, besides the Saturnalia. Likewise widely reported is the accompanying renewal of human rule, chiefly or kingly, upon submission to ritual humiliation by the god or defeat in ritual battle by the god's popular party. In Hawai'i, the erstwhile human king, heretofore in seclusion, comes in from the sea—he is thus a foreigner—to be ritually speared by a partisan of Lono, at which moment he becomes (again) the king. The ancient regime of the god gives way to human authority, but only on the condition of the submission of the latter to the former. The king rules by subjugation to the god.

A similar scenario of royal submission to the god occurs in Frazer's account of the old Babylonian New Year rite, the Akitu Festival, lasting eleven days, probably including Spring equinox. The Akitu ceremonies honored Marduk, the principal god of Babylon, and were focused on his great temple of Esagila in the center of the city:

> For here, in a splendid chamber of the vast edifice, all the gods were believed to assemble at this season under the presidency of Marduk for the purpose of determining the fates for the new year, especially the fate of the king's life. On this occasion the king of Babylon was bound annually to renew his regal power by grasping the hands of the image of Marduk in his temple, as if to signify that he received the kingdom directly from the deity and was unable without divine assistance and authority to retain it for more than a year. Unless he thus formally reinstated himself on the throne once a year, the king ceased to reign legitimately. (Frazer [1911–15] 2012, 9: 356)

In immanentist cultures, the gods, ancestors, and other metaperson denizens of the cosmos are not only occasional visitors; for all their distance and invisibility, they are also and ever present in human affairs, ever on call. People couldn't live without the immanent metaperson beings and forces that invisibly power their endeavors, making them efficacious or, too often, fruitless. If the gods are doing what people do, they are present, for all their distance, as an integral part of human existence, even as they manage their own affairs. Partible beings, the gods are present for all that they are distant; they are potent agents of humans' fate for all that they are unseen.

3

Metapersons

And by the trait of the human mind noticed by Tacitus, whatever these men saw, imagined, or even made or did themselves they believed to be Jove; and to all of the universe that came within their scope, and to all its parts, they gave the being of animate substance. This is the civil history of the expression "All things are full of Jove."

—GIAMBATTISTA VICO, *THE NEW SCIENCE*, 1744 (1968, 118)

THE COMPLEMENT OF human finitude is a spiritual multitude: "All things are full of Jove." Quite beyond Tacitus's put-down of the ancient Germans who see the "mysterious presence" of gods in groves and trees "only with the eye of devotion," Vico is speaking of an original age of religion in which whatever humans "saw, imagined or even made themselves" is made and animated by the agency of an indwelling divinity. But then "Jove"—the gods, the spirits—has the qualities of human persons, if also powers that exceed them. It is a world filled with other-than-human persons endowed with greater-than-human powers. Such is the enchanted universe of the cultures of immanence.

Here is a thought experiment that may help us, the presumably disenchanted ones, understand the enchanted universe of immanentist, enspirited cultures. Suppose all the "magical" things that make our current lives—all the appurtenances, meaningful and technical, whose substance and forces we did not make ourselves—were recognized by and as their humanized effects. Suppose they were proper subjects with real agency. Suppose the books and newspapers we read, the smart phones and computers we use, the radios we hear, the television sets we watch, the flags that distinguish us, the Michigan football team or Chicago Cubs baseball team whose wins and losses we can feel as our own, the turkey that makes our Thanksgiving and the spruce tree that makes our Christmas (some of us), the car that transports us, the ignition key that starts a powerful motor, the parents who though now dead come to us in dreams and in the house and the furniture they left us: suppose all these things and more that constitute our existence were known for just that, for their human or subjective influence rather than by their naturalistic attributes. The newspapers "teach" or "inform"" us about people and events in some distant place we did not see in a recent past we did not live, but all of which we imagine to be "real" and to have "really happened." That is what we call "myth" when peoples without newspapers do the like—perhaps even knowing that the narrative itself has the persons-powers to "teach" about what the ancestor-persons and god-persons did. We look at the television set which by some extraordinary powers brings us images of persons and things that we understand to be real existents, real persons and images—but as in René Magritte's surrealist masterpiece, even this is not a pipe. Subjectively speaking, how different is that from the people, things, and events we see in dreams—and are real enough when we are dreaming?

It is not as if we did not live ourselves in a world largely populated by nonhuman persons. I am an emeritus professor of the University of Chicago, an institution (cum personage) which "prides itself" on its "commitment" to serious scholarship, for the "imparting" of which it "charges" undergraduate students a lot of money, the Administration "claiming" this is "needed" to "grow" the endowment, and in return for which it "promises" to "enrich" the students' lives by "making" them into intellectually and morally superior persons. The University of Chicago is some kind of superior person itself, or at least the Administration "thinks" it is. Then there are corporations that have the legal qualities of persons themselves, with disastrous effects upon the body politics. I read in a recent single daily issue of the *New York Times* that: "Ruble hopes to join ranks of dollar and euro"; "G.O.P. weighs limiting clout of right wing"; "While Nepal's main political parties disagree fiercely . . . the embrace of democracy is now widely shared"; "Food companies claim victory"; "Iowa town's vote delivers rebuke"; "Rwanda has repeatedly spoken out against the Security Council"; and "[The Turkish government] is torn between its Islamist sympathies and its desire to become a member of the European Union." Or as the eminent Eduardo Viveiros de Castro once remarked, whatever is not marked for naturalistic explanation passes by default as anthropomorphism. There are persons everywhere. Long after the first Axial Age (800–300 BCE) and despite the transcendentalism of the second (15th–18th centuries), the world is still pretty much full of Jove; as Bruno Latour would say, we have never been modern (Latour 1993).

So it is in immanentist cultures: personhood is virtually everywhere and in almost everything. The universe is full of persons from whom emanate forces that constitute the world as objectifications of their intentions. Notice in our thought experiment that not only were things such as rubles or radios in effect animated by indwelling persons, but so were food companies, nations, and governments themselves active subjects and agents. Claude Lévi-Strauss retells an incident reported by Canadian ethnologist Diamond Jenness, apropos of the spiritual place masters or "bosses" known to Native Americans as rulers of localities, but who generally kept out of sight of people. "They are like the government in Ottawa, an old Indian remarked. An ordinary Indian can never see the 'government.' He is sent from one office to another, is introduced to this man and to that, each of whom sometimes claims to be the 'boss,' but he never sees the real government, who keeps himself hidden" (1966, 239n).

Not to forget, then, that spirits such as species-masters and Jove are themselves human in nature. The Christian God is three persons: God the Father who was never human; Jesus who was born and lived as a human before he was translated back to his Father in heaven; and the Holy Ghost, who may be literally a ghost-person or else a divine afflatus or spiritual power as such. Viveiros de Castro, speaking to his own field study of Amazonian Araweté people, notes the inclusion of "the various races of spirits" in the concept of *bïde*, whose principal meaning is

"human being," or "people." "There is no way to distinguish unequivo-
cally between humans and what we would call spirits, a notion that covers very heterogeneous beings." If it is necessary in certain contexts to
differentiate the spirits as nonhuman persons, one can so modify the
locution to mean "similar to humans." What characterizes all such beings
as we would call spirits, Viveiros de Castro observes, is that they have a
certain shamanic power, *ipeye hã*. Or is it not the other way around, that
the shamans have spirit-power? "Actually, since *ipeye hã* is inherent in
such beings, it may be better to invert the definition and say that the
shamans (*peye*) are endowed with a spiritual potency" (1992, 64).

What immediately follows here are notes on the variety of metaperson forms—animistic spirits, demons, ghosts and ancestors, species
and place masters, and high gods and others—commonly populating
the universe of cultures of immanence. As presented here, the catalog
is not complete, but it does include many of those spirit-beings prominent in the cosmos of these cultures. Many or all may well be co-present
in the same cosmic society. When all is said and done, it will be seen
that widely different cultural orders are similar in this regard.

Just so, the cosmology of the ancient Sumerians proves not that different from the universe of Inuit: "Ordinary kitchen salt is to us an inanimate substance, a mineral. To the Mesopotamian of the third millennium BC it was a fellow-being whose help might be sought if one had
fallen victim to sorcery or witchcraft. . . . As Salt, a fellow-creature with
special powers, can be approached directly, so can Grain. . . . Both Salt
and Grain are thus not the inanimate substances for which we know
them. They are alive, have personality and a will of their own" (Jacobsen
[1946] 1977, 130–31). Not only Salt and Grain, but any phenomenon in
the Mesopotamian world could be approached as a "spirit" as well as
humdrum practical object—a prime example of animism.

Animism

The Achuar do not see the supernatural as a level of reality separate
from nature, for all of nature's beings have some features in common
with mankind, and the laws they go by are more or less the same as

those governing civil society. Humans and most plants, animals, and meteors are persons (*aents*) with a soul (*wakan*) and an individual life. (Descola 1994, 93)

[Among Greenland Inuit there is] the belief that in every natural object there dwells a particular being, called its *inua* (that is, its owner)—a word which, characteristically enough, signified originally human being or Eskimo. According to the Eskimos, every stone, mountain, glacier, river, lake, has its *inua*; the very air has one. It is still more remarkable to find that even abstract conceptions have their *inue*; they speak for example of the *inua* of particular instincts or passions. (Nansen 1893, 225)

Report on the Australian wildfires of January 2010: "It's like the fire is a sentient being. It feels like it's coming to get us." (*New York Times*, 11 January 2020)

From the *New Yorker* magazine of the same date: "This is only one snapshot of the Haiti that will commemorate the tenth anniversary of its most catastrophic natural disaster this Sunday. For some Haitians, in addition to navigating the country's current and chronic problems, the anniversary might make them feel as though they're still being attacked, both literally and figuratively, by the soil. This is how one older family member who survived the earthquake once described the early, single-digit anniversaries to me. This is how I imagine one younger relative might have felt after losing several toes to part of a collapsed wall in the earthquake, only to nearly die again last year after being shot by another young man who wanted his motorcycle." (Danticat 2020)

As commonly understood, "animism" refers to cultural schemes of subjective presences in empirical entities. Within the physical bodies of things, whether animate or inanimate (by our lights), are indwelling somethings with more or less the same subjective capacities as human persons. The embodied presence generally goes by the same name and character of the human "soul"; or so Western observers have typically described the indigenous concept. The notion of "soul" here is more like

Aristotle's rational soul and might be even better described as "mind," involving such capacities as consciousness, intentionality, will, communicative abilities, and other such powers of intellection and volition. The aforementioned Inuit notion of the *inua* of "every object," as Franz Boas reports, referring to "the person" of the entity to which it is affixed, seems a better description of animistic subjectivity. Or as Knud Rasmussen characterizes the notion: "The personifications of such dissimilar things as fire, stone, a precipice, a feasting house and such like; these spirits are then referred to as the inua, the owner or lord, of the stone or house" (1929, 204). Animism is the personhood of things.

By the traditions of many Native Americans, some New Guineans, and several others, the various animal and plant species were human in origin; and although they subsequently acquired their current bodies, they remain human in essence. It is not unusual for animistic beings or things, even such as the sun or snow, to appear as humans in people's dreams and shamanic séances (e.g., Brown and Brightman 1988, 35, 37). Some are known to change into humans, and vice versa (e.g., Lienhardt 1961, 117). As it were, the person is the phenomenal thing in itself, the noumena, except that unlike this Kantian notion, the thing in itself is knowable precisely because it is a person. Not only a knowable, but also a sociable being with whom people interact in human terms—which is hardly mere fantasy. Thus dreamwork, indispensable to the success of worldy human endeavor, reveals the human dependency on what only the gods can provide.

In any given culture of immanence, virtually anything and almost everything may be a nonhuman person: not only animals and plants, but stones, streams, winds, fire, sun, stars, cliffs—any or all may have their inner *inua* (here used as a technical term). Indeed, it is said of Inuit that their cosmology "is an almost complete animism. Everything seems to have a soul-spirit. Geographical features, all the animals (except the dog, in some areas), lamp, entranceway and other items of structures and furnishings, tools, clothing, all have souls" (Lantis 1950, 320). There is a little soul in every part of a Greenland Inuit's body; if any part is ill, it is because the soul has abandoned it (Thalbitzer 1909, 450). The early twentieth-century Russian ethnographer Waldemar Bogoras cites a shaman of Siberian Chukchee to similar effect: "All that exists lives. The lamp walks around. The walls of the house have voices of their own. Even the chamber-vessel has a separate land and house. . . . The antlers lying on the tombs arise at night and walk in procession around the mounds, while the deceased get up and visit the living" (1904–9, 281). In the night, Bogoras was told, skins ready for sale turn into reindeer and walk about; trees in the forest talk to one another. "Even the shadows on the wall constitute definite tribes and have their own country, where they live in huts and subsist by hunting" (281).

One is reminded of Plato's famous allegory of the cave in *The Republic*, wherein Socrates discourses on the futility of human knowing. Humans are like prisoners chained in a cave facing the back wall, where all they see are the projected shadows of things passing in front of a fire behind them; and being so bound, they mistake the shadows for reality. Anthropologists, sensitive to the immanent character of the societies in question, are not Platonic philosophers who come to liberate people from their epistemological chains. To the contrary, as ethnographers we come to describe a cultural reality in which people know and relate to shadows and such as beings like themselves. We are the ethnographers of the caves, each a distinct world in itself.

Siberian shadows are a form of animism that Viveiros de Castro instructively describes in the Amazonian context as "perspectivism" (1998; 2004a; 2004b; 2015). The world

is peopled by different types of subjective agencies, human as well as nonhuman, each endowed with the same generic type of soul, that is, the same set of cognitive and volitional capacities. The possession of a similar soul implies the possession of similar concepts [that is, a similar culture], which determine that all subjects see things in the same way . . . What changes when passing from one species of subject to another is the "objective correlative," the referent of these concepts: what jaguars see as "manioc beer" (the proper drink of people, jaguar-type or otherwise), humans see as "blood." Where we see a muddy salt-lick on a river bank, tapirs see their big ceremonial house, and so on. Such difference of perspective—not a plurality of views of a single world, but a single view of different worlds—cannot derive from the soul, since the latter is the common original ground of being. Rather, such difference is located in the bodily differences between species, for the body . . . is the site and instrument of ontological differentiation and referential disjunction. (Viveiros de Castro 2015, 58–59)

Just so, Siberian mice are people living in underground houses, whose reindeer are what humans see as the roots of certain plants and the sleds they use for hunting are certain grasses. Chukchee say that by some power of transformation, the mice can suddenly become real hunters with real sleds, out for polar bear. But when it comes to carrying the game home, the sleds return to their original size and the bears become lemmings (Bogoras 1904–09, 283–84). We are not told what the mice make of their percepts of human hunting, but we do know that the "evil spirits" or ke'let that shamans attack, see shamans as ke'let or evil spirits themselves (295). Likewise, for the relations between Tifalmin and the kamiopmin, the "cassowary men" of the deep mountain forests, in the Mountain Ok region of New Guinea. "The Kamiopmin have a peculiar characteristic: though men perceive them to be cassowaries, in fact, they are actually human beings identical in society and culture to Tifalmin. They merely appear to human eyes as cassowaries. Reciprocally the Kamiopmin see Tifalmin as cassowaries, not with human form. Nor do they see Tifalmin villages" (Wheatcroft 1976, 154–55; emphasis original). Here as elsewhere the universe is peopled by different types of subjective entities—so many peoples, different in bodily hexis, united in a cultural nexus.

Although it may be said that "all that exists, lives," it need not be supposed, even of societies characterized as "animist," that personhood is necessarily universal, internal to all perceptible phenomena. This seems unlikely a priori, since it is humanly impossible to exhaust the description of a society's habitat, given the endless potential distinctions that can be made, and innumerable "objects" thus discerned. The trees may have their inua, their indwelling persons, but do the leaves, or the red or yellow leaves of autumn? Not all stones are alive, the Ojibwa man told the anthropologist, but *some* are (Hallowell 1960, 24). Moreover, some phenomena may have more personhood than others, may have more human attributes. Distant stars might be of little interest and proportionately little humanity; whereas shooting stars or thunder, in mediating between heaven and earth, are likely saying things to people (34). Among Rmeet, a Mon-Khmer people of upland Laos, the German anthropologist Guido Sprenger (2016) describes a continuum of diminishing person-qualities, from humans through buffaloes, pigs, chickens, and finally eggs (78). The scope of animism is thus relative to the cultural scheme. It is, as it were, a question of "personhood for all cultural purposes": not only practical purposes, of course, but also, ritual, medicinal, musical, social, political, and "mythical" purposes as well. Anything may be or become a person, and all those phenomenal entities meaningfully at play in the life of the given people are actually persons.

For Chewong of the Malay Peninsula, subsisting largely by hunting and gathering, the species of trees that have spirits (*ruwai*) with consciousness include: two that are among the tallest in the forest and are featured in "myths"; one or two used to make cloth and dart poison (the dart poison itself has a very strong spirit, or *ruwai*, that has to be protected from getting lost or killed); also the bamboo used for masculine blowpipes and another type for feminine quivers; and all leaves, roots, plants, and trees used for medicines. "It thus appears," Norwegian anthropologist Signe Howell (1989) writes in her excellent ethnography of Chewong cosmology, "that all plants which are somehow useful to humans are attributed with consciousness. 'They want to help us' (*to-logn*), it is said" (133).

In the same connection, Signe Howell speaks to the instability of the animist catalog, the contextual variation in the spiritual status of the elements, based on corresponding variations in their human values. Two important fruiting trees, for example, are spirits only when they are blossoming or fruiting. Also exemplary of the kind of variability, or indeed creative flexibility, of animist practices in many societies are Chewong "leaf people," the individual "spirit-guides" acquired in dreams, of whom most adult men have at least one. Taking the form of beautiful women in encounters with humans, these personages may be the spirits of species of plants, trees, or animals—or for that matter any thing one may experience. Howell heard of one man whose spirit-guide was a Japanese airplane (1989, 103).

Across the Pacific, the vision quests of Native American youths—famously in the Great Plains—could likewise lead to a lifelong alliance with the spirit-person of virtually anything. The Omaha scholar Francis La Flesche, the first Native American anthropologist, writing with the ethnologist Alice Cunningham Fletcher in the early twentieth century, reported of his people that the individual guardian spirit could be anything animate or inanimate. Characteristically also, the spirit was sent upon supplication to an all-pervasive greater power, here the well-known source of vitality and mobility, Wakonda (Fletcher and La Flesche [1911] 1992, 1: 128–33; 2: 597–600). And if anything in the human habitat may have the indwelling qualities of persons, then can we not say, following Descola's observation on Achuar, that humanity as a condition is the ontological ground of the phenomenal world? Even things which are not physical hosts of inner persons may be defined on the same grounds: that is, as individual nonpersons, literally and figuratively nonentities. (Which also poses an important question of immanentism as a cultural order: For all cultural purposes in the societies at issue, are there even "things"—as such? The implications for a cosmic economics marked by intersubjectivity are critical. We will need to rewrite economics itself, to describe an "economy without things," itself informed by the cosmic intercourse between humans and metahumans).

The question is made more intriguing by the presence of persons in things that are not their own spirit-selves but manifestations of encompassing metapersons, such as gods or totems. In traditional Hawai'i, certain plants, animals, cardinal directions, colors, clouds, days of the month, and much more were so many "myriad bodies" (kino lau) of one or the other of the ruling gods. Similarly, if in a mode of divine power as a free-ranging deity, the just-mentioned Wakonda of the Omaha was a universal source of vitality, capable of making anything, especially anything remarkable, into an enspirited agent. One might very well include these avatars of divinity in the class of animistic beings—in which case, insofar as the encompassing beings are also persons-in-themselves, the animism is doubled. For the most part, however, it will be useful to reserve the discussion of these variations on animism for later; here, I will speak to only one such complex of animist forms, mainly to give an initial sense of the metahuman plenitude of an enchanted universe.

It concerns a people already introduced in these pages, Manambu of the Middle Sepik region of New Guinea, as studied by the Irish anthropologist Simon Harrison. Here is a cosmology characterized by Harrison as "a systematic animism," comprising a thoroughgoing "human-ization of the conceived elements of the world. It projects notions of human identity and agency upon animals, plants, ritual objects and all the rest: they share kinship with human beings, have names, belong to subclans, marry and so forth" (1990, 58). The "conceived elements of the world" are thus explicitly fully human persons. All things of the world—mountains, rivers, plants, animals, and so on—have the names of ordi-nary people "*because those things are themselves in reality men and women*" (56, emphasis original). Nor is it evident who is the real namesake, the people or the things.

These are not the only persons indwelling in things. Supposing a man cuts down a breadfruit tree for its fruits, a clan magician proposed to Harrison, or that he harvested and threw the unripe fruits on the ground. "The fathers would see this and be angry, saying to themselves, why has he damaged the tree? It is not just a tree, it is a man. It has a name, and a father, a mother and a mother's brother, and the fruits are his children. . . . The fathers will call the [secret] name of the tree, and tell it to stop bearing" (48). Here is a third party, "the fathers," the invis-ible totemic ancestors of the subclans who created yams, fish, breadfruit trees, and everything else in the world—the trees and all being their own "metamorphosed forms" (44–55). The animism is doubled, and by the creativity of the totemic ancestors it is indeed, for all cultural pur-poses, universal. For the totemic beings effectively make and comprise the cosmos, including under that description the culture and the people. Such are totems: animal and plant species, tracts of land, ritual sacra, ceremonial houses and their architectural features, shamanistic spirits and other metahuman beings, winds, birds, the subclan wards of Avatio (the main village), the subclan slit drums, flutes, the sun, the moon, lagoons, the Sepik River, and so on and so forth. Each subclan thus possesses (or is possessed by) a section of the universe consisting of the bodies-cum-phenomena of its totemic ancestors. Each thereby becomes responsible for providing certain necessary means of existence for the others in the form of their own totem-being. By means of the jealously guarded secret names of their totemic ancestors, the subclans ritually solicit the latter to release into the world the respective foods, ritual paraphernalia, shell monies, and the like, that they exclusively control. Note that all this is a traffic in the bodies of persons. "There is a strong notion of consubstantiality between people and their totems, an idea that in allowing one another the use of their totemic resources they nourish each other with their own flesh. People often say, for instance, that when they eat yams they are eating human flesh and blood" (Harrison 1990, 48). The universe appears as a cosmic system of sublimated cannibalism.

Masters of Species and Spaces

[For Kwakiutl] the best way to mitigate the dangers of food-gathering is both by direct alliance with the individual food animal itself and through relationships to the chief of that species. Thus, a halibut is eased into the canoe to the accompaniment of a prayer both telling of the joy of the fisherman who has caught it and of the fact that the fisherman will perform the specific ceremonies needed in the halibut rituals (Boas 1921, 1320–27). At the same time, the fisherman has the right to fish for halibut only because the chief of his numaym ["house" or lineage] has a covenant with the chief of the halibut-people. (Walens 1981, 78)

At times it seems doubtful whether it is the [Māori] tribe who own the mountain or river or whether the latter own the tribe. (Gudgeon 1905, 57)

The greatest gods excepted, in many immanentist societies, everything that is a person has a master, a metaperson that governs all the beings of a given kind or a given habitat—although this is not necessarily true of human persons, who may have no chiefs of their own, though they have to deal with masters of game or lords of the forest. At the least these masters, or "owners" as they are most often described, are ubiquitous figures of the cultures of immanence. Complementing his description of Saulteaux animism—"each phenomenal entity has an animating principle, a soul (*òtcatcákwin*) and a body (*miÿó*)"— Irving Hallowell, the American ethnologist of Algonquin cultures, records that all natural entities and classes of entities, as well as certain human institutions, have their spiritual "owners" or "bosses." The owners of plants and animals control the individuals of their respective species, four brothers rule the winds, the Thunderbird controls thunder and lightning, the Great Hare is the "boss" of seismic phenomena (1934, 391).

In an illuminating survey of mastery and ownership in the cosmologies of South American peoples, Brazilian anthropologist Carlos Fausto (2012) cites, among many other instances, fellow Amazonian anthropologist Fábio Mura's observation that for Guarani-Kaiowá, "it is impossible to imagine the existence of places, paths, living beings and inanimate beings as neutral, autonomous and owner-less. All the elements composing the current Cosmos possess owners, constituting domains and reflecting an extremely significant logic in the Universe's hierarchisation" (Mura in Fausto, 35). The hierarchy in question is a form of the one and the many, and more specifically the one over the many, in which the singular master-being, by encompassing the individual members of the species or class, in significant ways controls their fate. Or as Fausto expresses it, the form involves "an interplay between singularity and multiplicity: the owner is a plural singularity, containing other singularities within himself as a body" (32). There will be further occasions in these pages to examine this categorical logic. Here the matter is the role of the master-being, who often as the parent of the individuals of its domain, cares for, protects, and otherwise disposes of their fate. And as this is most critical also for humans in regard to the plants and animals, so too do people come under the control of the species-masters, submitting to the rules imposed by the latter to gain access to the resources by which they subsist.

These metahuman masters are a diverse lot. They include:

- species-beings who are magnified forms of the animals or plants they control (Cree and other Algonquians);
- masters who are parents of animals or plants, or else the animals may be the pets of the master (New Guinea Highlands);
- anthropomorphic masters, perhaps of foreign ethnicity relative to the people concerned (the foreign Amerindian masters of caribou known to some Naskapi people);
- masters who are of different nonhuman species than their wards (the Moosefly tormenter of fishermen who is master of fishes, likewise Naskapi);
- original cultivators or autochthonous spirits of the land (common in Africa);
- collective masters of game or cultigens (Achuar mothers of game and goddess of garden plants) or the goddess of game animals (like Katu of upland Vietnam);
- masters of environmental domains (like Magalim, "boss" of the exo-social habitat of Min peoples of New Guinea, or the rulers of forests and waters in lowland South America);
- departmental gods who are owners of their domains (Hawaiian gods whose spheres are known by the same term [*kuleana*] used for rights in land); and still others.

What follows here are brief ethnographic notices of some of the major types.

Based on his own fieldwork on Rock Cree of Northern Canada and the narrative penned by David Thompson, a late eighteenth-century fur trader, Robert Brightman ([1973] 2002, 91–93) presents an archetypical account of individual species masters. In principle, as Brightman was told, "'for every kind of animal, they say that there's one big one. That's the one that can tell the others where they should go'" (91). In (modern) practice there are some exceptions, even of some economic importance, but as a rule each species—beaver, caribou, deer, moose, marten, wolverine, wolf, even beetle—has a master who is a giant exemplar of the form and regulates the movements, distribution, and numbers of the animals, as well as the access of human hunters to them: "'[The masters] tell an animal to help a hunter. Then that animal tells the hunter where he can find him'" (91). Such benefits to the hunters are contingent on their following the regulations required of them by the species masters. Hunters should refrain from wasteful kills. They should show proper gratitude by thanking the masters for successful kills and avoid their displeasure by offering various ritual respects, including appropriate sacrificial gestures. Absent these respects, the masters will withhold the animals by controlling their movements and failing to reincarnate them. An early incident related by David Thompson concerning woodland caribou suggested the species master resented any killing of his animals by human hunters—a local hint of the general predicament of peoples who live by slaying and consuming "people like us."

Not all species masters of northern Algonquian peoples, however, are magnified beings of an animal form, like those with whom Cree interact. Some are more literally "people like us." The caribou on whom Innu (Naskapi) of the Labrador Peninsula were heavily dependent—for food, clothing, and implements—were ruled by one or another anthropomorphic "Caribou Men," at least some of whom were erstwhile humans. Traditions tell of young hunters, seduced by doe caribou, whom they have tracked, thereafter marrying them and living with and as caribou, becoming their masters and regulating humans' access to them. "He who obeys the requirements is given caribou," goes a Caribou Man's song collected by Frank Speck, "and he who disobeys is not given caribou. If he wastes much caribou, he cannot be given them. . . . And now, as much as I have spoken, you will know forever how it is. For so now it is as I have said. I, indeed, am Caribou Man (*Ati'kᶜwape'o*). So I am called" ([1935] 1977, 81). Remark that Innu submit to metahuman authorities—*les rois des caribous*, the French-Canadian trappers call them—who in kind and in potency are without precedent among these "egalitarian" people themselves.

By contrast, for Mundurucú of the Amazon basin, the most important game mother, "the mother of all game," had no specific form of her own but manifested herself multiply in other beings of the forest (Murphy 1958, 14–17). She inhabited temporarily certain land tortoises and spider monkeys (*coatá*), and more permanently special stones visible only to shamans. These stones had the virtue of increasing the supply of the mother's animal children, as witness their placement where game was abundant—also by their own action, as they were alive themselves. The shamans propitiate the game mother by feeding her a special dish of sweetened manioc gruel; traditionally this was the central feature of major ceremonies in her honor. The individual game species also have their own mothers, but they are less frequently or only secondarily regarded in game rituals. (Note again the personified class logic or philosophical realism—here doubled—with the encompassing class-being standing as a distributed person in the individual instances.) Among the restrictions imposed on hunters by the game mother: the animal must be killed primarily for meat and the carcass should not be left to rot; and the animals must be respected and treated with decorum, accordingly it is forbidden to joke about, or make vulgar use of the parts of any slain animal. The game mother sanctions these rules by causing accidents to delinquent hunters, followed by intruding malignant objects in them, causing sickness or even death—unless forestalled or cured by shamans. There are also other mothers, although generally less marked, including a complementary mother of all water life, not only of fishes but of amphibians and aquatic reptiles, and also mothers of several species of rains and storms.

The Mundurucú pair of game and aquatic mothers is a version of the forest and water rulers widespread in lowland South America. The "culture heroes" of Tenetehara, Marana ýwa and Ywan, for example. "Marana ýwa owns the forest and all animals living in it, and Ywan owns the rivers and lakes and water life" (Wagley and Galvão [1949] 1969, 102). Protecting the creatures of their respective domains, they punish or reward people according to their regard for them. Animism is not a purely autonomous and set apart relation between humans and individual plants, animals, or "inanimate" things. The animistic beings are part of a hierarchical system from which their own powers are ultimately derived.

The individuals have their masters. The masters may well have their own masters. Animism is at least a dual system of the indwelling persons in things, consisting both of the *inua*, the animating spirit in and for it-self, and the manifest spirit of a greater power, with its overriding concerns and dispositions. The pioneer American anthropologist Paul Radin caught the general principle: "Among the Tlingit we are told that there was 'one principal spirit and several subordinate spirits in everything.' A similar conception exists among the Eskimo, the Asiatic Chukchee, the Winnebago, etc. . . . The *genii loci* of the trees were subject to the *genius loci* of all the trees within a certain area, etc." (1914, 361)—and it could hardly be special if the soul-spirit of all the trees was then subject to the god of the "certain area," most likely, the god of the forest.

The rulers of the Tenetehara habitat indeed approach godliness. Like Magalim, the serpentine "boss" and father of the creatures and features of the wild in the central Mountain Ok region of New Guinea. Father of all, he is himself autochthonous, the child of none and present from the beginning. In great part, the environments of Telefolmin, Feranmin, and Urapmin peoples are populated by the wards of Magalim—animals, plants, rocks, rivers, cliffs, and so forth—which are so many direct or variant forms of him. Some, marsupials and wild pigs, have species masters of their own, making a hierarchical system of personhood compounded through three levels: the individual animals, the species masters, and Magalim, the land. At the same time, all these beings, Dan Jorgensen was told by a Telefolmin man, had "many names . . . but in fact there was only one *masalai* whose true and secret name was Magalim" (1980, 351).

Just so, Robert Brumbaugh, ethnographer of nearby Feranmin, offers a segue between unity and multiplicity in speaking of Magalim, for not only are the manifold beings of the bush instances of him, but so are their powers "the same as his" (1987, 26). When offering a sacrifice to a local spirit (*masalai*), the Feranmin man says: "Tell your father [Magalim] to stop making thunderstorms—and not to send any earthquakes either" (26). Earthquakes and thunderstorms are hardly the only measures Magalim takes to defend his children against humans, as Jorgensen documented in his excellent compendium of Telefolmin studies. As all the creatures of his domain are "*Magalim man*, if you finish these things, Magalim . . . will repay it with sickness, or he will send bad dreams and you will die" (Jorgensen 1980, 352; emphasis original). Here, then, is another testimony to the predicament of people who live off people. Part of the elaborate respect rules concerning game and other things work to displace their subjectivity so as to free the body for human consumption.

In North America, the soul is thus separated from the body and re-incarnated; in parts of Amazonia, rather elaborate rules govern desub-jectification, freeing the body for human use. All the same, the perva-siveness of animism testifies to the ubiquity of cannibalism, at least its potential. Potential cannibalism has been as widespread as animism in the human species. Even today, among the transcendentalists, vegan people who shun meat do so on the same premises of the personhood of food.

Demons and Ghosts: Anti-Human Metahumans

When late in the fall storms rage over the land and release the sea from the icy fetters by which it is as yet but slightly bound, when the loosened floes are driven one against the other and break up with loud crashes, when the cakes of ice are piled in wild disorder one upon another, the Eskimo believes he hears the voices of spirits which inhabit the mischief laden air. The spirits of the dead, the tupilaq, knock wildly at the huts, which they cannot enter, and woe to the unhappy person whom they can lay hold of. He immediately sickens and a speedy death is regarded as sure to come. The wicked qiqirn pursues the dogs, which die with convulsions and cramps as soon as they see him. All the countless spirits of evil are aroused, striving to bring sickness and death, bad weather, and failure in hunt-ing. The worst visitors are Sedna, mistress of the under world, and her father, to whose share the dead Inuit fall. While the other spirits fill the air and the water, she rises from under the ground. (Boas, *The Central Eskimo* ([1888] 1964, 195–96)

Ghosts [of dead BaKongo in central Africa] are witches who have been refused admission to the village of the ancestors. . . . One I knew was said to have been "sent back for his identity card," as though the threshold were a military roadblock on the way to the city. Witches become "ghosts," not "ancestors," and are condemned to endless wandering in the trackless and infertile grasslands that lie between the forests and the cultivated valleys. . . . In the east these ghosts are *matebo* . . . "The *tebo* [ghost] is usually of short stature and very ugly. His skin is ashy, he has long red hair and exudes a revolting odor. Often at nightfall ghosts leave their haunt to pass by the villages, stealing chickens and goats, or perhaps cloths and other things. Sometimes they attack a man whom they meet on some lonely path, beat him severely and try to drag him to their lair to devour him. Human flesh is to these noxious beings what pork is to the ordinary Mukongo, the choice dish" (Van Wing 1959, 291). . . . [N]owadays such stories are apparently not common. (MacGaffey 1986, 73)

Alike as so-called evil spirits, ghosts share with demons a range of anti-human dispositions. For one, they are opposites of humans, taking "opposite" in the strict sense (as taught to me by the great linguist Floyd Lounsbury) that opposites (like sugar and salt) are things alike in all significant respects but one. In chapter 6 of *The Netsilik Eskimos* (1931), titled "Spirits and other supernatural beings that are not real men," the explorer Knud Rasmussen writes that the "air and sea and earth" around this Inuit people are "full of spirits, mostly evil spirits, very rarely good ones. All these invisible beings are dead people or killed animals who, on account of some breach of taboo, have not obtained peace after death" (239). More generally, in a great variety of societies as well, ghosts are the dead who have been separated and differentiated from their kin by some negative mark: their bad conduct in life; ritual neglect by their survivors in the matter of sacrifices or mortuary ceremonies; a bad death; or another such mortal fault. Ever jealous and vengeful with regard to the living, they become restless and nameless "free spirits," untethered to any specific group of people and dangerous to all. In such respects they are distinguished from ancestors properly so-called, who in death remain members of their households or descent groups, usually with some authority over the living members.

In his famous work, *The Ancient City* ([1864] 1980), the French classical historian Fustel de Coulanges made a deft comparison between the "sacred dead" of Greek antiquity, those properly buried and honored, and those neglected and without a tomb, condemned to become malevolent ghosts. After the taking of Troy, he relates, as the Greeks are about to return to their country, each takes with him a beautiful captive. Achilles, who is dead and under the earth, nevertheless claims his too, and he is given Polyxena, the youngest daughter of King Priam of Troy. By sharp contrast, a few lines later: "The soul that had no tomb had no dwelling-place. . . . [I]t must wander forever under the form of a *larva*, or phantom, without ever stopping, without ever receiving the offerings and the food which it had need of. Unfortunately, it soon became a malevolent spirit; it tormented the living; it brought diseases upon them, ravaged their harvests, and frightened them by gloomy apparitions, to warn them to give sepulture to its body and to itself. From this came the belief in ghosts" (9).

Demons are differentiated and estranged from humans, not only by their nonhuman or ex-human origins, but markedly so by their exaggerated or grotesque human forms. They are inhumans: anthropomorphic giants or dwarfs; persons with missing parts, gigantic penises, hearts outside their chests; hybrids of humans and animals; and other such fearful versions of humanity. (In the late medieval period, such inhumans were translated by transcendentalists into the immanentist peoples of *terrae incognitae*.) Also, like ghosts, inhumans are for the most part invisible, although they may make their terrifying presence known by suddenly becoming visible to unsuspecting humans or by changing into seductive and deceptive people. Shamanic beings themselves by their extra-human powers, sorcerers by their ability to steal people's souls, demons may be enlisted as helping spirits of shamans. Ordinary people know them for malicious dispositions worthy of their anti-human constitutions. Fright-and-escape is often the best story people tell of encounters with demons. Many are cannibals, or if they do not eat their victims, they cause them to suffer accidents, to fall sick, or to die by other means. It may happen to people traveling alone in the forest in broad daylight. For no good reason. Or on a dark night, when society is resolved into its familial particles, it becomes dangerous to leave the tent to answer a call of nature.

So Australian anthropologist Peter Lawrence (1984) describes the demons menacing Garia people in the low mountains west of Madang in Papua New Guinea:

> The role of demons is unambiguous. . . . [T]hey regard them as outside the moral order. It is impossible to have with them equivalent, mutually beneficial relationships based on "interest" and "concern," for their sole aim is to destroy, kill, maim, or cause disease. All men can do is to drive them away or keep them at arm's length. (233)

At funerals, pieces of the deceased's personal property are placed with the corpse to buy off the demons, as for example one notable monster who ambushes and devours the deceased's spirit on its way to the land of the dead; or else they engage in an aggressive ritual designed to frighten him.

> Finally, non-specific bush demons "wild men and women" . . . are habitually inimical, causing death, ill fortune, and epidemics such as the outbreak of dysentery that led to the disintegration of Uria village in 1950. There are no effective countermeasures: victims can do no more than withdraw from the scene, as did the Uria people when they moved to new settlements. (233)

Notice that, like more benevolent spirits who bestow a variety of benefits, from providing game to hunters, to the success of the gardener, to the propagation, health, and growth of people, the demons are all-purpose bad actors, causing any and all kinds of misfortune.

In the cosmology of many cultures of immanence, demons are the most numerous, diverse, and dangerous class of metahuman-cum-anti-human beings. There are twenty-seven different kinds potentially inflicting disease or death on Chewong of the Malay Peninsula, by Norwegian anthropologist Signe Howell's count—and she was still counting, even as Chewong might still be discovering new ones (1989, 107–12). Again, these demons are typically grotesque humans—"humans manqués" (104), as Howell puts it. They are the product of a primordial error on the part of the messenger sent by the creator hero to give breath to the two humanoid figures he had fashioned. Having succeeded with the first, the progenitor of human beings, the messenger lost his breath for the second, which instead of humans gave rise to this deformed and dreadful coterie of demonic beings called *bas*—beings that "though 'like us' are really quite different as well." These *bas* are usually referred to with shudder and fear: "'They want to eat us,' the Chewong say" (105). Many see the souls (*ruwai*) of people as meat. Many are very large and covered with hair and have eyes on the back of their heads. One kind that live in wild pandanus trees have one arm and one leg—a right arm and left leg or vice versa—coupled to the body of a dog: they bite and suck the blood out of people until they die. Another species has the body of an elephant and lives in a swamp, but ordinary people cannot see him. He eats human souls by attacking the body. If people step in his urine, they come up blistered. So many different varieties, living in so many different places, inflicting so many woes, from diarrhea to death.

Individual Guardian Spirits

Documented here are some of the more widespread forms of the dual spirit-powers of humans in which the complement of the inner social soul is an external being who largely controls the individual's life chances. Africa is known for these fateful external couples of individual persons, in forms ranging from particular animals to deceased former spouses. For West African Nupe, it is the external spirit twin that thus manages the vital character endowments of the inner "kinship soul" (*kuci*), the soul of a proximate ancestor that enters a child at birth (Nadel 1954, 23–6). As Nupe are markedly bilateral, the reincarnated soul may come from the mother's or father's people. Usually this kindred spirit had been a person of consequence and his soul reappeared in many descendants: he was thus a distributed person, whose grave became a shrine where various people sacrificed for diverse reasons. More continuously, each person had a twinned spirit-being, male for men, female for women, who from birth to death was responsible for "the luck and fate" of its human double. The twin was an autonomous being with its own dispositions, for which there was no accounting except God (Sokó), who created and empowered it. A marriage was successful or not depending on whether the doubles of the husband and wife were compatible. But success in life more generally depended on the twin one was given: "the 'good' spirit can give wealth, prosperity, and success in everything, at least as much as its strength permits; a weak spirit might well fail in all these attempts; while 'bad' spirits would intentionally make their [human] twins suffer nightmares, illness, and misfortune of all kinds" (29). Since there is no necessary correlation between a person's ancestral character, his or her kinship soul, and the dispositions of his or her twinned spirit, it will follow that whatever happens in life is spiritually determined. A great man must have had a great twin; witches are people whose own antisocial instincts are potentiated by their evil twins.

A large multicontinent class of personal guardians consists of individual animals or objects of various kinds, usually acquired in youth by a solitary quest in wild space beyond the bounds of human occupation, often as the consequence of vision or visitation induced by fasting and sometimes by self-torture. The animal or object appears to the supplicant while in a trance, dream, or altered state of consciousness. As a general rule, the guardian is gifted by a great god, and its lifetime powers of aiding its person are derived from the latter. External personal spirits of this sort have already appeared in these pages, as the Japanese airplane adopted by a Chewong man and the equally catholic visions that come to Omaha of the American Great Plains. In a detailed and most useful discussion of the phenomenon among Rock Cree people, Robert Brightman ([1973] 2002) cites the 1790 account of the Hudson's Bay agent, Edward Umfreville:

> His good or bad success in hunting, the welfare of his friends and family, his duration in the mortal state, &c., all depend on the capricious will and pleasure of some invisible agent, whom he supposes to preside over all his undertakings: for instance, one man will invoke a conspicuous star, another a wolf, one a bear, and another a particular tree; which he imagines influences his good or ill fortune in life. (77)

Called *pawākan* or "dream-spirit," the guardian is acquired by most males and many females in adolescence in a dream induced by days of fasting in an isolated place in the bush. Individual animals are the most common dream-spirits and of these predators, bears and wolverines are most powerful, but the *pawākan* can be virtually anything, including clouds, ice, rocks, winds, trees, and so forth. Cree call any encounters with spirits "dreams," and mostly their *pawākan* will appear as humans met in that state, although *pawākan* may also be summoned in an awakened and trance-like condition induced by drumming and singing. (The nearby Innu [erstwhile Naskapi] call this "spirit-power thinking.") By at least some accounts, these relations are effected through a person's own soul—"an animating and individuating force present in the human fetus at conception" (96)—hence another functional version of the inner-outer spirit dualism. By all accounts, the *pawākan* then does what the person is doing: "To others, and perhaps subjectively, the individual's ability to survive accidents and disease, enjoy long life, forage successfully, cure others, know and influence future events, and do anything with exceptional skill can be tangible signs of the strength and devotion of the *pawākan*" (88).

The dream-spirit is notable, too, for its ability to ward off and defeat adversaries—monsters, sorcerers, and in ancient times, enemies in war. Not that the *pawākan* is unrequited, as dream-spirits are known to be desirous of sacrifices, including tobacco, clothing, knives, food, and other such goods that signify their own essentially human condition; people are reported to call them as "my grandfather" or "the guy." And they refer to the gifts accorded in return by *pawākan* as "power." Which is to say again that differential human skills, as in hunting, or conditions as health or illness, or other fortunes or misfortunes, are so many metahuman qualities—so many enspirited capacities and effects.

Like the Cree familiars, the Omaha and Crow guardians are examples of what is traditionally known as the Native North American Vision Complex. Regarding Omaha, Fletcher and La Flesche write: "The vision, with its sacred call or song, was the one thing that the Omaha held as his own, incapable of loss so long as life and memory lasted. It was his personal connection with the vast universe, by which he could strengthen his spirit and his physical powers" ([1911] 1992, 131). Analogously to the Omaha vision, which was gifted by Wakonda, the Crow youth appealed to a higher power, the Sun, for a successful quest (Lowie 1935, 237–52). Perhaps because it also involved self-mutilation—cutting off a finger joint, tearing the flesh of the back with skewers, and so on—in order to provoke the god's pity, the Crow version became the most remarked of Plains vision quests. Also distinctive, the Crow youth was adopted by the Sun, who became his father—in the matrilineal kinship system of Crow, an affinal relative, a relative by marriage.

Ancestors

Each Manus man [of the Admiralty Islands, Papua New Guinea] worships his Father, not in Heaven, but in his house front rafters, not one Father for all, but each man his own. The skull of the father of the house owner has an honoured place in a finely carved wooden bowl hung high above, and just inside, the entry at the front of the house. The spiritual presence . . . guards the house and supervises the morals of its people. . . . The Manus put a price upon their devotion to their dead, but it is an impossible price. They want life, long life, and no accidents. (Reo Fortune [1934] 1965: 1, 20)

In short, living people [Trobriand Islanders] *are* their ancestors embodied. Thus when humans act magically, their incorporated spirit predecessors *as kin* are invisibly but effectively acting also. (Mark Mosko 2017, 57)

This strange practice of [Inca] is so reprehensible because they worshipped the bodies of the dead in spite of believing, as they did, that these bodies would never live again nor serve any useful purpose. It seems that if they were to consider this matter and let themselves be guided only by what they saw and held to be certain, they would stop worshiping the dead on purely reasonable grounds alone; they would realize that the service and care that they took in paying tribute to the dead was useless. But it is impossible to go into this matter among them without giving offense. (Father Bernabe Cobo [1653] 1990, 39)

"Ancestors" is another protean category of metaperson powers. At their minimal and maximal forms, ancestors come under the description of spirits of other kinds: individual guardian spirits at one extreme, and all-father and all-mother gods, ancestors of everything, at the other. The range of potent ancestral figures in between include: recent familial dead, heretofore called "kindred spirits"; descent group founders (of lineages and clans of various depth); the collective, corporate dead of descent groups; totemic beings; outstanding personages of recent memory, such as big-men of Melanesian clans; dynastic founders; and the chiefly or royal predecessors of current rulers.

Some of this variety has already been suggested in the earlier description of Manambu totemic ancestors. They are not the specific founders of descent groups but relatives thereof, hence classificatory ancestors of living Manambu. And not only classificatory ancestors of living Manambu, but creators-cum-ancestors of animals, winds, mountains, and everything else. Yet for all this variety of ancestors, the spirits here discussed under that designation have certain features in common—which distinguish them from asocial ghosts. Ancestors are the progenitors or heroes of specific groups, whom, having given life to these people, continue to be a potential source of their well-being: they continue to be life-givers, if now with metahuman powers. Along with kindred spirits, they are often, but not necessarily, well disposed to their descendants, and of all spirits the most concerned with their morality, especially with violations of incest taboos. However, insofar as the ancestors' kinship bonds with the violators are in conflict with their compassion for them, the ancestors may, by delegation or withdrawal of support, allow the punishments to be inflicted by evilly disposed spirits, such as demons.

As a rule, the most immediate ancestors, the kindred and lineage spirits have the most consequential influence on the living. Also as a rule, their powers are implicitly or explicitly derived from greater ancestors or godly sources, as the immediate dead may be ritually invoked as mediators to the higher powers. Accordingly, the benefits bestowed upon their descendants by ancestors of different orders—as between deceased fathers and clan founders, for example—are largely redundant. Any and all ancestors are likely to make their people's gardens grow and the fish bite, to create many children and keep them healthy, to guard against accidents and otherwise prosper and protect the living. They are, then, the object of prayer, sacrifice, feasting, ritual dancing, and other cultic practices, the physical counterparts of which are the "sacred" groves, shrines, images, graves, relics, bones, temples, and so forth, by means of which communication with the honored dead is established. By virtue of this deference and communication, then, the ancestors are everywhere their descendants are, "doing whatever men are doing."

Not, as I say, that they are always doing them good. On the contrary, they are often capricious and aggressive. What Meyer Fortes writes of West African Tallensi in this regard is not atypical:

> The relations between men and their ancestors among the Tallensi are a never-ceasing struggle. Men try to coerce and placate their ancestors by means of sacrifices. But the ancestors are unpredictable. It is their power to injure and their sudden attacks on routine well-being that make men aware of them rather than their beneficent guardianship. It is by aggressive intervention in human affairs that they safeguard the social order. Do what they will, men can never control the ancestors. Like the animals of the bush and the river, they are restless, elusive, ubiquitous, unpredictable, aggressive. (Fortes 1945, 145)

It is often remarked that the relationship of ancestors and their descendants is more or less explicitly contractual—and by the same token, more or less latently conflictual. By such means as sacrifice and its benefits, a certain reciprocity is established between the living and the dead. They may feed each other, a relationship often noted between people and the greater gods. Yet as already noted, given the asymmetry in powers, the relationship does not entail mutual support, as is commonly supposed, so much as it signifies the submission of the living. Note here that what often passes for reciprocity or gift exchange in sacrifice is more appropriately understood as tribute and deference, with the effect, moreover, of magnifying the person of the god by the conveyance of an offering identified with the person of the sacrificer. Neglect or violation of the rituals of the ancestral cult is almost a kind of *lèse-majesté*, evoking an ancestral wrath likely to be realized in the accidents, illness, or other misfortunes of their descendants. How the people respond to ancestral anger is culturally variable, as is their response to their forebears' failure to provide for their welfare even after they have respected all the taboos, sacrifices, or other demands of the cult. The people may be fatalistic. But some have been known to disavow the ancestral powers, to purposely neglect them, or even smash their skulls—and find someone else to reverence.

Traditionally, everything happens in the households of Manus, largest of the Admiralty Islands and home to an expert fishing people, as if the dead father were still alive. It is still his house, he is still the head. People talk to him almost as much as they do to fellow mortals. The New Zealand–born anthropologist Reo Fortune ([1934] 1965) translates his title (*Moen palit*) as the oxymoronic "Sir Ghost," but while the honorific is appropriate, for the named familial ancestor is treated with deference commensurate with his powers, he is anything but an asocial, untethered ghost. He is kindred spirit *par excellence*. "The power of Sir Ghost is absolute," writes Fortune, "and submission is made to it. If Sir Ghost gives life, a man lives; if Sir Ghost withholds life, a man dies. This is repeatedly said to Sir Ghost when a man addresses him" (5). The living father of the house honors "Sir Ghost" more than his own father, the grandfather of the house, who was disavowed as familial ancestor, his skull cast into the lagoon, precisely because he let his son die. But his own skull now enshrined in the rafters of the house, the deceased father survives his death, for he continues to be the person he was and to act as he had in life. If he were a community leader when alive, he is a leader among his fellow dead. If he were a "native constabulary" in the colonial era, appointed by the Australian Administration, he is still the policeman who receives the spirit–District Officer of a spirit-regime and collects spirit-taxes from the other household spirits. He may even marry and have children by a deceased woman of another house, for which purposes the two families engage in the appropriate exchanges of wealth in the names of the dead. The dead are the actual agents of the exchange. For all practical purposes, the ancestor is the active ruler of the household economy. Fortune speaks of a "compact" in which the living give their ancestor shelter, food, warmth, and an honored place, and he in return provides the people with good fishing, good health, and a fair wind for their canoes, beside guarding the house and supervising the morals of its members (12–21).

While it is true that the father is the all-around source of the people's well-being, the notion of compact ignores that the house providing warmth and shelter is his own, and he supplies the food for it. The house-ancestor brings in the shoals of fishes in their seasons and provides the daily catch upon which the family depends. Should they neglect him or morally shame themselves—notably by violating the virginity of a be-trothed young woman—he will visit punishment upon them. He can ruin the fishing by removing the "soul-stuff" of the house's nets and traps, ren-dering them impotent. He metes out hunger, poverty, sickness, and ac-cidents to the living for their delicts. Deaths, however, are usually inflicted by ancestors of other houses, when the father fails to protect his own. Not that there is necessarily justice in all this, as much depends on the temperament of the father and his relationship to other active dead folk.

Fustel de Coulanges relates that if the ancient Romans failed to pro-vide the dead with funerary repasts, the dead became malignant wan-dering ghosts who inflicted disease and sterility on the living. But if the family honored them properly, they became tutelary deities, continu-ously involved in domestic affairs on behalf of their descendants. "The dead were held to be sacred beings. To them the ancients applied the most respectful epithets that could be thought of; they called them good, holy, happy." More than that, "in their thoughts the dead were gods," an apotheosis Fustel de Coulanges backs up with Cicero. "Cicero says, 'Our ancestors desired that the men who had quitted this life should be counted in the number of the gods.'" Wicked or good, they were gods, even though the wicked were in death as they were in life. Of all the dead, says the moralist Cicero, "'consider them as divine beings'" ([1864] 1980, 13).

In practice, Fustel de Coulanges describes a patriarchal domestic cult not unlike Sir Ghost of the Manus, in which the benevolent actions of the dead are likewise the reciprocal of the ritual offerings, specifically the nourishment the living provide him. Fustel de Coulanges speaks of a perpetual interchange of good offices between the living and their dead. The ancestor receives a series of funeral banquets, "the only enjoyment that was left to him in his second life"; his descendants receive the aid and strength they need in this one. "Thus the ancestor remained in the midst of his relatives; invisible, but always present, he continued to make a part of the family, and to be its father. Immortal, happy, divine, he was still interested in all of his whom he had left upon earth. He knew their needs and sustained their feebleness." In the midst of grief, the living sought consolation from their dead; in danger, their support; and for their faults, a pardon ([1864] 1980, 28).

The sneezes of South African Thonga people, like our own, will draw sympathetic solicitations of divine blessings from those nearby, apparently to ward off the escape of breath-as-life, but for BaThonga it can also be the appropriate occasion to petition the ancestral gods for whatever might be needed. In his well-known tomes on Thonga culture, the Swiss missionary anthropologist Henri Junod (1912; 1913) cites a man's response to his own sneeze, beginning with a formulaic call on his ancestors collectively: "I pray to you! I have no anger against you! . . . Let me sleep and let me see life! [i.e., dream?] so that I may go by the road, I may find an antelope (dead in the bush), I may take it on my shoulders; or that I may go and kill 'ndlopfu bukene,' an elephant, (viz., meet with a girl and obtain her favour), etc. Now I say it is enough, you my nose!" (1913, 338). This is only a bit of what Junod calls the BaThonga's "ancestrolatry," their fateful reliance on a large collection of their own ancestors, both the paternal and maternal kindred spirits as well as the collective anonymous dead of the clan polities and the encompassing ancestors of the ruling chiefs.

Speaking of all these ancestors, even the recent dead, as "gods," Junod describes people's dependence on them in terms much like Trobriand Islanders and other Melanesians, West Africans, or Chinese. It is of the utmost importance to know what their gods think and do, as the very existence of the village, of the clan, and the welfare of every member of the clan depends on them. Is not Divinity [*Bukwembu*], "'the power of killing or of making alive, of enriching or of making poor?'" The ancestors are the masters of everything: earth, fields, trees, rain, men, children, even sorcerers. "They have a full control over all these objects or persons" (Junod 1913, 360). If a tree bears fruit, they have made it grow; if the crops are plentiful, it is because they forced shamans to increase them or prevented them from blighting them; if a tree falls, they directed it to fall.

Such being a common ethnographic case, here are noted only some more-or-less exemplary Thonga practices. An invocation accompanying the sacrifice on behalf of a sick child, as recorded by Junod, illustrates the role of named individual ancestors as mediators to the greater clan spirits. It also reveals an attitude toward the gods at once submissive and defiant—bawling them out for having let the child become sick; and besides, using the occasion to demand other benefits, notably riches.

> Bless this child, and make him live and grow; make him rich, so that when we visit him, he may be able to kill an ox for us. . . . You are useless, you gods; you only give us trouble [viz., the sick child]! For, although we give you offerings, you do not listen to us! We are deprived of everything! [Then, naming the god responsible for the sickness, the one to whom the offering was addressed:] [Y]ou are full of hatred! You do not enrich us! All those who succeed, do so by the help of their gods!—Now we have made you this gift! Call your ancestors so and so; call also the gods of this sick boy's father. . . . So come here to the altar. Eat and distribute amongst yourselves our ox [in fact, a chicken]. (Junod 1913, 368)

These are rich texts, from which Junod draws an instructive conclusion about the inherent ambiguity of the gods as the source of good and evil, and the corresponding ambivalence of the people toward them as submissive and dismissive. On one hand, the ancestor-gods are omniscient and omnipresent. On the other hand, "*they are still, however, but men!* They are not transcendent beings before whom miserable sinners tremble and offer prayers" (Junod 1913, 386; emphasis original).

Bystanders at most rituals invoking the gods talk among themselves, joke, even obscenely, while the invocation itself, as just noted, harangues the ancestral powers as much as it supplicates them. The ancestors are far from moral paragons. "Their *character*," as Junod describes it, "is that of suspicious old people, who resent any want of respect, or of attention, on the part of their descendants. They wish to be thought of and presented with offerings. It seems that they are not actually in need of anything, for they live in abundance, but they exact a punctual observance of the duties of their descendants in regard to them" (387; emphasis original).

Marked by lengthy genealogies that often reach into the heavens, the most elaborate ancestral cults in the cultures of immanence are those of kings and ruling chiefs. In collective ceremonies, as those of the New Year or the ruler's inauguration, and also at individual graves or shrines, the ancient potentates continue to ensure the welfare of the people and polity. And particularly also, their powers are enlisted in the service of their current successor, the living ruler. For the latter is otherwise vulnerable to an inherent process of entropy in aristocratic genealogies: the rulers of later generations being progressively distanced from, and subject to invidious comparison with the great achievements of the dynastic founders (David Graeber, personal communication; Graeber and Sahlins 2017, 9–11; 429–31). The new king or chief starts with nothing to brag about except his descent from illustrious predecessors. Hence the various documented means by which the living rulers assume the personage of the dynastic founder and the deeds of his predecessors as his own. The subjectivity of the king thus engulfs the kingship, its accumulated history and dominion. At his installation, the east African Shilluk king "becomes Nyikang," the ancestor of the ruling line—although Nyikang, as Evans-Pritchard shrewdly observes, is not the Shilluk king ([1948] 2011, 413–14; Graeber and Sahlins 2017, 63–64). The Kwakiutl chief inherits the name of the founding ancestor, and thereby the powers and deeds not only of the founder but of all prior incumbents of the chiefly name. The Kwakiutl chief is an "eternal individual," as Stanley Walens puts it (1981, 79). Indeed, he recites the great deeds of his ancestors in the first-person singular: "I conquered such-and-such a place;

I married princesses all over the world"—referring to events that occurred before he was born. The Danish anthropologist J. Prytz Johansen ([1954] 2012, 29–31) refers to comparable practices of New Zealand Māori chiefs as "the kinship I," embracing, as it does, not only the chiefly ancestors but the doings of their clan.

A more complex form of royal ancestrolatry, one also politically more problematic, is the famous Inca cult of the royal mummies, celebrating the twelve kings of the dynasty, the sons of the Sun, each of whom survived bodily with his wealth, lands, and entourage likewise intact and through the lineage (*panaca ayllu*) of his descendants who reverenced and served him, the dead ruler continued to exercise his life-giving powers in the empire of his living successor (Cobo [1653] 1990, 39–43; Bauer 2004, ch. 12).

Still, the conquistador and chronicler of early contact Pedro Pizzaro was expecting to negotiate with some living representative of the dead when in the mid-1530s he was sent by the Viceroy to request a woman from the Cuzco house of one such late king on behalf of an Inca notable in the Spanish service. "Then, I, who believed that I was going to speak to some living Indian, was taken to a bundle [like] those of these dead folk, which was seated in a litter, which held him and on one side was the Indian spokesman who spoke for him, and on the other was the Indian woman, both sitting close to the dead man" (Pizzaro 1921, 204–5). This was the usual condition of state of the royal dead, flanked by a man and woman who were his oracles. In this incident, there was a considerable period of silence and suspense following Pizzaro's request, presumably during which the oracles received the answer from the king, upon which both pronounced it favorable.

Surprising as it was to Pizzaro, the event was not out of the ordinary for the deceased kings who led more-or-less normal social and political lives, visiting and feasting each other as well as the living, counseling and sometimes frustrating their current successor, and in their own person or their statues being venerated on public occasions in public places. Father Cobo tells of a noble who sought to improve his chances of succeeding to the kingship by marrying off his mother to a deceased ruler, which presumably engaged the latter's *ayllu* in his cause as maternal kin.

The royal ancestors had their own plazas in Cuzco, kingly residences in or near the city, and country estates farmed by their lineage retainers. One late ruling Inca (king) complained that "the dead had the best of everything in his kingdom" (Pizzaro in Bauer 2004, 162). (Although periodically the late sovereigns were worshiped with large offerings of food, it was not because they were hungry, a notion Inca people considered risible [Cobo [1653] 1990, 41].)

Many of the powers of the royal ancestors, moreover, extended to their descendants, the senior members of whom constituted the greater part of the Inca nobility. Yet all these privileges and powers followed from and were enabled by the presupposition that neither the kings nor their divinity were diminished by their death—if anything they were enhanced. The prayers accompanying offerings to the statues and bodies of former sovereigns not only asked them to protect "these little children of yours so that they will be happy," but petitioned the ancestor to intercede on their behalf with the great creator god, Viracocha, to "bring them closer to him so he will give them the protection that he gives to you"—and "let all things remain in peace and let the people multiply; let there be an abundance of food, and let all things always be on the increase" (120).

The royal cult was an enhanced version of the ancestor cults of local Inca lineages (*ayllu*), which similarly featured a priestly medium conveying the dictates of a powerful founder. In historical memory, the lineage ancestor was generally a bellicose intruder who founded a town and expanded the terraced irrigation system, or else conquered the locale in question (Gose 1996, 389). Empire-expanding conquests were what the dead sovereigns were particularly famous for, and what, even in death, they enacted as mummies in funeral rites and statues carried into battle. Some of the deceased kings were especially renowned for their prowess in making rain, growing crops, or making women fertile. But as Canadian-born anthropologist Peter Gose (1996) observes, Inca "expected all of their sovereigns to live up to their divine billing as 'sons of the Sun', and therefore to go forth and conquer" (389). This warrior career was doubly enjoined on a new king by his initial poverty and, given the process of generational entropy, his lack of status and accomplishments compared to his royal predecessors. He was relatively poor because he inherited nothing: his divine father retained his royal estate—land, treasure, entourage, and all. Riches, followers, and royal dignity were all wanting at the beginning of the reign, and conquest was a principal means of acquiring them.

From Father Cobo's detailed description ([1653] 1990), it seems that the New Year Festival (*Capac Raymi*), the most important of the year, was designed to overcome the deficits of a new reign and launch the king's imperial career (126ff.). The principal festival of the annual ritual cycle, lasting for an entire month, it would provide wealth from the tributes of the provinces—received by "the attendants of the king and the *guaca* [deities]" (127)—and the backbone of a fighting force in the large number of noble youth who were knighted as warriors in protracted ceremonies. Moreover, judging from the first day's proceedings on the plaza of the Temple of the Sun, the rituals were also meant to signify the superiority of the king over his deceased predecessors and their encompassment in his sovereignty. On a low ornamented bench in the plaza were placed the images of the great gods: Viracocha, the Sun, Moon, and Thunder. Before the reigning Inca appeared, the former rulers and entourages came and were arranged in order of seniority. Then the king made his entrance and sat on the bench next to the gods, while his court attendants made a tight circle around him. In the ensuing days, the young knights-to-be went through the tribulations of their initiation, involving processions led by the insignia of the king and pledges of loyalty to him.

But all this is to anticipate the last chapter of the book, on the cosmic polity—which, like the ceremonies of the Inca, essentially consists of the human usurpation of the gods.

Gods: "Divinity Is One"

The Dinka Divinity is spoken of as both single and manifold. All the sky-Powers are said to "be" Divinity; yet Divinity is not any one of them, nor are all of them merely subnumerations of Divinity. They are also quite distinct from each other, though considered together in relation to men they have a reality of the same kind. The Dinka assert with a uniformity which makes the assertion almost a dogma that "Divinity is one." (Lienhardt 1961, 156)

Above and beyond the dichotomy between forest and village stands Pleng (literally, "Sky"), the supreme power in the Katu [of highland Vietnam] cosmos. . . . Pleng is the ultimate source of life and fertility, but also the master of death and misfortune. As the source of life-giving rain, light and heat, Pleng is beseeched for blessings and prosperity; as thunder and lightning and final cause of death and disease he is feared and placated. Arbitrator of life and death, he commands the legions of spirits populating the earth—the benevolent ancestors and house spirits as well as the dangerous spirits of the forest. . . . As the mightiest of spirits, and comprehending them all, Pleng is usually invoked first at every act of worship, followed by the whole array of other spirits in the Katu pantheon. Pleng is usually called upon in conjunction with Katiec (literally, "Earth") . . . as if the two were as-pects of a single whole, a dual and androgynous deity appearing in human perception as Sky and Earth. (Århem 2016b, 96)

The Saulteaux [or Anishinaabe, a western branch of the North American Ojibwa] world proper is . . . roughly stratified in terms of a hierarchy of powers which parallel terrestrial, meteorological and celestial phenomena in an ascending series. The Winds and Thunder, e.g., are of a higher order of power and importance than most, if not all, terrestrial phenomena and kadabéndjiġet or k'tci mä´ni tu, the "owner" of the world, is both the most remote (highest?) and power-ful of all beings. . . . In my opinion [Hallowell writes,] the notion of a High God [of the Saulteaux] is indubitably aboriginal. And one in-trinsic bit of evidence may be offered here. This is the modesty of knowledge which the Indians exhibit in respect to the positive char-acteristics of the Great Boss. If their concept were due to missionary influence, I doubt whether this would be true. For Christians—and particularly missionaries—claim a much more intimate and positive knowledge of their Deity than any Pigeon River Indian. (Hallowell 1934, 390–91, 403)

Why not call them gods? Why deny they are indigenous? To deny that metahuman beings such as Manitou of Algonquians, or Sedna of Inuit, are indigenous gods, is to impose a transcendentalist understanding of religion. Viveiros de Castro, speaking of the celestial *bïde* powers of Ararweté and Amazonian gods in general: "I know the term 'god' is rarely, if ever, used by anthropologists in referring to superhuman beings of Amazonian cosmologies—perhaps because of an affected anti-ethnocentrism which ends up subscribing to the Western conception of Divinity" (1992, 343n17). But then there are also Pleng of Katu; Himself the Above and other Sky People of Melpa; Nhialic of Dinka; the Holy People of Navaho; Afek and Magalim of Mountain Ok Peoples; Taku Skan, Wakonda and such "Great Spirits" of Souian peoples; Nzambi of BaKongo; Mairu of Amazonian peoples; Sokó of Nupe; Chidô and Ama of Jukun; Rangi and Papa of Māori; Sangalang Burong and Pulang Gama of Iban, and so on and so forth.

The intolerance and reticence about indigenous peoples' gods takes one or both of two forms, which when thus combined are self-contradictory. On the one hand, reports of these high gods are dismissed because they do not have the transcendentalist characteristics of the Judeo-Christian God, are not a detached, relentlessly moralistic metaperson who has abandoned the world, and whose greatest concern is the salvation and damnation of individuals. You might think, with Hallowell, that this is a good reason to suppose these immanentist gods are indigenous, precisely because they don't match the description of the missionary's God. Unlike the latter, these gods are often bisexual or in context male or female; or, instantiating heaven and earth, they may be a sexual couple who give rise to a family of gods. Their own sexuality is a condition of the possibility of human fertility. In any case there are commonly a number of them, and also unlike the Christian God, they are as responsible for evil as for good—since they are responsible for everything. But inasmuch as our own monotheistic Paragon is incomparable, these other, immanentist gods are too often dismissed as in effect "false gods"—thus reinforcing the missionary's transcendentalist point that there is only One.

On the other hand, the intolerance and reticence about indigenous peoples' gods takes a second form. Inasmuch as many of these societies lack any such human authorities yet nevertheless have high-god concepts of some sort, it must be because they have been influenced by Christianity, Islam, or the theology of some other "high civilization." How could they conceive of gods when they don't even have chiefs or kings? Clearly, this argument rides on the transcendentalist premise that the concepts of divinity are "superstructure," ideal reflexes of the real-political and real-social order. But as has already been put into evidence here, in immanentist regimes the cosmos of metahuman powers is as an all-around infrastructure, pre-posed to human relations and actions, and comprising fateful powers of weal and woe unknown to people on their own. The human polity is no match or model for the cosmic polity.

I risk, yet again, in the Leachian sense: supreme gods—more often plural than singular—are universal in the cultures of immanence, no matter how "egalitarian" or loosely organized the human society itself. (No relation, however, to the claim made famous by the Austrian linguist-priest Wilhelm Schmidt [1912–55] that revelatory traces of the Christian God are to be found the world over.) Again, the raison d'être is human finitude. People are dependent on powers that are extra-human in nature and fundamental for their existence: "extra-human" precisely because human-being *as such* is not self-sufficient. Gods are hypostatized forms of the alien sources of people's life and death, necessarily other-than-human in such respects, if necessarily persons in relation to humans.

Typically, the gods were never human (like Pleng of Katu or Wakonda of Sioux) or else they are ex-humans (like Sedna of Inuit); they may also be strangers to their people (as in Tikopia)—even as they are often their "mothers" or "fathers," or ancestors of chiefs or kings. Gods are nonhuman persons who are the ultimate sources of the cosmic powers encompassing and governing human fate. As in Peter Lawrence's (1965) notice of Parambik, creator of the earth, and other gods of Ngaing people in New Guinea's Rai Coast District, Madang Province:

They are believed either to have always existed as deities or to have been originally men and women who became deities under special circumstances. They are conceived to be the same as human beings in one sense, having similar physical attributes and emotions, but different in another, having infinitely superior powers. Although normally human in form, they can turn into birds, animals, fish or insects at will; and they can travel long distances and do things beyond human capabilities. Yet they live on earth with men, generally in their own special sanctuaries within striking distance of human settlements. (203)

As eternal beings present from primordial times, the gods encompass their human dependents temporally. As lords of the skies, the oceans, the underworld, or the earth, they encompass their human dependents spatially. Thus extra-human and encompassing, the gods by these twinned attributes convey the meteorological, physiological, botanical, zoological, and other conditions of people's vitality and mortality. "Supernatural power," as Irving Goldman (1975) writes of Kwakiutl,

> must come from an outside realm, from an outer cosmological zone or from another type of being. This principle of acquisition is pervasive and fundamental. It lies at the foundation of Kwakiutl lineage exogamy, of ritual exchange and antagonism, and it lies at the heart of the shamanistic Winter Ceremonial [where initiates repeat the original acquisition of powers from animal spirits by human ancestors].... In fact, we are dealing with a Kwakiutl version of a universal principle of acquisition of powers. (197–98)

True also of the people of Bellona (Mungiki) Island, a Polynesian outlier in the Solomon Islands, whose pre-Christian (before 1938) religion was chronicled in two detailed monographs by the Danish cultural sociologist Torben Monberg (1965; 1966). Their gods ('atua), he noted, were not related to humans: they had no ties with people; they were generally considered "different classes of beings" (1966, 36). The gods, however, lived like people: they ate and drank, married, had offspring, loved and hated, did good and were malevolent. But they had power ('ao) over nature and the means of human existence. They "sent" the fruits of the gardens, the animals of the bush and fishes of the sea, the rain and storms. "They had the power to make people prosper or wither."

And for all their differences, humans and gods could communicate through mediums and even "become identical in the rituals in which gods spoke through certain officiating priests" (1966, 42).

Like East African Dinkas' Nhialic ("Divinity"), gods are one in essence and multiple in forms. Not simply the one and the many, but the One over and in the Many. Dinka Nhialic is a partible or distributed person: in being—and/or in power, to put a fine point on it—present in all the "spirits," great and small. "Divinity is one." Or as in Evans-Pritchard's (1956) oft-cited description of the analogous and neighboring Nuer god Kwoth, the various spirits of the air, the ancestors, and other powers are so many "refractions" of Kwoth, the one deity in other manifestations: "Nuer do not conceive of lion-spirit as something separate from God. . . . Lion-spirit is thought of as Spirit in tutelary relationship to a particular social group. *It and God are the same thing differently regarded*" (93; emphasis mine).

Similarly, in Central Africa, Wyatt MacGaffey writes of Nzambi Mpungu, the high god of BaKongo people as he was known in the nineteenth century: "He was the most general spiritual entity, made less remote by being implicit in all the others, all of which (including man) might at times be regarded as *nzambi*" (1986, 78). The others are in such respects *nzambi*, but Nzambi is not the others. Further, for all that Nzambi is abstract and remote, he is no *deus otiosus*, as "'he' participates in and is presupposed by all the lesser forces or entities, the 'spirits,' the dead, and the living" (262n13).

Likewise for West African Nupe, as reported by the Austrian-British anthropologist S. F. Nadel: they commonly say, "'God is far away.' Yet in a different, more mystic sense he is present, always and everywhere." Even so, "he is hidden and cannot be seen" (1954, 11). One does not approach Sokó, "God," directly, yet almost every ritual involves some blessing invoking him. Mainly the mysterious ways of Sokó are realized through ancestral souls who, while awaiting reincarnation, act as guardians of their descendants. Still, the god is the agent: the ancestral soul (*kuci*) has "no power of its own," but acts "in some fashion through Sokó" (24).

This same theme of great gods as the agents in the cults of lesser divinities who mediate their powers is widespread on the African continent. About Chidô, supreme god of Sudanese Jukun, the colonial administrator and anthropologist C. K. Meek writes: "So far is the Jukun from regarding him as a distant and listless god that they think of him as being ever present and ever-working, either directly or through [his consort goddess] Ama and the host of minor deities. The religious rites centre round the latter; [and so] . . . a casual onlooker might conclude that Chidô is of small account" (1931, 189). There is no contradiction between the two claims that, on the one hand, "the work-a-day religion of the Jukun is the cult of the ancestors," that "the ancestors are, in fact, the dominating influence in the life of a Jukun" (217–18); and, on the other hand, "Chidô is the ultimate cause not merely of the life of man but also of his resurrection and immortality, just as he is the giver of seed and the cause of the perennial re-birth of the crops" (189).

The rule in immanentist cultures is that the high gods are at once the most remote and the most powerful of beings—as Irving Hallowell says of the quite different and distant deity of Saulteaux. Everywhere too, the apparent contradiction between the great distance of the gods—including their abstract character, lack of cult, and so on—and their great power is resolved by the fact that the ancestors, demons, *genii locorum*, or other metapersons who immediately determine the human fate are acting under the direction or with the referred power of the supreme deities. Not only are the gods doing what men do, but the great gods are doing what the lesser gods do.

This same sense that all lesser powers are greater powers is conveyed in Hermann Strauss's observations, noticed previously, that the various "spirits" (*kôr*) of the Mount Hagen cosmos, including those animating human beings, do not act on powers of their own "but from a hidden source." The spirits of the dead "are not powerful *per se* . . . but are capable of using hidden power very effectively to benefit or harm those whom they have left behind. And this is the case with all other *kôr*: they do not have their own power, they merely have greater access to power than human beings, and are able to exploit it in a way which normal human beings are not" (Strauss 1991, 113). Strauss does not indicate in this passage whence the "hidden power" derives; but an earlier discussion of "Himself, the Above" (or simply "The Above"), the personification of the class of primordial celestial deities who gave rise to territorial clans in Mount Hagen, apparently identifies the ultimate source of all potencies. "The Above" is the cause of disasters afflicting the whole clan-community—famines, epidemic illness, drought, defeat in war—and also untoward misfortunes of individuals—a youth dies suddenly, a couple is barren.

When a great number of children die, Mbowamb (Mount Hagen people) say, "'He himself, the above, is taking all our children up above.'" When a young man falls in battle or dies unexpectedly, people say, "'He died so suddenly because the *Ogla* [the above] himself covered him.'" Yet the Above may not have been involved directly; he may have delegated the evil to lesser powers. For if many are killed in battle, they say: "'He himself, the *Ogla*, gave away their heads' . . . ; the heads were 'given away' to spirits and demons, who were thus able to kill people because the *Ogla* had placed them in their power." Likewise, in the event of an unexpected defeat, people say, "'Can't you see that he himself, the above, made openings (i.e., openings for evil powers of magic, the spirits, etc.) . . . which led to their defeat?'" Not that the Above is only punitive: if a man survives a fierce, hopeless battle, "people say, 'He himself, the above, did not take him out . . . and did not hand him over.'" More generally, "they say, 'Just as the sun stands up above (and sees everything), so he himself, the above, is always watching everything we are doing!' . . . And in good times one may hear, 'He himself, the above, hands down our fruit and food at every harvest; that's good!'" (Strauss 1991, 38–9).

That the power of the lesser metapersons is referred from higher powers is often indicated by the implicit or explicit presence of the latter in the invocations of the former, most commonly the presence of high gods in sacrifices addressed to the ancestors. Consider the perennial presence of the goddess Afek, mother of people and the staple taro, in the Mountain Ok region of New Guinea, who is always implicit if not explicit in the major sacrifices. In the Telefolmin region, writes Robert Brumbaugh, "Afek remains present and accessible. Taro fertility is a visible sign of her power, just as her bones are the visible signs of her presence. . . . Thus the Falamin [Feranmin], when addressing the local ancestors in ritual, consider that they are heard by Afek as well. When stronger reassurances are needed, the local ancestor is bypassed, new personnel take charge of the ritual and Afek is invoked directly" (1990, 67). The god is the Power of the powers.

To speak of West African Nupe again, the Austrian-British anthropologist S. F. Nadel makes the same point in another, useful way in noting that "the Nupe creed seems without economy" (1954, 30). Different divine agencies explain the same human phenomena, thus overlapping in their concerns and actions. One sacrifices to spirits, twins, kinship souls, and through rituals, to God (Sokó); or else one uses medicines, customarily empowered by God, to do so for the same reasons: to secure prosperity, protect oneself from illness, or safeguard the fertility of people or natural things. The observation could be duplicated many ethnographic times over—and to the same conclusion: the gods are the First Cause of the powers of the spirits.

And returning to Dinka and Nuer in East Africa, and expanding the perspective to include the other Nilotic peoples—Acholi, Anuak, and Shilluk—Godfrey Lienhardt notes that all have a term that, translated literally would be "Divinity High" or "the above"—who is more or less among these peoples the subject of a cult. Among all, however, Divinity High "represents the most generalizing concept of its class. Even among the Nilotes for whom the high divinity is the most otiose—the Anuak and the Acholi—and whose attention is primarily directed to divinity with other more specialized attributes, 'Divinity High' is not simply one among equals of the same kind. . . . It is true that among many, perhaps all, of these peoples, creation and birth, and certainly death, may also be attributed to other 'spiritual agencies'; but even so, in these cases the more specific agents are often closely connected with 'Divinity High'. Whatever other agents may be conceived of as the sources of special instances of creation or destruction, 'Divinity High' among the Nilotes is ultimately Creator and Destroyer" (1997, 46). Yet something more is implied than "Divinity is one." In effect, so are good and evil.

Lienhardt goes on to observe that it is difficult for peoples with more dualistic ideologies (Christianity notably) to grasp that for Nilotic peoples there does not seem to be "a *conflict* between two opposing principles" (46; emphasis original). They don't instantiate good and evil in two antithetical deities, like god and the devil. Rather, the high gods do both, they are all-purpose creators and destroyers. They are essentially amoral, a help to humans who properly defer to them, but also the source, directly or indirectly, of all human travails. Of all the metapersons involved in human affairs, the ancestors are most likely to act as moral agents, especially in regard to crimes against kinship, and most especially in regard to incest. The ancestors are kinsmen, but by the same token they are often reported to be reluctant to punish the offenders, instead delegating that to malignant spirits or exposing the delinquents to the same fate by withdrawing their protection. Thus the metahuman ethical spectrum from amoral high gods to malevolent, essentially immoral demons and ghosts, perpetually dangerous to humans.

The Phenomenology of Divinity: Entity and Quality

In Standard American English and other European languages, terms like "spirit" and "power" alternately designate a definite metapersonal entity—"a spirit" or "the spirits"—and a metapersonal quality or active principle of such beings, their efficacy as "spirits." So Lienhardt writes of the aforementioned *Nhialic*, the Dinka people's encompassing notion of divinity: "*Nhialic* is figured sometimes as a Being, a personal Supreme Being even, and sometimes as a *kind* of being and activity which sums up the activities of a multiplicity of beings. . . . 'Divinity', like *nhialic*, can be used to convey to the mind *a* being, a *kind* of nature or existence, and a quality of that kind of being" (1961, 29–30; emphasis original). But whether these two aspects of divinity, entity and quality, are differentiated, and whether metahuman powers are hypostatized and distributed to persons and other non-spirit-beings varies complexly among immanentist cultures.

In the matter of Dinka *nhialic*, the metahuman being and its characteristic actions are bound together, a single compound under a common name; as Lienhardt observes, they may be contextually relevant either as entity or quality. Apparently this cannot be for the "hidden powers" of spirits in Mount Hagen, New Guinea, as described by Hermann Strauss (1991), which as hidden, unnamed, as well as inseparable from spirit-beings, would simply be presumed when speaking of the actions of the latter—be they the celestial gods from which these powers derive, kindred spirits, collective ancestors, stone shrines, cult houses, the anima of trees or other metaperson entities. In such forms as Dinka Nhialic and Mount Hageners' "hidden powers," neither the godly source nor his or her powers are free elements that may be imparted to ordinary things or beings: the Mount Hagen big-man is not himself enspirited, though he gains access to the spirits by sacrifice and other ritual means. By contrast, one may speak of certain Cree persons as "manitou-men," that is, as embodied manifestations of the supreme deity, Manitou, instances of his distributed person and powers.

The Wakonda of Sioux peoples and the Manitou of Algonquians are alike in this respect, and the former, as documented in the classic monograph on the Omaha by Fletcher and La Flesche ([1911] 1992), offers an exemplary illustration of the enspiriting of things, including some people. Apparently only vaguely anthropomorphic in form but anthropo-psychic in character—with will, consciousness, and other cognitive qualities—Wakonda is, like Dinka "Divinity," the Power of lesser powers. The guardian spirit acquired in the wild by a fasting youth is an animal of appropriate gifts sent by Wakonda. Wakonda is the force of success in the important annual buffalo hunt, he makes the maize grow, and he is generally responsible for the food supply—as well as the calamities the people suffer, individually or collectively. He may be described as a creator quite like Australian Aboriginals' totemic ancestors: as one old man explained: "'All forms mark where Wakonda has stopped and brought them into existence.' ... Each 'form' was the result of a 'stop,' where there had been a distinct exercise of will power, an act of the creative force Wakonda performed" (600). But as then implied, Wakonda projects himself into things, which as enspirited by him as versions of his person, are thereby motivated by his powers. The world is filled with Jove. The ethnographers explain:

The Wakoⁿda addressed in the tribal prayer and in the tribal religious ceremonies which pertain to the welfare of all the people is the Wakoⁿda that is the permeating life of visible nature—an invisible life and power that reaches everywhere and everything, and can be appealed to by man to send him help. From this central idea of a permeating life comes, on the one hand, the application of the word *wako^{n}da* to anything mysterious or inexplicable, be it an object or an occurrence; and on the other hand, the belief that the peculiar gifts of an animate or inanimate form can be transferred to man. The means by which this transference takes place is mysterious and pertains to Wako^{n}da but is not Wako^{n}da. So the media—the shell, the pebble, the thunder, the animal, the mythic monster—may be spoken of as wako^{n}das, but they are not regarded as *the* Wako^{n}da. (599; emphasis original)

Or in another iteration: "The object, be it thunder-cloud, animal, or bird, seen and heard by a dreamer, may be spoken of by him as a *wakonda*, but it does not mean they are *wakonda*" (Fletcher in Radin 1914, 346). Again, the god as distributed person.

This is not the "animatism" expounded by the early British ethnologist R. R. Marett (1914, 14); nor is it the analogous "magic power" claimed by his German-American contemporary Franz Boas ([1908] 1974, 259ff.), consisting of an impersonal extraordinary force in itself, inherent in things and creatures of nature. What is missing is the animating spirit-being in and of such power. Arguing against this godless concept from his experiences with Winnebago and Ojibwa peoples—hence both Siouan and Algonquian concepts, *wakanda* (*wakonda*) and *manito* (*manitu*) respectively—Paul Radin (1914) writes:

> The term always referred to definite spirits, not necessarily definite in shape. If at a vapor bath the steam is regarded as *wakanda* or *manito*, it is because it is a spirit transformed into steam for the time being; if an arrow is possessed of specific virtues, it is because a spirit has either transformed itself into the arrow or because he is temporarily dwelling in it; and, finally, if tobacco is offered to a peculiarly-shaped object, it is because either the object belongs to a spirit, or a spirit is residing in it. . . . If a Winnebago tells you that a certain thing is *waka* (i.e., sacred), further inquiry will elicit from him information that it is so because it belongs to a spirit, was given a spirit, or was in some way connected with a spirit. (349)

Robert Brightman helpfully alerted me to a Cree text collected by the respected linguist Leonard Bloomfield in which he translates a verb derived from the noun *manitōw* variously as "be a manitou person," "be of manitou power," or "have manitou power" (Bloomfield 1934, 225, 227). After mutual discussion of this and other texts, and having intensively studied Cree culture himself, Brightman writes in a recent personal communication: "If I take this right the Manitou qua Deity is compounded entity + qualit(ies) and it is a dyadic compound and not solely the quality constituent that distributes hierarchically 'downward' to spirits, humans, animals, etc." As said before, what is entailed is the deity's "enspiriting" of things, giving them the power of his own being. But equally critical are the contingencies of *wakonda* and *manito*: the "temporarily dwelling" of the spirit-being in this or that worldly entity, his coming and going, clearly as a matter of the pertinence at the moment of the arrow or the conjurers' vapor bath to the human person or persons concerned—"for the time being." Or again, as the early American and indigenous anthropologists, Alice Fletcher and Francis La Flesche ([1911] 1992, 599) observe, there is "on the one hand, the application of the word *wakonda* to anything mysterious or inexplicable, be it an object or an occurrence; and on the other hand, the belief that the peculiar gifts of an animate or inanimate form can be transferred to man." Wakonda appears and disappears in and as things according to their relationships to human endeavors—with effects for better or worse. Particularly in this potential and relative sense is Wakonda the motivating force of whatever there is.

But Wakonda is hardly the only force in things, which may also have their own indwelling persons: beings with their own will and their own fateful presence in human affairs. Like the four kernels of "sacred" red seed corn distributed by a certain designated clan to each Omaha family and mixed with their own seed for planting. "It was believed that the sacred corn was able to vivify the seed and cause it to fructify and yield a good harvest" (Fletcher and La Flesche [1911] 1992, 262). Or consider the famous "sacred pole" of the Omaha, with its capacity of unifying the people as a whole—as it were by opposition to a hostile metaperson power. The pole was fashioned from a miraculous tree, cut down and attacked as an enemy, and then, as the chiefs worked on it, "they trimmed it and called it a human being" (218). The name of the pole included a prefix that indicated it had "the power of motion, of life" (219). Indeed, the ethnographers, citing the red seed corn and other life-giving powers, make the broad observation that everything lived and partook of man's qualities, that the idea of "personality" was dominant in the culture, and that "the force within this personality was recognized as that of the will" (609). In sum, Omaha may experience both the inherent person in things as well as the god in things, perhaps in the same things. It is hardly unique: recall the Manambu totemic ancestors who are manifest in all manner of phenomena—rivers, mountains, winds, the position of the sun, and so on—which are at the same time forms of embodied human persons.

Pause, then, for an analytic résumé. At issue here are metahuman beings that manifest or inhabit worldly phenomena of human experience, by contrast to "free spirits," such as ancestors, ghosts, and the like. One can distinguish two such embodied forms of spirits: (1) the so-called owners or indwelling spirits who are persons in themselves and for themselves, like the *inua* of the Inuit; and (2) those enspirited by the deity, whose powers they thus manifest, like the Wakonda of Siouan peoples. *Inua*-beings intervene in human life in terms of their own cognitive and volitional capacities, albeit these capacities are originally acquired from the gods; *wakan*-beings, if they may be so-called, enact the intentions and dispositions of the deity. The distinction is between spirits who are persons in their own right, and those that are avatars of the god. This is often a difference too between the fixed presence and constant influences of the spirit-persons in things by contrast to the pro tempore and pragmatic presence of the god in unusual and fateful events—a bad accident, a defeat in war, a bountiful harvest, an untoward death, a needed rainfall. Here again, the great gods are characteristically the most remote and yet most powerful of spirits, though the more proximate *inua* and other lesser powers have more continuous and effective influence in people's everyday existence. There are, however, societies where the great gods, as conditions of the possibility of the hierarchical human order, often take precedence over the lesser spirits of things.

Māori of New Zealand, for a revelatory example. The British colonial ethnologist Elsdon Best explains in typical colonial language:

> When the Māori walked abroad, he was among his own kindred. The trees around him were, like himself, the offspring of [the great god] Tane; the birds, insects, fish, stones, the very elements were all kin of his, members of a different branch of the one great family. Many a time when engaged in felling a tree in the forest, have I been accosted by passing natives with such a remark as: "*Kei te raweke koe i to tipuna i a Tane.*" ("You are meddling with your ancestor Tane"). (Best 1924, 128–29)

Māori people often overrode the intermediate spirit-beings—lesser gods, clan ancestors, the "souls" (*wairua*) of things, for all their importance—to invoke Tāne or another of his divine brothers in contexts of technical activities, planting and harvesting, births and deaths, and many life-giving or death-dealing situations. It is the archetypal god who is active, indeed whom the human actor becomes. The god is the paradigm. Whakatau was the first to take vengeance, so "whenever vengeance is wreaked on somebody again, Whakatau again does his deed in the shape of the avenger" (Johansen [1954] 2012, 148). In the tradition of the creation, heaven was raised from the earth and put on poles by Tāne, thus making human existence possible; "but this creation is not an event which ended long ago; it is constantly repeated. Therefore, a father may sing to his son: 'It was he (viz. Tane) who put poles under heaven above us; then you were born to the world of light'" (150). Encompassing the cosmos in time and subsuming its myriad persons, human and metahuman, in his own being, Tāne, the ruling god of man, becomes ever more enspirited in the lives of the people. He progressively dominates and replaces the lesser *inua*-divinities acting in terms of their own capacities.

This sort of pantheistic move, this takeover of the cosmos by the supreme god or gods, is well known elsewhere in Polynesia. It appears clearly in the pages of Valerio Valeri's *Kingship and Sacrifice* (1985), his magisterial study of the cosmology of the traditional Hawaiian polity. Here is a universe encompassed in the persons of four great cosmocratic deities—Kū, Kane, Kanaloa, and Lono—each ruling a domain (*kuleana*) consisting of living humans, anthropomorphic images, and a multitude of cultural activities and natural phenomena. The gods are respectively manifest in colors; directions; days of the week; periods of the day; natural and inorganic phenomena, such as thunder, light, seawater, and so on; plants; animals; seasons; certain smells; cloud formations; a particular number; birdsongs; and more (15ff). All these entities are so many of the god's "myriad bodies" (*kino lau*), forms in which the deity is instantiated in legend, cult, and ritualized practices that constitute human politics and economics.

As Valeri shows, a certain logic motivates the multifarious contents of the god's domain, namely the metaphoric and metonymic connections of these phenomena to the person-attributes of the god or the cultural practices over which he presides. The god Kū governs activities pertaining to and performed by human males: war; fishing; the construction of canoes, temples, images, and so forth. Many natural manifestations of Kū are signs of these activities, of materials involved in them, or of their places in space and time. The dog, hog, and game fish are bodies of Kū, as they metaphorically evoke the warrior and his ways. All the plant species that instantiate Kū are those used in the rituals or technical activities of war and fishing: the woods of canoe construction, for example; the *kauila* tree used for making spears; the *lehua* tree from which an important Kū image is carved—and metonymically as well, the birds whose feathers adorn the god images and are notably captured when the *lehua* blooms. Things that evoke virility because they are erect or straight—the word *kū* itself means "erect, straight"—are manifestations of Kū: high mountains, the digging stick, the high, hard, and straight *koa* tree, "everything that is straight, vertical, high, or deep in nature tends to be associated with Kū." So is the period of the month devoted to Kū ritual, as well as the month of the year when the war temples are opened. It goes on (11–12). All these elements and acts, as instantiations of the god, are thus empowered by him. "By transforming himself into different but interchangeable bodies," Valeri writes, "by his power of metamorphosis, the deity accomplishes wondrous 'miracles' (*hana mana* [works of *mana*])" (12).

What from one vantage is the *deification of the human world* is, from another, the *human appropriation of divinity*; and either way, it is a process promoted by that force familiarly known as *mana*. Here is a third form of the phenomenology of divinity consisting of the hypostatization of godly power as a quality divided off from deity itself and proliferating as a force of vitality and mortality within human society. Most distinctively, *mana* is acquired one way or another and to some extent or another by privileged humans who thus assume the divine ability to make gardens grow; rainfall, fish, and game appear; enemies die; women fertile; people wealthy; witches perish; epidemic sickness end; and other such potencies of divine origin and character. In effect, humans usurp the powers of spirits, bringing heaven to earth and potentially making a large part of human society itself full of Jove. Māori may thus speak of that *mana* of human beings (*mana tangata*) by contrast to the *mana* of gods (*mana atua*) (Smith 1974, 62). (Not worthy of further discussion here is the abundant abuse of "mana" in popular discourse—joining the pidgin anthropology of "totem," "tribe," and "culture"—where the ethnographic iterations of the concept typically degenerate into go-anywhere, all-purpose notions of mystical efficacy.)

Oceanic *mana* is the classical locus of the form, or more specifically Melanesian *mana* as described by Bishop R. H. Codrington ([1891] 1972), based on his experiences over twenty-five years in the region during the late nineteenth century. But Oceanic *mana* is only one, if often taken as paradigmatic, of a large family of divinely imparted powers, including the *nawalak* of Native American Kwakiutl people; *semengat* and its cognates of Malays and Indonesian islanders; *kuti* of West African Nupe, *ipeyé ha* and its cognates among Araweté and other Amazonians; *guruwari* of Australian Walbiri; *monova* of Trobriand islanders; *hasina* of Malagasy in Madagascar; as well as Islamic *baraka*, and even *charisma* in its original Weberian sense of divine inspiration—not to mention the similar potencies locally known to numerous other peoples.

Of course, there are significant differences in the humanization of divine powers among these societies, as Bishop Codrington already noted among Melanesians, but several of the generic similarities he

determined remain valid cross-culturally even as they provide a frame-
work for assessing the nature and measure of the variations. For one, the
necessary derivation of *mana* from a divine source, from what Codrington calls "spirits" or "ghosts," meaning gods or ancestors. Too often
mana has been described as an "impersonal force," even by Codrington
himself, but as it is the divine quality or potency of some determinate
deity, imparted as such to human beings or things, it remains indisso-
ciable from the godhead. "This power," as Codrington writes, "though
itself impersonal, is always connected with some person who directs it;
all spirits have it, ghosts generally, some men" ([1891] 1972, 119). *Mana*
is in this regard a personal quality of divinity selectively transmitted to
humanity. "No man, however, has this power of his own; all that he does
is done by the aid of personal beings, ghosts or spirits; he cannot be
said, as a spirit can, to be *mana* himself, using the word to express a
quality; he can be said to have *mana*, it may be said to be with him, the
word being used as a substantive" (191). (Arguments have been made
that divinely endowed persons can indeed be *mana*; albeit as divine, the
quality is not that of the person as such.)

   "The Hawaiian case," writes Valeri, "confirms that mana is a quality
of divine origin. It is therefore predicated most often of gods and of the
persons or things that are closest to them: ali'i [chiefs], priests, prayers,
temples, sacred houses within the temples . . . images of the gods . . .
ritual objects, and omens" (Valeri 1985, 98–99). The analogous *guruwari*
power accessed by Walbiri people is explicitly that of their primordial
Dreamtime totem-ancestor; the original *nawalak* of a Kwakiutl chief
likewise was acquired by the lineage ancestor from a godly theriomor-
phic being; so does a Tikopia chief receive *manu* (*mana*) from his clan
gods through a series of chiefly predecessors. Or, the god at issue may
be identified by the kind of power some exceptional human person has
manifested: a successful Māori warrior has been endowed with the
mana of Tu-matauenga, fierce ancestor of men; or the priestly expert
who brings a successful harvest of sweet potato has acted with the *mana*
of Rongo-maraeroa, the god who, in a feat of derring-do, brought the
crop from the legendary homeland of Hawaiki.

The power in these instances, as in the classic Melanesian forms, is indeed a substantive. *Mana* is literally handed down as a substance by the god to the Tikopia clan ancestor, and thence to the chief, in return for the offerings and deferential prayers of solemn kava rituals. And as Raymond Firth (1950) reports: "Natural phenomena *work* as they do in a normal course to a large extent through the *manu*, the supernatural power of spiritual beings, stimulated and canalized through the qualities and acts of chiefs" (89; emphasis mine). Again, the acquisition of godly qualities by privileged persons may be abiding, as with the *mana* Hawaiian ruling chiefs inherit by divine descent. Or the divine efficacy may be performative and temporary, like the *guruwari*-power of the Walbiri ancestor acquired by initiated men in ceremonies that maintain the fertility of the landscape and the foods it provides—the landscape and foods also being the ancestors gone to ground in ancient times. In certain Walbiri traditions, *guruwari* is shaken like soft white fluff from the Dreamtime ancestor's body (Munn 1973, 30n18), whence it enters into the phenomenal world, including into human infants, as an invisible fructifying force; or again, in the form of representative graphic designs, *guruwari* can be ritually made to bring ancestral power into human affairs.

Most notable in the Melanesian instances cited by Codrington is the apparent after-the-fact attribution of *mana* to those who achieve economic or political success by their own talents and efforts. But as the good bishop insists, *mana* is a post-factum attribution only because it is an a priori conviction. Accordingly,

all conspicuous success is a proof that a man has *mana* . . . he becomes a chief by virtue of it. Hence a man's power, though political or social in character, is his *mana*; the word is naturally used in accordance with the native conception of the character of all power and influence as supernatural. If a man has been successful in fighting, it has not been his natural strength of arm, quickness of eye, or readiness of resource that has won success; he has certainly got the *mana* of a spirit or of some deceased warrior to empower him. . . . If a man's pigs multiply, and his gardens are productive, it is not because he is industrious and looks after his property, but because of the stones full of *mana* for pigs and yams that he possesses. . . . [A] canoe will not be swift unless *mana* be brought to bear upon it, a net will not catch many fish, nor an arrow inflict a mortal wound. (120)

In these enspirited societies, human political relations are metahuman relations, and human political authorities are cosmic persons. They introduce into human society as their own powers the potencies appropriated from the cosmic host, as the next chapter will suggest.

4

The Cosmic Polity

What we could call "natural world," or "world" for short, is for Amazonian
peoples a multiplicity of intricately connected multiplicities. Animal
and other species are conceived as so many kinds of "people" or "societies," that is, as *political entities*. . . . To be sure, we too—by which is
meant us Westerners . . . think, or would like to think that we think,
that it is only possible to be human in society, that man is a political
animal, etc. But Amerindians think that there are many more societies
(and therefore also humans) between heaven and earth than are dreamt of
in our philosophy and anthropology. What we call "environment" is for
them a society of societies, an international arena, a *cosmopoliteia*. There
is, therefore, no absolute difference in status between society and
environment, as if the first were the "subject," the second the "object."
Every object is another subject, and is more than *one*.

—DANOWSKI AND VIVEIROS DE CASTRO 2017, 68–69
(EMPHASIS ORIGINAL)

IN A STATE OF IMMANENCE, human society is a fractional part of a
much larger, cosmic society populated by a multiplicity of different
kinds of persons, many organized in their own societies, and all more
or less ordered, empowered, and encompassed by the greatest of
them, deities of this cosmic polity—this *cosmopoliteia*. From all
around the world come anthropological calls to go beyond the

perspective of society by and for itself, beyond the usual anthropo-centrism, and instead to see the human order as integrated in the universal order. The arguments are broad, as when Danowski and Viveiros de Castro (2017) speak of the cosmic societies of Amazonian and Amerindians in general; or particular, as when the latter says of Araweté, "Society is not complete on earth: the living are one part of the global social structure, founded on the alliance between heaven and earth. The cosmology of the Araweté is its sociology" (Viveiros de Castro 1992, 218).

Also broadly for an array of immanentist cultures, beginning with Australian Aboriginals, the British structural-functionalist Radcliffe-Brown comments that the personification of species and natural phe-nomena "permits nature to be thought of as if it were a society of per-sons, and so makes of it a social or moral order" (1952, 131). As Mervyn Meggitt writes more narrowly of Australian Walbiri:

> the totemic philosophy asserts that man, society and nature are in-terdependent components of one system, whose source is the dream-time; all are, therefore, amenable to the law, which is co-eval with the system. . . . The care of sacred objects by the men of one patrimoiety, the sexual division of labour, the avoidance of mothers-in-law, the mating of bandicoots, the rising of the sun, and the use of fire-ploughs are all forms of behavior that is lawful and proper. (1962, 251–52)

Across Northern Asia, "the realm of the social does not end with human beings; rather, it knows no ending. So, to put it rather simply, instead of having one nature encompassing many human societies, we are con-fronted with one society of both humans and nonhumans encompass-ing, as it were, many natures" (Pedersen 2001, 415). Or, in a general comment on animism in Southeast Asia, the Swedish anthropologist Kaj Århem writes:

> animist cosmologies assume a "social" cosmos populated by human and non-human persons (animals and plants), communicating and interacting with each other as autonomous subjects in an intersub-jective field of relations. In this cosmic society, subjectivity and

intentional agency constitute the ultimate ground for being and order. (Århem 2016a, 5)

In particular, in the Malay Peninsula "the human social world is intrinsically part of the wider world in which boundaries between society and cosmos are non-existent" (Howell 2012, 139). But then, as French political anthropologist Georges Balandier writes of African political systems: "Every society links its own order to an order beyond itself, and, in the case of traditional societies, to the cosmos" (1970, 101).

As said, however, the cosmos is not only a universal society composed of diverse species of persons, but a hierarchical arrangement of them, a cosmic polity whose higher divinities empower the lesser beings, among the least of whom figure the needy and subordinate humans. So does Kaj Århem (2016a) describe the cosmology of Southeast Asian hill peoples:

> An outstanding feature of hill-tribe cosmology is the proliferation of spirits—nature spirits, ancestors and ghosts of all kinds. . . . The universe of spirits tends to be hierarchically ordered with a Supreme Being—a transcendent subject—at the apex. It is typically part of a more comprehensive ontological hierarchy, comprising living physical beings and things, including humans, inserted between the spirits of the Upper World and the beings of Below (the dead, ghosts and spirits of wild animals and plants). (19)

Not that "transcendent" here would mean more than extra-human in origin and nature of the deity. In Århem's own contribution (2016b) to the same volume on Southeast Asian animism, concerning Montagnard Katu of Vietnam, "the supreme power in the Katu cosmos," Pleng, "Sky," "is the continuous source of life and fertility, the master of death, disease, and misfortune, and the provider of rain, light, heat, thunder, and lightning. "He commands the legions of spirits populating the earth—the benevolent ancestors and house spirits, as well as the dangerous spirits of the forest" (96). Pleng is usually invoked first in every act of worship, followed by the whole array of lesser powers—thus acting under the authority and by the allocated potency of the god. Århem notes in this connection that "the Katu explicitly compare the spirit hierarchy to the army and the state administration" (97).

Given the longstanding relations of hill peoples with Shan states, one might justly suppose that the high gods such as Pleng, together with the spiritual bureaucracy over which they preside, were borrowed from lowland civilizations. Judging, however, from similar cosmologies from, say, the middle of New Guinea or the Central Arctic, it could well be that what were borrowed by Southeast Asian hill peoples were state-system terms to describe their indigenous universe. What remains, then, from the comparison is the somewhat remarkable finding that the cosmic polity has the lineaments of a state, even among peoples who would themselves qualify as "egalitarian societies." From which it is plausibly further concluded that the state is prefigured in cosmology before it is known in society.

Hierarchy in Cosmology, Equality in Society

Even societies with strong egalitarian values profess a world view structured by hierarchy. The Buid of Mindoro, whose central social value derives from the equality of husband and wife, are "obsessed with hierarchy," as Gibson (1986, 185–8) notes, referring to relations with animals, spirits and neighbouring groups. This consideration of outsiders and non-humans renders Southeast Asian cosmologies hierarchical. . . . even without recognizable political or economic dimensions stabilizing them. (Sprenger 2016, 41)

Take the Montagnais-Naskapi (Innu) hunters, crudely described by American ethnographer Frank Speck ([1935] 1977) in a condescending way that even in 1935 must have seemed problematic within the emerging notions of cultural relativism:

[They] sheltered only in draughty caribou-skin or bark tents, clad in caribou-skin raiment, using mostly bone and wooden implements, and professing neither political institutions nor government. . . . One may account for lack of government and other social institutions by visualizing the sparsity of population and its scattered manner of living in family groups. (5–6)

One gets the point: this is a classically "egalitarian society," perhaps, like many, egalitarian in the negative mode of resenting any who would pretend to rule them rather than voicing isonomia as a value. They obeyed no chiefs nor any instituted authority with the partial exception of "conjurers" or shamans—whose own powers in any case were not human but came from their spirit familiars. For all that equality, however, they did obey and respect Moose-Fly and his instantiations as stinging moose-flies, on pain of not catching any fish.

Moose-Fly is the "overlord, or master" of fishes; or in Naskapi idiom, *təpə-nəmə´k nəmə´c*, "he who governs fish," the dispenser of the fate of the fish tribes, specifically those of salmon and cod. Implicit in Speck's description is the common master-spirit conflation of the one and the many: the Moose-Fly as a divisible and distributed person is present in the moose flies who appear when fish are taken in the summer. In their individual forms, he comes "to witness the treatment of his subjects by the fishermen—his [Moose-Fly's] inclination to torment them by his stings . . . being an indication of his custody over the fish and a warning against wastefulness of the flesh. Then, to the observant and economical fish catcher the ration of flesh will be continued, while wasteful fisherman will sooner or later be punished by deprivation" ([1935] 1977, 118–19). Note that Moose-Fly is a doubled master, the species-master of moose-flies, as well as a generic master of fishes. A Naskapi elder in 1924 explained Moose-Fly's powers to Speck:

> *Məsəna´kʷ* I am called, the one who is master of the fish. I support them. You Indians will be given fish; you who do as is required are given fish, not him who wastes them. He who takes fish and wastes them will not henceforth secure anything. And likewise he who laughs at the fish on account of his big eyes here, will not catch fish. And he who ridicules the way fish are formed will not be happy for they will not be given my fishes. Whoever wants to take fish must do right; after this, fish will be given him. For I am master of the fish. And as I say, so it will happen here as I say. I the moose-fly, *məsəna´kʷ*, so I am named. (Speck [1935] 1977, 120)

To note the obvious, which is the present point, Moose-Fly, as master of fishes, is thus master of Naskapi people—in a notably vital way, as master and dispenser of their means of subsistence. Whether Naskapi fishers catch any salmon or not depends on their obedience to certain rules mandated by the Spirit-Power who supplies the fishes. For all that, Naskapi people have no such authorities of their own, for all that, they are "egalitarian" themselves—they know and submit to such ruling powers as a condition of their survival. Of necessity, they are subordinate members of a hierarchical society. And to speak of economics as well as politics, their technical success in catching fish is a function of their relationship to the species-master of the fishes and of the higher powers.

Achuar of Amazonia, practicing a mixed economy of hunting and slash-and-burn agriculture, are likewise subject to hierarchical relations beyond any they know themselves. Descola's (1994; 1996) description of their situation is instructive philosophically as well as ethnographically. Socially, Achuar start from somewhere near zero, or as Descola puts it, "a near caricature of zero-degree social integration," lacking chieftainship, village communities, and unilineal descent groups (1994, 8). Yet the animal-persons they hunt and the manioc persons they cultivate have near-equivalents of these institutions, cosmic forms of society in which Achuar themselves participate. The animals that men hunt are controlled by spiritual "game mothers"—the animals are in effect their children—with whom Achuar have to negotiate hunting agreements. More importantly, the peccaries, monkeys, and other prey have their own species masters, an outsized personage of the species type with whom the hunters, through the spells by which their souls communicate, are often in intense relationships. Here again, the game-persons are under the authority of chiefly figures who determine the access of human hunters on the condition that they too acknowledge the game masters' authority—and yet by negotiation they finally become predators rather than supplicants.

The same kind of engagement in cosmic hierarchy marks Achuar women's gardening, for their success depends on concourse with the goddess Nunkui, the mother of manioc and other crops—which are individually so many personages and instantiations of Nunkui. Again, by appropriate spells, harmonious and constant commerce between women gardeners and Nunkui is required at every stage of the agricultural process in order that the plants will grow and bring forth abundant yields of her offspring. By a complex interplay of voices, metaphors, and subject positions, the spells empower the women to assume the identity of Nunkui and nurture the plants as their own children (Taylor 1996; 2017). Notable here: on some occasions the gardeners are translated into daughters of Nunkui, in effect creating a burgeoning cosmological matrilineage of three generations—Nunkui, her gardener daughters, and their many plant children—without precedent in the human society itself (Karsten 1935, 128, 133).

How is it the people can conceive such relations of authority in regard to species-masters and other cosmic persons that are inconceivable within the community of human persons? "Conceive" is the apt word, for as Descola writes, the species master "is the ultimate incarnation of the species' aptitudes and their emblematic representative, rather in the manner of the essential forms of Platonic philosophy that exist forever in the empyreum of ideas, like so many models for the elements of the world" (1996, 126). Descola's ethnography is not only about Platonic shadows but rests on Platonic ideas. Perhaps an Aristotelian realism of class as the common empirical "essence" of all instances of the kind—the "tableness" of all tables, hence "table" as an existent—is more appropriate to the ontologies of immanence at issue here.

At issue here is that in any commonplace categorical or class realism, the relation of type to token, as of Moose-Fly to moose flies, is in itself a model of hierarchical relationships. Already by the usual interpretation, the Platonic form is said to participate in its worldly particulars, which is to say, the form is distributed in its instances but indivisible—as has been said more than once in these pages of the relations of spirit-being to its worldly manifestations. It only needs to be added that class-form, by encompassing its empirical instances, amounts to "hierarchy" in the sense that French anthropologist Louis Dumont gives it in his influential *Homo Hierarchicus* (1970). Class is the topology of hierarchy. Just so:

the Achuar tend to think of Nunkui as a single being, but endowed with the gift of ubiquity which allows her to multiply her appearances and to be present in all gardens in which her services are explicitly called upon. This apparent contradiction between unity of being and multiplicity of concrete manifestations is entirely characteristic of the way the Achuar see the existence of mythic beings. (Descola 1994,196)

One is reminded again of Evans-Pritchard introducing *Nuer Religion*: "It is in the nature of the conception of spirit . . . that what is distributed in a number of beings is, though different, yet the same and, though divided, yet a whole" (1956, 52). This organization of the one and the many is virtually a universal characteristic of the relations of higher metapersons to lesser ones in their domain.

Homo hierarchicus: hierarchy is built into the human way of thinking the world; it is ontological, insofar as the elements of the world are classed or categorized. And insofar as the universe for other necessary reasons is populated by other-than-human persons (metapersons), it is a more or less systematic cosmic polity, ruled by greater and lesser beings, the latter generally by delegation of the former. Introducing his own volume on Hawaiian religion, Valerio Valeri, quoting André Lalande's (1960) definition and echoing Plato, considers a "type" as a "'*concrete* being, real or imaginary which is representative of a class of beings' because it . . . 'presents the most characteristic and perfect form thereof'" (1985, ix; translation mine). Accordingly, "since as types the deities personify classes of moral, social beings, I consider them as moral, social species as well. In sum, 'concept,' 'type,' and 'species' can all be used, depending on the context, to designate what the deities stand for" (ix). Or, to be reminded of the deity of the African Kongo Nzambi: "much more than an abstract conception, he participates in and is presupposed by all lesser forces or entities, the 'spirits,' the dead, and the living' (MacGaffey 1986, 79). And again Magalim, god of the wild at the confluence of the Sepik and the Fly headwaters in New Guinea: "Despite a diversity of appearances and haunts, Telefolmin hold that all *masalai* [wild spirits] are in fact one being with many aliases whose true nature is Magalim. Magalim is identified with the earth and its powers and is held to be the master of wild animals and the forest" (Jorgensen 1998, 103). In Fausto's (2012) already noted study of master/ owner concepts in Amazonia, he speaks of them as "a singular image of a collectivity," "a magnified singularity," and "a form of encompassment, expressed as a relation between containers and contained" (32–33).

The same categorical structure functions in relations between Amazonian chiefs and their followers. The chief stands *pars pro toto* for the community—a phenomenon familiar to students of many Oceanic societies, among others, where chiefs or big-men use the first-person singular in speaking of their lineages or clans. Indeed, the same categorical realism of type and token is the topology of totemism and lineage organization itself. Totemism is essentially a segmentary form of species-master concepts, consisting of an emblematic form (bear, lion, etc.) of living instantiations (bears, lions, etc.), differentially associated with and identifying the constituent groups of a given society. As for descent groups such as lineages, consider this keen observation of Alfred Gell in *Art and Agency* (1998):

> The notion of genealogy . . . is the key trope for making plurality singular and singularity plural. Any individual person is "multiple" in the sense of being the precipitate of a multitude of genealogical relationships, each of which is instantiated in his/her person; and conversely, an aggregate of persons, such as a lineage or tribe, is "one person" in consequence of being one genealogy: the original ancestor is now instantiated, not as one body, but as the many bodies into which his one body has transformed itself. (140)

(That well said, "lineage" as the participation of the ancestor in the bodies and identities of living persons—as by the transmission of "blood," "bone," or "soul"—is a spiritual condition as much as it is a hierarchical order. Not simply that the ancestor stands for the lineage the way "manioc" stands for plants of a certain nature, but more as the goddess Nunkui is the mother of manioc. Divinity is no more imaginary or less real than kinship.) In sum, as a categorical notion, "class" is a hierarchical order of things, a symbolic topology of token and type, which when hypostatized in a world of immanent person-beings generates structures of authority and power far superior to humans, and to which they must submit—and endeavor to appropriate.

The prominent British anthropologist and specialist of Southeast Asian cultures, Rodney Needham, deftly undermines Durkheim's argument that the notion of "class" originated as a representation of the fact that people organized themselves into groups, when he observes that a notion of class was already required in order for people to organize themselves into groups, one distinct from another (1963, xxvii). Class, of course, was only one of the Aristotelian or Kantian categories—like cause, time, space, and so forth—for which Durkheim would claim a sociological origin rather than an a priori intuition. Thus, "the first logical categories were social categories; the first classes of things were classes of men, into which these things were integrated" (Durkheim and Mauss 1963, 82). Without going any further into the tempting epistemic murk of the existence of a transcendental subject in a world of immanent subjectivity, what is of greater relevance here is the lack of any necessary correspondence between the human social order and its supposed collective representations, notably the metahuman or spiritual order, as Durkheim envisioned it.

As said earlier, well beyond Durkheim, this sense of "religion" as an imaginary epiphenomenon of real sociopolitical relations, mirroring or inverting them in ways that functionally sustain them, is our native common average normal social science, including virtually every variety thereof from classical Marxism to neoliberal economism, by way of garden varieties of anthropology, history, political science, sociology, and cultural studies. Like Marx in his *Theses on Feuerbach* (1845/1888; in Wood 1988, 80–81), where he agrees to a point with Feuerbach's critique of religion as the secular world detaching itself from itself and establishing itself in the clouds, thereby creating an imaginary religious duplicate of the secular order. Only that Marx as anthropologist insists that this version of religion was an ideal form of a society in which a ruling capitalist class expropriated and victimized the greater population of working people.

Anthropology itself has an interesting history with this issue, marked early on by the Scottish folklorist Andrew Lang's objection to E. B.

Tylor's reflectionist theory of religion as society transported into the clouds. Tylor, the pioneer British evolutionary anthropologist, writes:

> Among nation after nation, it is still clear how, man being the type of deity, human society and government became the model on which divine society and government were shaped. As chiefs and kings are among men, so are the great gods among the lesser spirits. . . . With little exception, wherever a savage or barbaric system of religion is thoroughly described, great gods make their appearance in the spiritual world as distinctly as chiefs in the human world. (1871, 2:225)

"Very good," comments Lang, but "whence comes the great God among tribes which have neither chief nor king, nor any distinctions of rank, as among Fuegians, Bushmen, and Australians? . . . This theory (Hume's) will not work where people have a great God but no king or chief; nor where they have a king but no Zeus or other supreme King-god, as among the Aztecs" (1898, 179). Lang is on good ethnographic ground, as will be confirmed presently. By contrast, the radical separation of the "spiritual world" from the "human world," of "divine society" from "human society," or the "religious" from the "secular" in the various celestialization-of-society theories reveals their own cultural ground in a society where God has gone away. The transcendentalist paradigms of the Wise Men fail to comprehend the immanentist practices of the Bushmen.

Yet it was wrong to say that there is no necessary relation between the structure of human society and the morphology and potency of the encompassing cosmic polity. As a general rule, the closer the human society comes to a "zero degree of social integration," lacking chieftainship, stable settlements, corporate descent groups, and so on, the greater the disproportion between the organization and powers of human and metahumans. Hunters-and-gatherers as a general rule are far outnumbered by a multitude of spirits, which for their part are more or less systematically ordered in a hierarchy dominated by inclusive spirits on the order of gods. We have seen the like among Algonquian peoples, but just to refresh the memory, this notice by Robert Brightman of Rock Cree: "Differences in the degree and character of a person's skills and powers derive both from the number and the identity of the dream guardians they possess. This implies a more or less systematic hierarchy of animate beings in terms of their relative 'power' (M. Black 1977). Bears, the game ruler entities, thunderbirds, clouds, the sun, the moon, the morning star, and the beings associated with the four winds and directions are today identified as especially powerful agencies" ([1973] 2002, 87).

It only needs adding that the lesser metapersons of the Cree cosmos acted with powers (the multitude of *manitōw*) devolved from a figure (Kicimanitōw, Manitōw) with the dimensions of a ruling god. David Thompson, the late eighteenth-century fur trader who sojourned in Rock Cree territory, here following Brightman ([1973] 2002), "described the rulers as occupying a node within the cosmogonic design of the deity Kicimanitōw who granted human beings autonomy but placed other kinds of living things under the guardianship of 'manitos' over which it in turn exercised control. Of the functions of the rulers in relation to their species, Thompson's clients emphasized control of migration" (92). This in a society where the "most power to control others' decisions and behavior was limited to the authority of men and women over their unmarried junior relatives" (11).

Note that where the authority of chiefs and kings significantly affected the behavior of the population at large, it also then reached to the order of the cosmos, since it was fundamentally the other way around. The power that men had learned to exercise over their fellows was derived from and sanctioned by gods of the kind that already ruled over peoples who themselves had no rulers. Anu, the Sky, supreme god of Sumerian and Akkadian civilizations of the third millennium BC in Mesopotamia, was the prototype of all fathers and "as the 'pristine king and ruler,' he was the prototype of all rulers" (Jacobsen [1946] 1977). His were the insignia in which the essence of royalty was embodied— the scepter, headband, shepherd's staff, and crown—and from him the king acquired them. These insignia antedated the kingship; they were in heaven even before Anu. "And when the king commands and the command is unquestionably and immediately obeyed, when it 'comes true,' it is again the essence of Anu which manifests itself. . . . It is Anu's power that makes it immediately efficacious" (139). What men do, the gods are doing, even (or especially) when it is the king.

Durkheim was certainly right about this: power is a religious idea. But the point here is anti-Durkheimian, as Viveiros de Castro (1992) deftly shows in his landmark ethnography of the Araweté:

> How to account for the coexistence of, on the one hand, a "loosely structured" organization (few social categories, absence of global segmentations, weak institutionalization of interpersonal relations, lack of differentiation between public and domestic spheres) with, on the other hand, an extensive taxonomy of the spiritual world . . . [and] an active presence of that world in daily life, and a thoroughly vertical, "Gothic" orientation of thought? Societies such as Araweté reveal how utterly trivial any attempt to establish functional consistencies or formal correspondences between morphology and cosmology or between institution and representation (2–3) . . . [E]very attempt at sociological reduction brings us back to cosmology, or where there is no way to privilege the sociological codification because we risk finding almost nothing—or something else: the gods, the dead, and discourse. (27)

Societies such as Araweté would include other peoples of Amazonia, native Australia, northern North America, southern South America, much of New Guinea, upland Southeast Asia and Indonesia, Siberia, and parts of Africa: I mean so-called tribes without rulers or egalitarian societies. For all of them, it would be futile to claim a correspondence between morphology and cosmology.

There are no egalitarian societies. Yet as ruled by cosmic authorities, these societies have a deep experience of subjection to persons essentially like themselves. "We are surrounded by enemies," the Chukchee shaman told the revolutionary Russian writer and anthropologist Waldemar Bogoras in the early twentieth century. "'Spirits' always walk about invisibly with gaping mouths. We are always cringing, and distributing gifts on all sides, asking protection of one, giving ransom to another, and unable to obtain anything whatsoever gratuitously" (1904–9, 295). Greed and exploitation may also be religious in origin.

The spirits are generally more venal as well as more powerful than the people they sustain—for a price in deference if not also in substance.

But to the main point: even societies approaching a zero degree of integration themselves are embedded in a hierarchically organized, cosmic polity, in which they occupy a dependent, solicitous, deferential, and vulnerable position. We need something like a Copernican revolution within anthropological perspective: from human society as the center of a universe upon which it projects its own forms—that is, the received transcendentalist wisdom—to the immanentist condition: the ethnographic realities of people's dependence on encompassing life-giving and death-dealing powers, essentially persons like themselves, who rule earthly existence. Something like the state, the cosmic state, is the general condition of humankind—even in the state of nature.

The Cosmic State

[In Sumerian cities and their Akkadian successors of the third millennium BCE], the Mesopotamian universe did not, like ours, show a fundamental bipartition into animate and inanimate, living and dead matter. Nor had it different levels of reality. . . . In the Mesopotamian universe, therefore, everything, whether living being, thing, abstract concept—every stone, every tree, every notion—had a will and character of its own. World order, the regularity and system observable in the universe could accordingly . . . be conceived of in only one fashion, as an order of wills. The universe as an organized whole was a society, a state. (Jacobsen [1946] 1977, 149)

Thus the Danish historian Thorkild Jacobsen in 1946 saw the lineaments of a state in the cosmology of Mesopotamian civilizations of the third millennium BCE. He describes the human society as part of a larger, universal society, and the larger society as a political state. The description poses the question: Is there anything in this cosmology, any kind of metahuman being or spiritual hierarchy, we haven't already seen the planet around, even among peoples without rulers and no such claim to the pretentious status of "civilization"? To compare great things with

small ones: for all the differences in scale and cult, the Sumerian cosmology is not that much different in structure than the universe of Central Inuit or New Guinea Highland peoples. True that Sumerians had
notably great gods, An, Enlil, and others, while notably for Central Inuit
almost everything has its *inua*, its inner "person." For their part, Central
Inuit are ruled by powerful high gods, Sedna, Sila, and Moon, while
Sumerians had their share of animism. Both have extensive and complex
"rules of life" sanctioned by the gods and enforced by lesser metahuman
powers. If Sumerians were encompassed in a cosmic state, so are Iglulik
people. Given that cultural range, it seems safe to say that, taken in its
cosmic totality, the state is a universal human institution.

What follows here is a more or less detailed description of the com-
parables in the Inuit and Sumerian cosmologies, with added notes from
New Guinea and elsewhere.

To begin, we have to rehearse the outlines of the Central Inuit cosmic
scheme. The triad of gods—Sedna, Sila, and Moon, deities respectively
of the Sea, the Atmosphere, and the Heavens—were known across the
Arctic from East Greenland to Alaska, if under different local designa-
tions and in varying relations of prominence. The Sedna-figures are supreme in the central region, Sila in Greenland, and Sila or Moon Man
in Alaska. The wide distribution and local differentiation of this divine
triad, coupled to the elaborate rules of human conduct sanctioned by
the gods, amount to persuasive testimony of their antiquity and indigenous status.

The present discussion focuses on Central Inuit, whose remoteness
and limited contact with Euro-Americans are still further warrants of
the aboriginal rule of great gods over pretty much anarchic people.
From Coronation Gulf to West Greenland, as American anthropologist
Edward Moffatt Weyer puts in a vintage text, "All groups of Eskimos . . .
perform ceremonies that characterize their religion in one way or another as belonging to the cult of the Sea Goddess" (1932, 355–56). Sum-
marizing several nineteenth-century Western reports, Franz Boas (1901)
writes similarly of Sedna's authority in the region: "This woman, the
mother of sea mammals, may be considered as the principal deity of the
Central Eskimo. She has supreme sway over the destinies of mankind,

and almost all the observances of these tribes are for the purposes of retaining her good will or propitiating her if she has been offended" (119). Sedna holds sway over human destinies as the mother of the sea animals that are the essential condition of an Inuit existence: notably the seals, whales, and walruses upon which people depend for food, clothing, heat, and light. (By some accounts, she is also the mother of land animals and humankind.) From her large stone house at the bottom of the sea, she makes the animals available to hunters, or else withholds them and threatens people with starvation, according to their respect or disregard for "all the observances of these tribes" as aforementioned—and as will be further considered momentarily. First, however, to consider the rest of the Inuit pantheon with its "spiritual bureaucracy," which is largely engaged in carrying out Sedna's will.

Taken together, Knud Rasmussen's (1929; 1931) intimate accounts of Iglulik and Netsilik peoples indeed convey the sense of a *cosmopoliteia*, with greater gods commanding lesser spirits, down to the myriad "evil" spirits of the dead, to uphold the elaborate divine order, the "observances" or "rules of life," imposed upon the human population. Known in Iglulik as "the woman down there" (Arnâluk Takánâluk), the Sedna-figure, writes Rasmussen, "plays by far the most important part in everyday life." She is, "if one may use such an expression, the principal deity, with power in some respects over both Sila and Tarqeq, these latter acting as agents to see that her will is obeyed" (1929, 62). Not that Sila and Moon Man are mere servants of Sedna. They are semiautonomous, able to detect and punish human delicts on their own, sometimes through their own lesser agents. While Sila is a dangerous Storm spirit, as Air he can be celebrated as a universal life-giver, source of humans' breath-soul. The Moon, a great hunter in the sky and benefactor of human hunters, is also a power of fertility; by shining on the genitals of barren women, he makes them conceive. Sometime protector of people against Sedna or Sila, Moon Man is regarded as the most sympathetic of the great deities. Still, Rasmussen reports, when a transgression of the "rules of life" is detected, the Sea Goddess, if she does not act directly, acts through the other deities. "The moon spirit helps her to see that the rules of life are duly observed, and comes hurrying down to earth to punish any instance of neglect. And both sea spirit and moon spirit employ Sila to execute all punishments in any way connected with the weather"—such as severe and prolonged blizzards, preventing men from hunting (Rasmussen 1929, 62–63).

No doubt this is generally understood *post factum*. There is a blizzard, that's Sila, so someone has broken the rules. Moon sees it because from up in the heavens he can see everything. But although the action of these two gods is, as it were, deduced empirically, the intercession of Sedna is not. The intercession of Sedna is rather axiomatic: she is the Prime Mover of the Inuit Cosmos, the will and power in the action of the other spirits. Indeed, in Rasmussen's (1931) ethnography of Netsilik people, the great multitude of "evil spirits" is also engaged on her behalf in enforcing the "rules of life." Here, too, the Sedna figure, Nuliajuk, is accounted the primary source of a universal governance:

> The powers that rule the earth and all the animals and the lives of mankind on earth are the great spirits who live in the sea, on land, out in space and in the Land of the Sky. There are many, and many kinds of spirits, but there are only three really great and really independent ones, and they are Nuliajuk, Nârssuk [aka Sila] and Tatqeq [aka Moon Man].... and the most powerful of them all is Nuliajuk, the mother of animals and mistress of both the sea and the land. At all times she makes mankind feel how she vigilantly and mercilessly takes care that all souls, of both animals and mankind, are shown the respect that ancient rules of life demand. (Rasmussen 1931, 224)

At this point, the description of the structure becomes complex. Nuliajuk rules, Rasmussen says, through *toṅrät*, both "the ordinary *toṅrät* and *toṅrät kiglᴐrigtut*: evil spirits" (224). These are not further defined, though cognates of *toṅrät* usually designate spirits in general; hence I take Rasmussen to mean ghosts and demons, the former the innumerable souls of people and animals who "have not obtained peace" because of a bad or neglected death (239), the latter the disfigured humanlike ogres that haunt Inuit settlements. These spirits are said to make the animals available to hunters or to withhold them, according to Nuliajuk's will. The same spirits are said to influence wind and weather, although apparently through Narssuk, the Sila figure, and one of his subordinate spirits. And recall Boas's vivid description of Sedna's rule of the myriad evil spirits during the raging storms of early autumn (Boas [1888] 1964, 195–96). But when a great shaman manages to harpoon Sedna, like a seal through the ice, she withdraws and all the dangerous beings with her. In sum, while the Inuit cosmic hierarchy seems clear enough, from great deities and their attending spirits through ghosts, demons, the *inua* of things, and the name-spirits of persons, in practice the system is marked by overlapping and duplicated powers. And since, as will be seen, all the complex rules of human life are said to express the will of Sedna, as would their sanctions as imposed by whatever spirit-power, in that respect, for Inuit too, Divinity is one.

Scholars perennially agonize over whether to consider the likes of Sedna as "gods." Too often some promising candidate is rejected for failing to closely match our own ideas of the Deity, with all His transcendental, judgmental, and beneficent qualities. But as the psychoanalyst and scholar Daniel Merkur remarks of the Inuit Powers, "To deny honorific status as 'god' to the Sea Mother, the Indweller in the Wind [Sila], and the Moon Man is a pedantic nicety devoid of humanity and religious tolerance" (1991, 37–38). Sedna, Sila, and Moon have the essential divine qualities of immortality and universality, even as they are the sources of human life, prosperity, and death. Only that, as immanent "indwellers," they *are* the phenomena so governing the human fate. In this connection, it is notable that they are not humans themselves, for all their attributes as persons. Precisely they are erstwhile humans who have been translated to divine status, over and above the human population, by breaches of the norms of humanity—specifically by crimes against kinship. Various versions of Sedna's origin depict her as an orphan, as mutilated in sacrifice by her father, and sometimes as responsible for his death; the Moon Man's divine career featured matricide and incest with his sister; Sila left the earth when his parents or adopted parents, who were giants, were killed by humans. Musing and amusing: the Inuit cosmological traditions (aka "mythology") rehearse a classical Western-scholarly formula of state-formation, the progression "from kinship to territory." Leaving their kinship status, the gods become ex-humans, and achieve a kind of territorial sovereignty, each in and over their own domain and the phenomena therein.

Above all, the deities, particularly Sedna, motivate and enforce the vast, complex, and intimate array of rules that control people's behavior down to whether a woman may comb her hair as long as a newly captured seal has not yet been cut up. "From birth to death, human beings have to regulate their lives according to the powers that control human weal and woe, and whose anger can give rise to suffering and hardship" (Rasmussen 1929, 169; cf. Weyer 1932, 367). Although often referred to as "taboos," the regulations include many prescriptions as well as proscriptions, hence the adoption here of Rasmussen's designation, "rules of life." There must be some hundreds if not a thousand such rules in the long chapter of Rasmussen's monograph on "The Intellectual Character of the Iglulik" (1929)—chapter entitled "Precepts or Rules of Life and Conduct for All Occasions." The rules, as he says, apply "under all conditions of life," and given their scope, he can only offer a kind of extensional definition of their principal kinds: they apply generally "when help is most needed," during pregnancy, birth, infancy, transition to womanhood (menstruation), illness, death, "and last but not least in hunting" (169).

The great majority of the rules, even for hunting, have no evident (Euro-American) rational ground, whatever they may have had in their original context; and many have no apparent meaningful relation either to the activity at issue. The barest explanations have to do with interest of the deities, again Sedna especially, in the project: like the taboos regarding the treatment of bearded seals, which are many because bearded seals are a favorite of Sedna's. That said, for Inuit in general the rules of the hunt "elicit the favor of the spiritual forces presiding over [the] food supply. . . . [T]he taboos are directed toward the spirits of the game animals themselves or toward their protecting deities" (Weyer 1932, 367). Here, for illustration, are a few more of the Iglulik rules of life, recorded separately by Rasmussen in the 1920s, and before him, Boas:

- A man who has lost his wife may not drive or strike his dogs for a year after. (Rasmussen [1927] 1999, 135)

- A pregnant woman must never go outside without her mittens on. (Rasmussen 1929, 170)
- A newly born infant is cleansed by being wiped all over with the skin of a . . . small snipe; water must not be used. (171)
- The marrow bones of animals killed by a firstborn son are never to be eaten with a knife, but must be crushed with stones. (179)
- A man suffering want through ill success in hunting must, when coming to another village and sitting down to eat, never eat with a woman he has not seen before. (182)
- Persons hunting seal from a snow hut on sea ice may not work with soapstone. (184)
- Young girls present in a house where a seal is being cut up must take off their kamiks and remain barefooted as long as the work is in progress. (185)
- If a woman is unfaithful to her husband, while he is out hunting walrus, especially on drift ice, the man will dislocate his hip and have severe pains in the sinews. (186)
- If a woman sees a whale, she must point to it with her middle finger. (187)
- Widows are never allowed to pluck birds. (196)
- [A woman whose child has died] must never drink water from melted ice, but only water from melted snow. (198)
- On sleeping in a new snow hut for the first time, one must not sleep overlong, or poor hunting will result. It is necessary to show the souls of the animals that one is eager to capture them. (191)
- A woman who has a newborn child, and has not yet recovered, must eat only of seals caught by her husband, a boy, or an aged man; else the vapor arising from her body would become attached to the souls of other seals, which would take the transgression down to Sedna, thus making her hands sore. (Boas 1901, 125)

Sedna punishes hunters who disrespect the sea mammals because, as their mother she is consubstantial with them. By traditions well known across the region, these animals were derived from Sedna's finger joints, severed as she clung to the gunwales of a boat from which she had been thrown overboard to calm a storm. In the most popular accounts, her own father had so sacrificed and mutilated her; in other versions, she was an orphan, devalued and thrown in the sea for lack of kindred support. The animals "being part of herself," Sedna is a distributed person, one over and in the bearded seals, walruses, and other hunters' game—animals that besides have their own indwelling persons (*inua*).

Accordingly, hunting seals involves a triad of souls or *inua*—of animal, god, and hunter—as Boas (1901, 120–21) relates in an account of the fate of the hunter who violates the rules. For its part, the hunted seal in Boas's text is endowed with greater powers than ordinary humans. It can sense that the hunter has had illicit contact with a corpse by the vapor of blood or death he emits, breaking a taboo on hunting while in such condition. The revulsion of the animal is thereupon communicated to Sedna, who in the normal course would withdraw the seals to her house under the sea, or perhaps dispatch Sila on punishing blizzards, thus making hunting impossible and exposing the entire human community to starvation (120). The punishment thus comes down on the whole community, which is why a great premium is put on public confession. The offense exposed, a powerful shaman (*angakok*) may undertake the hazardous task of placating or coercing Sedna into releasing the animals, or confronting Sila to calm the weather. Great shamans have been known to beat the god into submission.

Note that in many anthropological treatments of animism, inasmuch as they are reduced to individualistic or phenomenological reflections on the relations between humans and animals, these interactions are characterized as reciprocal, egalitarian, or horizontal; whereas often in social practice they are at least three-part relations, involving also the master-person of the game animal concerned, in which case they are hierarchical—with the offending person in the client position. Or rather, the entire Inuit community is thereby put in a subordinate position, since the sanction also falls on the fellows of the transgressor; and as the effect is likewise generalized to all seals.

In apparent contrast to Iglulik people west of Hudson's Bay and Netsilik people in North Baffinland, in South Baffinland many of the demonic beings (*tuurngait*) who are helping spirits of shamans are also masters of game animals, with whom, moreover, they are identified by nature. A manuscript written by the Anglican missionary Edmund James Peck—in the region from 1894 to 1905—recently discovered and analyzed by Frédéric Laugrand and colleagues, catalogs some 347 spirits of various description from human and humanoid to animal by way of hybrid creatures (Laugrand et al. 2006, 419–68). (These are of the character discussed elsewhere as "monsters" or "demons.") Known as the "owners" of various species, many of these powerful spirits make caribou, seals, and other prey available to hunters through the ritual action of their associated shamans.

Many indeed are the indwelling *inua* of game, places, or objects, which for the *inua* of species entails the right to give their animals away, or in some instances to exclusively hunt them. Accordingly, the ethnographers prefer to speak of the guardian *tuurngait* as "owners" rather than "rulers" of game, in contradistinction to Franz Boas, who used both terms in his Baffinland work—appropriately, I believe, for the clear sense of dominion involved. In any event, as with Sedna and seals, "ownership" here is a class relation of master-to-individual, including the sense of bodily encompassment of the individual animals in the personified species-being, the *tuurngait*. "Animals, objects, and places have an *inua* that has to be respected. . . . The *inua* of a dog is its owner and he can give away the dog. The *tuurngait* as described by Peck often appear to hold a similar position towards animals: they can give them away. This notion of ownership seems to imply some sort of identity between the animal and its owner. . . . [T]he notion of ownership implies . . . a close relationship between owner and owned (as in 'my own body')" (Laugrand et al. 2002, 39).

In sum, the cosmic totality, if largely ruled by Sedna, consists of a variety of beings: on one hand, the indwelling persons of things (*inua*), including the great gods indwelling their domains, game masters, the enspirited people, and the significant objects of their existence; on the other hand, the "free spirits," the multitudinous ghosts of animals and people, and the many forms of demons, most of them dangerous to people. Writing of Nunamiut of Northern Alaska, anthropologist Nicholas Gubser (1965) puts the matter of *inua* in a way that makes interesting reading in comparison with Sumerian concepts of the nature of divinity, to be presented shortly:

> The Nunamiut regard "most, or possibly all, animate objects (people, mammals, birds, fish, and insects) and most inanimate objects (lakes, mountains, the moon, directions of wind, and the atmosphere as a whole)" each to have an *inua*. . . . "Without a spirit [*inua*], an object might still occupy space and have weight, but it would have no meaning, it would have no . . . real existence. When an object is invested with an *inua*, it is a part of nature of which we are aware." (Merkur 1991, 26–27, quoting Gubser 1965, 199)

Otherwise said, when an object or phenomenon makes a meaningful difference in the cultural scheme, such that we become aware of it, it has an *inua*. In the event, the physicality of the phenomenon—the body in the case of objects or the sensibility in case of thunder or winds—is inseparable from its interior spirit. The physicality of the thing is not its spirituality, but the two are one. (Which is also to say it is not a "thing.") Accordingly, for Central Inuit again, "Divinity is one;" or as Boas put it, everything from stones to the moon has its *inua* ([1908] 1974, 276). Note the Moon man is a god; Sila, the atmosphere, is commonly spoken of as "Sila Inua"; likewise, the sea goddess: "The *inuat* [pl] of the sea, the moon and the air could be considered the spiritual owners of their respective territories" (Oosten 1976, 27). Considering, then, Sedna's sometimes control over these divine and lesser *inua*, as well as demons and ghosts, in enforcing the prescribed rules of human life with penalties ranging from accident and illness to starvation and death, everything happens as if Inuit people were the subjects of a polity of cosmic dimensions—indeed, a cosmic state.

Impressed by the ubiquity of *inua* and the rule of the numerous demons by a single master, the early Danish geologist and explorer Henry Rink in 1875 depicted the universe of West Greenland Inuit as a "general government of the world":

> Inasmuch as we are allowed to consider almost every spot or supposed object a special dominion with its special inua ruling within

certain limits, we might also be led to imagine several of those do-
minions as united, and made subordinate to one common ruler, by
which means we would have a general government of the world
under one supreme head ready organised. . . . Still, on looking at the
whole religious views of the natives, they do seem to presuppose a
single power by which the world is ruled. (Rink 1875, 38–9)

"Government" would seem exaggerated, but the observation of a unitary
power is accurate: a metaperson host under a triad of supreme authorities enforcing complex "rules of life" with rewards and punishments
ranging from prosperity to death. Thomas Hobbes famously speaks of
the state of nature as all that time "men live[d] without a common
Power to keep them all in awe" ([1651] 1991, 88); Knud Rasmussen reports the Netsilik people had more than enough such awesome power:
"Life on earth is a constant alternation between evil and good, between
mankind and the universe. . . . Mankind is held in awe through its fear
of hunger and sickness" (1931, 224). "We do not believe, we fear," Aua
the Iglulik shaman said to Rasmussen (1929), a statement often repeated
in anthropology circles:

> We fear the weather spirit of earth, that we must fight against to wrest
> our food from land and sea. We fear Sila. We fear dearth and hunger
> in the cold snow huts. We fear Takánakapsâluk [Sedna], the great
> woman down at the bottom of the sea, that rules over all the beasts
> of the sea. We fear the sickness that we meet with daily all around
> us. . . . We fear the souls of dead human beings and of the animals we
> have killed. (54–56)

No doubt these fears are constant, but they are often only latent,
belied by visitors' reports of the amiable and even cheerful dispositions
of Inuit people. As the midcentury anthropologist Margaret Lantis puts
it, to some extent they are living a "dual life" (1950, 318). Aua, the same
shaman who recounted the litany of fears to Rasmussen also led him to
Kublo's house nearby, where a small blubber lamp flickered, giving virtually no heat, and two cold children lay under skin rugs. Aua looked at
Rasmussen: "'Why should it be cold and comfortless in here? Kublo

has been out hunting all day, and if he had got a seal, as he deserved, his wife would now be sitting laughing by her lamp, letting it burn full, without fear of having no blubber left for tomorrow. The place would be warm and bright and cheerful, the children would come out from under their rugs and enjoy life'" (1929, 55).

As I say, to juxtapose Inuit to Sumerians of the third millennium BCE and their Akkadian successors is to compare small things with great ones. Sedna is no Enlil; the *angakok*'s hut is no priestly temple; no Inuit god is One over as Many manifestations or in-personations as the family of An/Anu. Yet in the principles as well as the varieties of divinity, the two immanentist systems are fundamentally alike, beginning with the Vichian fact that "what men do, the gods are doing." As the decisive agents of human achievements, the cosmic manifold of metahuman powers amounts to an all-around cultural infrastructure:

> [E]verything seems to indicate that the ancient Mesopotamians viewed the functioning of the universe—its never-ending routines as well as more or less abrupt turning points, the functioning of nature as well as that of the society of human beings and of each individual— as only the continuation of creation. Once the world appeared and began to exist, everything that occurred in it, like the origin itself, was wholly due to the gods' intervention alone, and it was the only determining cause. (Bottéro 2001a, 90; cf. 104)

The point is that culture itself is a divine creation—as set forth in a famous Mesopotamian text from the late third or early second millennium BCE, on "Enki and the World Order" (J. Black 2002; Averbeck 2017).

The great god Enki fashioned the human order, from the institution of kingship to the system of irrigation ditches and dikes on down to the standard shape of brick molds, acting by delegation from his brother Enlil (then ruling under their celestial father, An):

> When father Enki goes forth to the inseminated people, good seed will come forth. When Nudimmud goes forth to the good pregnant ewes, good lambs will be born [*ll.* 52–60]. . . . At my [Enki's]

command, sheepfolds have been built, cow-pens have been fenced-off. When I approach heaven, a rain of abundance rains from heaven. When I approach earth, there is a high carp-flood [*ll.* 89–99]. . . . He organised ploughs, yokes and teams . . . he opened up the holy furrows, and made the barley grow on the cultivated fields . . . Enki, responsible for ditches and dykes [*ll.* 318–25]. . . . Enki placed in charge of all this the king [*ll.* 358–67]. . . . He demarcated borders and fixed boundaries [*ll.* 368–80]. (Black 2002)

For each of these things or activities, Enki placed a lesser god "in charge"; hence a great panoply of gods (*dingir*) was engaged in the great panoply of human social practices—here again, an all-around cultural praxis. An observation of Jacobsen's on temple workers indicates what being "in charge" entailed:

> Since man, as the Sumerians saw him, was weak and could achieve no success in anything without divine assistance, it was fortunate that all these human workers in and outside the temple could invigorate themselves with divine power. Each group of human toilers had human overseers; but above these there were divine officials to direct the work and infuse success into human efforts. (1976, 81; cf. Vanstiphout 2009, 30)

Another Vichian principle thus follows, the rule of *verum ipsum factum*: since human cultural practices were made by the gods, they alone could know them; and most particularly, they knew the hidden and recondite forces that made the grain grow when the farmer planted it, the spear fly true when the warrior wielded it, or the reed flute sound when the musician played it.

All this is to say that the gods are immanent in human affairs, whether directly, by their manifest or distributed persons, or by delegation to subordinate gods—the lesser gods "in charge," the demons, ghosts, or indwelling persons of things. Contrasting Mesopotamian immanentism with biblical transcendentalism, students of the Ancients such as Henri and H. A. Frankfort make the point in terms particularly relevant here. The Frankforts open their conclusion to the important work, *The Intellectual Adventure of Ancient Man* (Frankfort et al. [1946] 1977) with a striking critique of biblical discourse on God's work as totally inappropriate to ancient Near Eastern conceptions—blasphemy, even:

> When we read in Psalm 19 that "the heavens declare the glory of God; and the firmament sheweth his handiwork," we hear a voice which mocks the beliefs of Egyptians and Babylonians. The heavens, which were to the psalmist but a witness of God's greatness, were to the Mesopotamians the very majesty of godhead, the highest ruler, Anu. . . . In Egypt and Mesopotamia, the divine was comprehended as immanent: the gods were in nature. . . . The God of the psalmists and the prophets . . . transcended nature. . . . The mainspring of the acts, thoughts, and feelings of early [Near Eastern] man was the conviction that the divine was immanent in nature. (363)

Fair enough, except that as American Assyriologist Francesca Rochberg (2016) documents at length, ancient Mesopotamia was "before nature," a functioning and intelligible ontological order that existed before the Greeks' *physis* and its subsequent elaborations. Composed essentially of divine subjects, of metapersons, the cosmos for Mesopotamians was not a "natural" realm of impersonal "objects," operating by their own laws—any more than it thus implied a transcendent category of the "supernatural."

> Because of the absence of nature as a meaningful category in the cuneiform world, the problem of "apparently irrational beliefs," usually associated with explanation by recourse to supernatural agency, must be addressed differently. Indeed, to invoke supernatural agency presupposes a conception of the order of nature, and to base causation upon a supposed category of the supernatural distorts the evidence of cuneiform magical texts that do not operate on the basis of such ideas. (Rochberg 2016, 13; cf. Rochberg 2009)

Hence the gods were not "in nature," as the Frankforts put it. Nor should we accept the commonplace, equally oxymoronic alternatives, such as the gods "are nature," "all of nature is divine," or the world is populated by "nature spirits." In the anthropology of most of humanity, "nature" is not natural.

Thorkild Jacobsen also draws upon the Old Testament—Exodus 3:1–5, on Moses and the Burning Bush—in order to make clear the contrast with Mesopotamian immanentism. In so doing, moreover, he characterizes Mesopotamian divinity in a way that could equally stand for the *inua* of the phenomenal world of Central Inuit, not to mention the cultures of immanence generally. What, he asks by way of introduction to the biblical passage, makes Mesopotamian religion "specifically Mesopotamian"? He proceeds to answer:

> One cannot but note a tendency to experience the Numinous as immanent in some specific feature of the confrontation, rather than as all transcendent. The ancient Mesopotamian, it would seem, saw numinous power as a revelation of indwelling spirit, as power at the center of something that caused it to be and thrive and flourish. (Jacobsen 1976, 5–6)

So God calls out from the midst of the bush, and says Moses, "Here am I." But, opines Jacobsen, this God is not the bush; he is calling from the bush, "but he is altogether transcendent, and there is nothing but a purely situational, ephemeral, relation to the bush" (6).

A Mesopotamian would have experienced the event much differently. The numinous power he saw and heard was "power of, not just in, the bush, power at the center of its being, the vital force causing it to be and making it thrive and flourish. He would have experienced the Numinous as immanent" (6). (In any event, Sumerians did not "hear" divine speech so much as they perceived it in omens and divination; not a big Inuit technique, but elaborated nearby on the Labrador Peninsula [cf. Rochberg 2016, 170].) And, a few pages later, Jacobsen observes that "bringing the phenomenon into being was therefore also and necessarily bringing into being its power and will; and the creation of the outer form, the external habitation, was inviting—or magically enforcing—the presence of the power within" (Jacobsen 1976, 14). The implication is, when Enki made the barley or the plough, he made the efficacious spirit-person of and in them—in Sumerian and Akkadian, the "god" in them (*dingir*; Akkadian: *ilu*).

It seems to be an academic sport among students of ancient Mesopotamia—on the model of some ancient Mesopotamian professors?—to count the number of their "gods," although since the number of spirits is countless, and could run into the many thousands and include such "gods" as rivers, chariots, parts of temples, demons, and date palms, the effort is fruitless. Especially since all these were being equally labeled "gods," *dingir* in Sumerian, *ilu* in Akkadian, typically because they explicitly carried the Sumerian or Akkadian determinative for "Heaven" prefixed to their name; or because they demonstrated "godlike behavior"; and/or because they received the kinds of offerings presented to other *dingir/ilu*—"and this occurs in Mesopotamian texts from almost every period and region" (Porter 2009b, 163).

Why do modern scholars not speak of a generic term for "spirit" or "supernatural being" in the manner of the good, out-of-date anthropology of Raymond Firth? Firth defines the analogous Tikopian term *atua* in his Tikopian-English dictionary: " n. 1. Supernatural being in gen.; spirit; ghost," which he then declines into nine subtypes of different ranks, origins, and powers—and one verb meaning "take as a guardian spirit . . . [as in] when his grandfather died he made a guardian spirit of him" (1985, 24–25). The Sumerian *dingir* likewise covers a range of differentiated forms—quite like the Inuit complex of metapersons—including the four or seven high gods that "determine the fates"; the fifty great gods of a so-called divine assembly (perhaps many of whom rule kinds of things or activities); a great host of monsters, demons, and ghosts; the indwelling spirits of phenomena such as mountains, rivers, and ploughs; and individuals' kindred spirits and guardian spirits. In the case notably of divine phenomena, including the indwelling of certain great gods to their cosmic domains, if all spirits come under the same designation (*dingir*, "god"), it is not only because their potencies are metahuman, but they all have the same composition. Basically, the Mesopotamian cosmos is a hierarchical assemblage of similar forms; as for Inuit, it is *inua* all the way down.

Otherwise said, Divinity is one. In his well-regarded text on *Religion in Ancient Mesopotamia* (2001a), Jean Bottéro moves tortuously to the same conclusion about the universal and animistic sense of the *dingir* concept—especially for Sumerians. (One gets the impression throughout the work that Bottéro holds the Sumerians as relatively "primitive," coming out of a fourth millennium or earlier state thereof, leaving it to their Akkadian successors to refine the Mesopotamian pantheon, among other things.) Hence the somewhat awkward description of the "doubling" of the Sumerian universe by "supernatural personalities" on the human model, while at the same time denying that there could be any "confusion" between the objective phenomenon and the "god" who is nonetheless identified with it as its motivating force. "What is at first surprising," Bottéro writes, "is the strange collection of beings bearing this [Heaven's] sign who made up the pantheon" (2001a, 45). The great majority of these beings bear Sumerian names, for the Sumerians more than any others "had the idea of doubling the visible world by an entire invisible, explicative, and directive world and must have been responsible for the recognition and 'discovery' of such a multitude of gods, which they transmitted with their culture to the Akkadians" (45–46). Before writing and history, Bottéro explains, the "resolutely polytheistic and anthropomorphist" Mesopotamians, "in order to dispel the innumerable secrets behind things," conceived of them as imaginary figures like themselves, though far more potent, each such figure responsible for certain natural phenomena like its driving force—all this based by Bottéro on the tried and untrue theory of finding god ("the supernatural") when the human enterprise is uncertain (2001a, 44).

In other words, Bottéro writes, "the ancient Mesopotamians doubled their universe with a parallel universe of supernatural personalities" (44). Yet as he states in another work: "Although a naive view [of whom?] could easily identify the gods with the objects of their authority and care, there was not the slightest confusion between them. The gods were concealed within them, rather like the motor inside the machine it sets in motion; each area was merely the domain they gave life to, 'created' and organised by them" (2001b, 186). From all evidence, however, the better way to express this would be that the gods are distributed persons, such that the particular beings they gave birth to are indeed forms of them, hence treated as their persons, whatever else these things are in their individual selves. As a distributed person, the god is the class of which particular beings are instances, that is, forms or bodies of the god, such that the goddess of grain and reeds, Nidaba, is the grain, is the reed. As this passage by Barbara Porter demonstrates:

> Nidaba, the goddess of reeds, grasses, and grain, is addressed anthropomorphically in one hymn as "the housekeeper of An, lady" and then extolled with the words, "Milady, you are the food of (the temple) Ekur, you are the drink of (the temple) Eanna . . . Nidaba, you are the beer." (Porter 2009a, 5)

"You are the beer"—what else makes it intoxicating? What makes beer, for beer is not the man who makes the beer? Finitude.

Jacobsen ([1946] 1977) has a useful summary of the principle entailed in this concept of the god as a singular multiplicity, the one in and as the many—with the bonus of an insightful notice of Nidaba in her reed manifestation. As in cultures of immanence the world over, the Mesopotamians were hardly nominalist but instead practiced a form of philosophical realism, which identifies the class being as an encompassing individual. Any phenomenon that the Mesopotamian met was alive, Jacobsen notes, endowed with a personality and a will, a distinctive self-animated self. But the self of a piece of flint was not limited to itself. It was itself, and yet also a greater self, a class being, behind it, permeating it and giving it the character of flint, which it shared with other flint. "And as one such 'self' could permeate many individual phenomena, so it might also permeate other selves and thereby give to them its specific character to add to the qualities which they had in their own right" (134). If the species-character of flint includes its willingness to flake easily, that is "because it had once fought the god Ninurta, and Ninurta had imposed flaking on it as a punishment" (131). Likewise reeds have their own "mysterious power," including the ability to grow luxuriantly in the marshes and other "amazing things," such as making the music that comes out of the shepherd's pipe. Found in every reed, these powers were "combined for the Mesopotamian into a divine personality—that of the goddess Nidaba" (132). A later text has a more extended collocation of the goddess's mysterious powers:

> Nidaba is in the reeds, essential for rebuilding houses and cities. She is in the reed when it is fashioned into a reed stylus, making it work well and fulfill its purpose; and she is in grains providing sustenance for the temples and bread . . . for the gods. With abundance and plenty she insures a stable reign for kings. The building of cities and palaces, stability of rule, offerings for the gods—even the simple pleasure of the shepherd's pipe—depend on her presence, her will and power cause reed and grain to be, flourish, and thrive in their full potential. (Jacobsen 1976, 10–11)

For Jacobsen as for Bottéro, however, there is a caveat. True, that Nidaba "was one with every reed in the sense that she permeated it as an animating and characterizing agent; but she did not lose her identity in the concrete phenomenon and was not limited by any or all existing reeds" (Jacobsen [1946] 1977, 132). The reed is Nidaba, but Nidaba is not the reed. Jacobsen makes the difference too radical by supposing the reed as an individual "concrete phenomenon" is just and only that. Nidaba is the reed, but the reed is not Nidaba. What this ignores is that some reeds make better-sounding flutes than others, as some flints flake more easily and truly than others. In Jacobsen's own terms, there is some will, personality, and agency of its own in each reed, each flint original. Flint and reed are at once species-beings, typically in the person of a god, and individual instances of the god as well as their own persons. We have seen this kind of dualism of divinity and animism before: something like Sedna and the seals generated from herself, who have their own *inua* as seals.

Of course, Sedna, Sila, and the Moon are hardly comparable to the great Sumerian gods, except that they are essentially the same in nature. Like An, Enlil, Enki, and Ninhursag, the immortal Inuit gods are original sovereigns of the universe, not merely as the rulers of their extensive wordly realms, but inhabiting and permeating them as the motivating being of them—cosmic *inua*. Still, the differences are complicated by what often seem to be conflicting and overlapping perspectives in modern scholarly descriptions of the Mesopotamian high gods. Indeed, the gods historically existed in two versions: an original Sumerian and enduring Mesopotamian system of cosmic figures, genealogically and hierarchically organized, who created, divided, and ordered the universe, notably including human society and culture; and a decentralized system involving the same high gods and others as patrons of city-states, who in that partisan capacity would usurp the position of supreme deity, even as they redundantly take on the cosmic functions of the other gods, sometimes even their body-parts, thus making a local version of the overall pantheon. It is clearly the universal Sumerian-cum-Mesopotamian cosmology that Sumerologist Samuel Noah Kramer has in mind when he speaks of a fourfold universe of heaven and earth, sea and atmosphere, each realm created by a specific deity who likewise created and controlled all the entities existing therein (1963, 115).

Hence the ideal-typical description by Kramer and others of the great gods as a cosmic family with An, the Sky and father of all the gods and supreme among them; his son Enlil, the air or atmosphere (who replaces An as ruling god around 2500 BCE); Enki, younger brother of Enlil, god of the fertilizing sweet waters, male fertility, and wisdom; and Ninhursag, earth-mother, fertility goddess, sometimes said the consort of An. (In a Mesopotamian cosmogony of the kind known to many from ancient Greeks to New Zealand Māori, Heaven [An/Uranus/Rangi] mates with Earth [Ki or Ninhursag/Gaia/Papa] giving birth to the gods, one of whom [Enlil/Cronus/Tāne] separates the parents, brings light to the world, and ultimately makes humanity possible.) It is particularly in this pan-Mesopotamian cosmic mode that the great gods are essentially like the Inuit deities—among many others appearing in these pages. Their cosmic powers are the same, as Sedna is of the sea, Sila of the air, and Moon of the heavens. Consider, then, this enlightening discussion of Anu, Enlil, and Ea (Akkadian forms of the Sumerian An, Enlil, and Enki) by Francesca Rochberg, which I quote at length:

> The gods, being conceived of and imagined, not observed, may be differentiated from natural (perceptual) phenomena, yet the gods

seem to have been viewed as immanent and active in the world of phenomena, as many instances of divine agency are preserved in Sumero-Akkadian mythology. For example, as forces over the basic parts of the physical world, the three great gods, Anu, Enlil, and Ea were said to "inhabit" specific regions of the cosmos in their myths. Thus, in the myth of *Artra-ḥasīs*, the divine trinity cast lots, divided the universe, and came to be identified with heaven, earth, and the subterranean waters of Apsû, respectively. Through this narrative account, the character of the principal Sumerian deities, An, Enlil, and Enki, is shown as that of forces within or over various parts the world, such as the sky, the winds, the foothills, and the sweet waters. Celestial gods, such as Nanna, Utu, and Inana, similarly are made manifest in the luminaries and as the personalized powers in those natural phenomena. (2009, 50–51)

If you will, cosmic *inua*.

Together with the four supreme gods, the last three mentioned—Nanna or Sīn, god of the moon and wisdom; his son Utu, god of the Sun and justice; and Inanna, his daughter or daughter of Enki, goddess of sexuality—make up the aforementioned seven who in the all-Mesopotamian pantheon "determine the fates." But insofar as various gods were often in lethal competition with each other, that is in the form of the city-states of which they were the rulers, the traditional Mesopotamian pantheon stood to be revised in their favor. The city's own god could take precedence over An or Enlil as supreme and universal ruler. Indeed, various temples, kinship groups, and even individuals, in the supplications to their tutelary deities, might well exalt them over all others. Bottéro speaks of "henotheism," under which description he offers many examples of lesser gods usurping the titles of the ancient cosmic hegemons (2001a, 41–43). If Anu was "the prince of the gods," so was Sīn. So were various gods "the ruler of Heaven and Earth," "sublime throughout the universe," "unequaled." "Ištar 'dons the lordly tiara' and 'gathers to herself all rites,' all powers." Note, "all the powers": presumably the favored god became something of an all-god, taking on the various functions of the great ones she or he had displaced; "it seems that in Mesopotamia . . . a profound tendency toward religiosity pushed the faithful in a certain way to encapsulate all sacred potential into the particular divine personality whom they were addressing at a given moment" (41–42).

All these superlative epithets and generalized powers, moreover, were not only applied interchangeably among the greatest divinities, such as Anu, Marduk, Enlil, or Enki, they were accorded to many lesser popular gods too, such as Ninurta, now "the first of the gods"; or Shamas, "the god of gods" (Bottéro 2001a, 41). C. Leonard Woolley, the archaeologist of Ur and Mesopotamia, has a clear and succinct description of this divine *primus inter pares* contest. "All the gods," he writes, "originally had their functions": Enki was lord of waters and wisdom; Enlil, rain and wind; Nergal, plague; Shamash, justice; Ishtar, love; and so on (Woolley 1965, 121–22). But insofar as each city was subject to rain, wind, and plague, and sought justice—in brief, required the whole menu of divine functions—each of them tended to usurp the provinces of others, perhaps under similar gods differently named, perhaps under a god of many functional parts, and notably by subsuming the other gods under its own.

Again, on an exponentially lesser scale, something similar is afoot among Inuit groups, judging from the shifts in dominance among Sedna, Sila, and Moon, the latter taking precedence in Alaska, Sila in Greenland. For certain inland, caribou-hunting Barren Grounds Inuit, the eclipse of Sedna altogether is a practiced matter of complementary opposition, as all sea meat is strictly taboo, and many of the hunters had never seen the sea (Rasmussen [1927] 1999, 72). Rather, Sila, broadly characterized by Rasmussen as "the universe; the weather, and . . . intelligence and wisdom," is here the supreme deity—as the One in Many, a singular plurality. In the generalized form of Silap Inua—"the Lord of Power, or literally, the one possessing power"—Sila is greatly involved in people's fate. "Often also, the term Pinga is used, this being a spirit in the form of a woman, which is understood to dwell somewhere in space," whom all fear, especially for her watch over people's dealings with animals, for she is the mistress of game. "She is omnipresent, interfering as occasion may require," and is the reason for the many taboos regarding the respectful treatment of animals (81–82). (There seem to be quite a few part-Silas and metaperson aspects of Sedna in Baffinland [see Laugrand et al 2002; 2006].) Up in heaven, the Moon—"Lord of Heaven, Tapasum Inua"—is master of the souls of the dead, which on the dark nights he sends down to earth in the form of humans and animals. "'So we see that life is endless,'" said the shaman (*angakok*) to Rasmussen, "'only we do not know in what form we shall reappear after death'" ([1927] 1999, 80).

Back in Mesopotamia, for all the partisan claims of this or that god to cosmocratic supremacy, in the traditional all-Sumerian/Akkadian pantheon, An/Anu was father to them all. All the gods are *anuna*, "[offspring] of An," and in that respect, inferior to and dependent on the heavenly source of divine power. *The source*: once again, divinity is unity, *dingir/ilu*, such are the potencies of lesser gods referred from An—who is thus ultimately responsible for what happens in the human world, however remote in space, unregarded in cult, or upstaged by Enlil. "All things and forces in the polity that is the universe conform to An's will" (Jacobsen 1976, 97). As noted before, this cosmic polity would have something of the following hierarchical order. Under An are the other six supreme powers, and below them the "fifty great gods," apparently including those, such as Nidaba, Nudimmud (the one who begets cows), and others to whom Enki "charged" with specific things or functions. Then the plenitude of demons, monsters, or evil spirits, so-called.

"We do not know much about most of these monstrous, fearsome, dangerous, and evil anthropomorphous or zoomorphous beings" (Bottéro 2001a, 187). We do know that, as An was father of all the gods, "he likewise fathered innumerable demons and evil spirits" (Jacobsen 1976, 95). We also know that these spirits were directly under orders of greater gods, who delegated them to inflict illness and other travails on humans who defied them, forbearing to punish such transgressions themselves, though they were ever implored to call off the evil ones. For the Mesopotamians knew what was, in effect, an extensive taboo system, whose rules, decreed by the gods and enforced by demons, included prescriptions apparently as arbitrary as any of the Inuit gods required.

The catalog of the divinely inspired Mesopotamian "rules of life," *mutatis mutandis*, could have come from reports of the Fifth Thule Expedition on Baffin Land in the 1920s—some of the rules are almost interchangeable. The principal compilation is a late second-millennium Akkadian document, the *Shurpu*, an exorcist text featuring an extravagant list of "sins," as the Mesopotamian scholars are wont to call them (Reiner [1958] 1970; Bottéro 2001b, 249–54). (In fact, in Reiner's admirable translation, certain proscriptions are designated "taboo," itself only one of a number of distinct technical terms referring to the act and its violation: "sin," "crime," "blasphemy," "error," etc.) As Jean Bottéro informs us: "Sin, the disobedience of divine will, of which we have lists of dozens of examples in all realms of behavior, was at the very center of the religious consciousness of the Mesopotamians beginning at the latest at the turn of the third millennium, and remained until the very end" (2001a, 188). But I demur.

"Sin" is a transcendentalist concept having to do with individual morality, and like "higher religion" is an analogue of the ethnographer's "taboo"; but the term is misplaced in this Mesopotamian context, where, much more like Māori *tapu*, it refers to conduct promulgated and sanctioned under an immanentist regime of metahuman powers. The effect is another transcendentalist distortion of an immanentist cosmology. "Sin" is a concept of individualistic and soteriological dimensions, precisely involving divine punishment of transgressive persons in "another world" for moral breaches in this one. What ethnographers describe as "taboos" or "rules of life," while likewise offenses against god(s), are sanctioned in this earthly life by illness, accident, death, crop failure, the disappearance of sea mammals, and the like, often on a community scale, for offenses perhaps committed by others. The rules at issue are often of no particular moral content; rather, fundamentally entailed in their breach is the disobedience of the god—as by Inuit women who point at whales with their middle fingers.

Unlike sins, then, where "the punishment fits the crime," in the case of these rules of life, there may be no necessary or evident proportion between the delict and the effect—as witness the poor Inuit who will suffer a dislocated hip if his wife is unfaithful while he is hunting walrus

(Rasmussen 1929, 186). Deference and obedience are singularly at stake, relationships that are even better served by "irrationality" than by logical motivation. Blind obedience. Like the Inuit duties to Sedna, the Mesopotamian literature has a fair quotient of such "sins."

For a good number of the injunctions in the aforementioned *Shurpu* text

> apparently have nothing to do with religious, social or personal duties; they seem to be customs derived from fairly irrational representations, probably dating from time immemorial and no clearer to the ancient Mesopotamians than to us when, for example, we bless someone who has just sneezed. (Bottéro 2001b, 250)

"The gods governed all people," Bottéro observes:

> It followed that all the prescriptions that ruled human existence—as much on the strictly religious level as on the political, administrative, and "moral" ones, including those folkloric constraints inherited from a distant, forgotten past and those obscure routines that everyone respects without knowing why—were believed to emanate from the "governmental" will of the gods. (2001a, 188)

Amusing that the gods and rules all preceded the kings and city-states that for Bottéro, as for so many Mesopotamianists writing in the conventional Durkheimian mode, are where divine authority is modeled on the human polity. However, citing a study of the Babylonian Akitu Festival by the Danish orientalist Svend Aage Pallis [1926], Jacobsen ditches the usual reflectionism to endorse a more arresting theory of the human political relation to the gods—the one that's in this book:

> Man—in the person of the leader of the community—represents the god, literally re-presents him, for by acting the god, by presenting his external form, he becomes the god, the form fills with its content, and as the god he performs the acts that fulfill the divine will with all its beneficent results for the community. (1976, 14)

The *Shurpu* compiles over 250 "sins," including the many offenses against civil and religious order: counterfeiting money, adultery, theft, diverting an offering promised to a god, and the like, punishing "who has eaten what is ta[boo] to his god, Who has eaten what is taboo to his goddess" (Tablet II.5; IV.2; in Reiner [1958] 1970, 13, 25). But then there are "a good number" that have no evident functional or logical ground. Among them:

- pointing at a lamp [even sounds Inuit] (Bottéro 2001b, 250)
- lighting a fire in the presence of a third person (250)
- drinking from a cup made of unfired clay (250)
- putting one's finger on the wound of a sheep that has had its throat cut (250)
- refusing or asking for something in bad weather (250)
- plucking blades of grass on the steppe or reeds in the marsh(250)
- pulling a reed from one's boot (250)
- urinating or vomiting in a stream or river (250)
- to drink water from an unfired (clay) cup (Tablet III.21; in Reiner [1958] 1970, 19)
- to sit on a seat facing the sun (Tablet III.23; in Reiner [1958] 1970, 19)

For Bottéro (2001b), "the most astounding feature of the *Shurpu* catalogue" is that these heterogeneous injunctions, from the political and moral to the seemingly irrational, are intermingled willy-nilly as having the same force and scope, any and all of them visiting illness or other evils on those who transgressed them:

> Viewed from this aspect, these rules were all equally important, because it was not a matter of the gravity of their repercussions on social life, but their intrinsic dignity and their nature as expressions of divine will. Those who, by violating them, rebelled against the gods, resisted or neglected them and, in short, scorned them, deserved to be punished by those same gods. (251)

But not by *these* high gods. As Sedna or Sila might delegate the punishment of Inuit offenders to multitudinous ghosts and demons, so did Enlil, Enki, or others of the great gods order the many and monstrous "evil spirits"—who were also gods (*dingir*)—to inflict misfortune on the violators of their divine will (Bottéro 2001b, 166–67; 2001a, 186–89).

Such were the "demons, evil gods, evil spirits—who were inimical to man" (Jacobsen 1976, 12). Thorkild Jacobsen illustrates these punitive spirits from the vast corpus of Babylonian cuneiform texts:

> They are gloomy, their shadow dark,
> no light is in their bodies,
> ever they slink along covertly,
> walk not upright,
> from their claws drips bitter gall,
> their footprints are (full of) evil venom. (Jacobsen 1976, 12)

And again:

> Neither males are they, nor females,
> they are winds ever sweeping along,
> they have not wives, engender not children,
> know not how to show mercy,
> hear not prayer and supplication. (12–13)

In ancient Mesopotamia too, "that land which admitted familial and collective responsibility" (Bottéro 2001a, 188), the fault may not have been one's own. The offender could have been some close kin, upon which, beseeching Marduk, one prayed: "Let no guilt of my father, my grandfather, my mother, / my grandmother, my brother, my sister, / my family, kith and kin, / Approach my own self, but let it be gone!" (147). And where the Inuit relies upon the shaman (*angakok*) to drive off the demons or calls upon gods to do so, the ancient Mesopotamians had their exorcists whose methods for doing the like were not all that different. The *Shurpu* is largely given to exorcists' incantations for treating a sick person. "Blasphemy against god and goddess, the evil (effect) of sorcery . . . evil machinations / may they be released for you, absolved for you, wiped off [you] today" (Tablet VIII.81–2; in Reiner [1958] 1970, 43).

Perhaps unlike the Inuit *angakok* who didn't "believe" but "feared" the spirits' malevolence, the Sumerians did both. Or so I judge from modern scholars' frequent invocation of the terrors. C. Leonard Woolley, for example: "The fact is that throughout the religion of the Sumerians is not one of love but of fear, fear whose limits are confined to this present life, fear of Beings all-powerful, capricious, unmoral. Somehow or other virtue does not appeal to the gods" (1965, 125). (Not to take this convergence with Central Inuit in the matter of relations to the gods as a general attribute of immanentist peoples. More often the ethnographers are impressed by the lack of reverence and awe, even in the course of ritual proceedings, when bystanders may be joking and commenting critically on the performance [Firth 1967, 84, 145; Viveiros de Castro 1992, 122; Meggitt 1962, 291].) What can be generalized from these observations is the often capricious and amoral character of divine action, and, as noted earlier, the people's ambivalence to gods who are the root of all evil as well as the source of their well-being.

There were not only gods, demons, and taboos in old Mesopotamia, but *inua* everywhere, indwelling persons, a classic animism that not only constituted a subjectivized physical world but involved many things that people ostensibly made. When Bottéro speaks of Mesopotamians doubling the visible world with invisible personalities, and Jacobsen similarly pronounces that flint, grain, everything was alive, it took them into a territory of divinity they found remarkable, namely "gods" of apparently mundane character whom Bottéro in particular is quick to devalue by comparison to the likes of An, Enlil, and Enki. (As noticed earlier, for Bottéro, these worldly phenomena were animated by greater divine patrons, with whom they were not to be conflated—which is something less than half true, as will become apparent momentarily.) By all evidence, however, here were such remarkable "gods" (*dingir/ilu*) in their own right: rivers, mountains, fire, wild animals, stars, sun, moon, planets, rain, storms, bodies of water, not to mention "the fertile powers of nature, for example, the growth of sheep . . . and the growth of grain" (Bottéro 2001a, 64,184–86).

As I say, classic animism. Or perhaps the more up-to-date versions observed by Philippe Descola and Eduardo Viveiros de Castro, who are among the primary inspirations of anthropologist of religion Anna Perdibon's recent book, *Mountains and Trees, Rivers and Springs: Animistic Beliefs and Practices in Ancient Mesopotamian Religion* (2019). In

Perdibon's finely observed work, rivers or tamarisk trees hardly come off as lesser beings; they may be related to the gods and enspirited by the gods, but by virtue of their own agency and will, they are not only proxies of the god.

> The rivers Tigris and Euphrates recur as deities *per se* in several con-texts throughout the different periods and sources. They are some-times explicitly referred to as gods through the divine determinative [ᵈIDIGNA; DINGIR], but more often their identity is manifested by being recorded among other gods in myths, incantations and ritu-als, god lists, offering lists and personal names [as personal gods?].
> (Perdibon 2019, 117)

Well aware it seems that the Tigris and Euphrates were formed by Enki's semen, Perdibon has a fine understanding that this is a complex, hier-archical animism—of which there are several other ethnographic ex-amples in these pages, including Sedna's presence in seals and Baffin Land demonic game masters of particular species that also have their own indwelling *inua*. (I repeat an earlier query: Is there really any other kind of animism, say, one consisting of masterless other-than-human persons?) Consider the tamarisk, "the bone of divinity," as Perdibon testifies, which when ritually consecrated provides households with im-ages that protect against epidemic diseases. In pre-Sargonic times, the roots of the tamarisk were referred to as Enki and Ninki, and its neck as Enlil. As in another incantation:

> Tamarisk, firm tree, tree of Anu;
> Its roots toward the underworld
> (are) Enki and Ninki;
> From its branches
> (it is) Anu, the princely gudu-priest. (Perdibon 2019, 148)

The tamarisk as a whole and in its separate parts incorporates the persons of multiple gods, among them some of the greatest, while the tamarisk is an agent in its own right, a numinous being in and for itself. More generally, Perdibon astutely observes: "a tree comprises a multi-layered combination of meanings: it is considered kin to humans, and as an 'other-than-human' person, while also being closely related to divinity, and the perfect medium between the worlds, human and divine, below and above, earthly and heavenly" (152). And as she also says, although her study focused on the animism of mountains, trees, and rivers, it could well have been extended to minerals, animals, plants, and hybrid creatures.

> The Mesopotamian religious framework features a complex and fluid picture in its notion of what lies beneath the category of "god": along-side the gods with their anthropomorphic features, natural elements are considered living beings, often defined through the category of d i n g i r/*ilu*, thus partaking of the divine community and acting as persons within the animate cosmos of ancient Mesopotamians. (170–71)

This is a rich work. I would only try to complement it with notices of some other kinds of entities that received the titles, deference, and offerings of gods in old Mesopotamia, as culled from the essays edited by Barbara Porter, *What Is a God?* (2009a): thrones, chariots, daggers, musical instruments, scepters, branding irons, quivers, animals, fantastic creatures, lion-men, date palms, parts of temples, including the pipes running in from the fermenting vat, city gates, winds, ziggurats, leaders' staffs, lapis lazuli necklaces, incense, fire, drums, platforms on which gods stood, stones, lyres, weapons, and so on and so forth—a regular Borgesian Chinese encyclopedia.

If the animistic beings evoke scholarly surprise at the everyday things that are deemed "gods," the Mesopotamian people's so-called personal gods might be hard-to-believe for the opposite reason: namely, that they are characteristically significant gods, like Nidaba, or even supreme gods, like Enki. People's familiar helping spirits are among the most powerful beings in the cosmos—even as, however, they are related to one in the most intimate way, as "father" and "mother." (It's like Lien-hardt says of East African Dinka: only the god creates the child, the human parents just beget it [1961, 39–40].) Jacobsen is again the key source on this, and here is the key passage:

A common way of referring to the personal god is as "the god who 'created' or 'engendered me' or 'the divine mother who gave birth to me.'" To see more precisely what these terms imply we must realize that the personal god dwelt in the man's body. If his god "removed himself from his body," the body was open for evil demons of disease to take over and "possess" the man. (1976, 158)

Actually, Jacobsen writes of two gods, a male god received from the human father's side, and a goddess from the mother.

We are already familiar with the kind of guardian spirit-powers they afforded Mesopotamian persons, as they are quite like their counterparts in other societies mentioned here, including the name souls of Inuit. Generally speaking, the god is responsible for the person's fortunes, his or her achievements in life, "so much so that one might almost say that the god was a personification of the power for personal success in that individual" (Jacobsen 1976, 155). As implied by the threat of demons, also stressed was the role of the father-god as protector of the person: a lot of the inscriptions concerning invocations of the god are about relieving the person from attacks coming from malevolent outside powers.

Another central intervention of the personal gods offers an irresistible clue to the kinship system of the ancient Mesopotamians. Just as the god and goddess acquired from one's human parents engendered the person and then came to dwell in him or her, those same personal gods are "present and active in the most decisive and necessary achievement of fulfillment for the ancient Mesopotamian, that of engendering a son" (Jacobsen 1976, 158). That is to say, a son will have the same parental god as his human father and the same goddess as his mother; but so would his son, and all the male descendants thereafter. This Jacobsen was able to confirm from dynastic genealogies: "father and son invariably had the same personal god and goddess. The god passed therefore from the body of the father into the body of the son as generation followed generation" (159). Since succession is evidently patrilineal, what is here signified is a system of patrilineal lineages—or more generally, patrilineal descent groups—whose men

prescriptively marry women from the same outside group, thus complementing their own divine father with the same goddess-mother bestowed by their matrilateral kin.

(That said, something more can be said about it. There are just two
major kinship constitutions in which a patrilineal line of men is invariably paired with women of a different lineage: a dual organization of
exogamous moieties, with the men of each moiety marrying the
women of the other [fig. 1(i)]; and matrilateral cross-cousin marriage,
in which a series of patrilineal descent groups are linked in a hierarchical chain, each being wife-giver to some groups and wife-taker from
others [fig. 1(ii)]. The moiety system is unlikely in Mesopotamia:
involving reciprocal exchange, it is basically egalitarian, hardly appropriate to the kingly ordered Mesopotamian city-states and empires.
Matrilateral cross-cousin marriage, however, differentiates descent
groups according to the circulation of women between them, wife-
givers as life-givers usually being superior to wife-takers—but not
always, as alternatively, wife-taking from inferiors may be a matter of
chiefly privilege. So I risk: the ancient Mesopotamians were organized
in ranked patrilineal groups, related to and hierarchically differentiated from each other by the normative practice of matrilateral cross-
cousin marriage.)

Yet at the same time the divine polity is engaged in the kinship
system of a hierarchical human society, the gods in their intimate relations to individuals are the principals of a guardian spirit complex
hardly distinguishable, structurally, from some native North American hunters: an external spirit-power, complementary to the ancestral
human soul, that differentially governs an individual's life chances, as
in the name-soul guardians of Central Inuit. Recall the elements of
Inuit name-soul practice: the name the child acquires with the reincarnation of the soul of an important kinsman, a soul that carries the
"magic power" that is "with him, work[s] inside him, keep[s] danger
away and become[s] his guardian spirit" (Rasmussen 1931, 219–20).
Although the Inuit don't have lineages like the Mesopotamians, they
do live under organizations of that description prefigured in their cosmology. Indeed, one acquires the powers of the generations of the
same name:

(i)

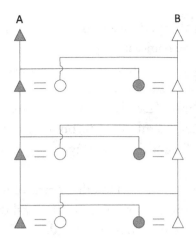

(ii)

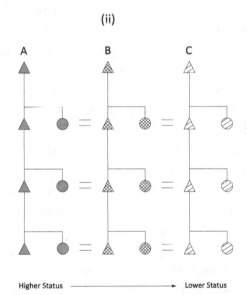

Higher Status ⟶ Lower Status

(i): Direct or symmetric exchange of women between two patrilineages, A and B. Although the diagram represents sisters of A marrying men of B (and vice versa), these are often "sisters" in a classificatory sense, resulting in regular matrimonial alliance between two clans or moieties. This arrangement is typically egalitarian, lacking in hierarchy.

(ii): A system of indirect or asymmetric exchange between patrilineages (A, B, C, . . .). Here, men of a lineage (B) regularly receive wives from another lineage (A), and in turn supply wives to another (C). A status hierarchy obtains, since wife-givers as life-givers are typically (but not always) superior to wife-takers. Thus, lineage A has higher status vis-à-vis lineage B, but B has higher status vis-à-vis lineage C. Men in such a system marry their mother's-brother's-daughter (often "classificatory"), so in technical parlance this is known as matrilateral cross-cousin marriage.

Source: Diagrams by Frederick B. Henry Jr.

A person's name is always derived from that of someone deceased, and carries with it the namesake's qualities; one becomes, indeed, a member of the great community of all who have borne the same name back to the ultimate distant past. Each living human being is thus attended by a host of namesake spirits, who aid and protect him as long as he is faithful to rule and rite, but may become inimical on any transgression. (Rasmussen [1927] 1999, 132)

The namesake spirit is an external familiar spirit of higher status and greater powers who is the individual's protector and the agent of one's achievements—provided one does not offend.

What to make of these similarities? Leaving aside the radical differences in organization and cult, at the bare bones, the fundamental structure of the ancient Mesopotamian pantheon, including the relationships among the powers, hardly had it over the Inuit. Both live under a hierarchical regime of high gods and their associated divine helpers, species masters, demons, ghosts, a broad animism of the phenomenal world, kindred spirits, and personal guardian spirits. Also the bare bones of the Mesopotamian universe is constituted by the same principles of cosmic order as the Inuit. In both societies, the metahuman hosts are immanent in human affairs; the gods are doing what the people do. As the agents of human success and failure, life and death, the spirits "determine the fates." Both peoples also know the principle of the unity of divinity, according to which the lesser spirits acted by the referred power of the original supreme gods, who thus governed the universe by their will if not by their own act. In both cosmologies the hierarchical order is magnified and centralized by distributed personhood, the greater spirit as a singular plurality, manifest in the encompassed others of the class, in arrangements ranging from species masters to the god in and of multitudinous phenomena. The entire cosmos is a universe of interacting subjects, notably the indwelling persons of sensible things. For all its identification with the origins of civilization, the Mesopotamian cosmology appears not to be very different from a range of immanentist cultures from great civilizations to modest hunter-gatherers.

So double the question: What to make of these striking parallels, and why, of all peoples, choose the Central Inuit for comparison to ancient Near East civilizations?

It is not simply to shock the professors of conventional wisdom by the similarities in the cosmologies of peoples as radically different culturally, and especially politically, as Inuit hunters and the denizens of Sumerian city-states and Akkadian empires. It is also a conditional something else. I chose Central Inuit to make the case that, given their isolation, the cosmological correspondences cannot be written off as the influence of Christian missionaries or the pantheon of any high civilization. Too often, the received anthropological and historical wisdom writes off the presence of supreme gods in societies such as Inuit hunters as acculturation effects. Totally improbable, according to received theory, that people who would not brook others telling them what to do could be subalterns in a cosmic state ruled by gods with the power to run their lives. Doesn't make sense. Superstructure is totally out of joint with infrastructure. Gods are supposed to be the celestial imitation of kingship; the cosmology in general is supposed to be ordered on the model of human society.

Among scholars of Mesopotamian antiquity, this is still the fair common average theoretical position: An, Enlil, & Co. are supernaturally hyped metaphors of Sumerian kingship, if they were not also given a boost into universal sovereignty as ideal projections of the empire of Sargon of Akkad. Like expert Assyriologist Samuel Noah Kramer, who, incidentally, in vaunting that *History Begins at Sumer* ([1956] 1981), claims that there had begun also "man's first cosmology" (75), in which, "on analogy with the political organization of the human state, it was natural to assume that at the head of the pantheon was a deity recognized by all the others as their king and ruler" (Kramer 1963, 114). Or:

> Before the rise of empire, the existence of autonomous city-states engendered special gods who were venerated locally as the protectors of their hometowns; whereas, with the rise of empire, certain local gods assumed a nationwide importance they had not previously enjoyed. (Bertman 2003, 115)

Or, in the third millennium, "the ruler metaphor was extended to the gods. Nature gods were transformed into city gods or heads of state" (Nemet-Nejat 1998, 179). In the same spirit,

> [German Assyriologist] W. von Soden's authoritative introduction to ancient Mesopotamia . . . bases its account of Mesopotamian religion on the premise that "the terrestrial world was carried over to the primarily heavenly world of the gods." [French historian] G. Roux's handbook, *Ancient Iraq* (1966), still a staple of introductory courses, states simply that in early Mesopotamia, "divine society was conceived as a replica of human society." (Porter 2009a, 4)

Bottéro is a big fan of this theological reflection theory, especially in connection with the supposed transition from a fourth millennium religion of disparate "nature spirits" to an ordered pantheon calqued on the Sumerian polity of the third millennium: "The innumerable gods and their initially disorganized world were transformed into a supernatural reflection of earthly political authority. Like that authority, the world of the gods had its supreme representative, a king and his ancestors" (2001a, 51).

In sum, here are so many transcendentalist moves on Mesopotamian culture, a veritable cosmic coup d'état, stripping the gods of their power by impoverishing them to the status of Idea. Thus removed from society, the quondam rulers of all become the imaginary servants of the real, human sovereigns. Enlightened social science sucks the substance out of divinity, turning the gods literally into nonentities, phantom creatures of Thought, in the service of the human powers that be to validate their legitimacy and consecrate their authority. The masters of the universe are reduced to political servitude.

For Sumerians, as noted, it was quite the other way around. They and their successors were organized and acted on the axiom that kingship was created by the gods, and that the gods were doing what the king did. The initial caution in selecting such a remote group for comparison as Inuit, for fear of acculturation effects from some "high civilization," was misplaced. Everything indicates that the cultural influences were running in the opposite direction: not that the "tribals" got their gods from ancient "high civilizations," but that the civilizations inherited theirs from the tribes. A cosmic polity governed by supreme gods is commonplace in immanentist cultures, perhaps everywhere among nonliterate, non-state hunters, herders, and slash-and-burn gardeners. Given also the certain supposition that the great civilizations of the Near East, India, China, and the Americas developed out of some such peoples, it follows that their hierarchical cosmologies were already in place from their beginnings. It also follows that—as the ancient Mesopotamians said—kingship came from heaven to earth, not the gods from earth to heaven. The human polity appropriated the cosmic polity.

Afterword

I GO BACK TO THE BEGINNING, the all-around, existential finitude of the human condition. The communities of Inuit—but also Australian Aborigines, New Guinea Highlanders, Amazonian Achuar, and others of their kind featured in these pages—may be small in scale, only more or less integrated, and lacking institutional authorities; but the conditions upon which their existence depends, and of which they are not the authors, are many, varied, and cosmic. From the most intimate aspects of life—people's own bodies, their implements, plants and animals on which they subsist—to the state of the world affecting everyone, raining on the just and unjust alike, they live and die by forces of which they are well aware, but which are not their own. Beside the intimate powers of daily life, potencies of universal, encompassing dimensions make the weal and woe of all the people collectively—rain and shine, seasons, epidemic disease, the running of the salmon, migration of the caribou, the growth of sweet potatoes.

Without ambitions to rule others, people submit to a world of powers that are acting among them, immanently and at all times, to determine their fate. Hence, it would be a mistake to say that the people "invented" the "spirits," that they created the gods in their own image, or accord them some such ultimate power over the Powers. *People did not create the gods out of thin air; they only hypostatized the forces that were already conditions of their existence. I repeat: humans did not imagine the gods, they only objectified, or more precisely, subjectivized, the extra-human forces by which they themselves lived and died.* The forces were already there. They were not imagined. They were real, empirical, life-giving and death-dealing forces. People only gave them substantive qualities that made them negotiable, or at least intelligible—consciousness, understanding, volition, and intention. They hypostatized these existential forces as persons, hidden souls with whom their own hidden powers or souls might communicate, but who, as the instantiation of these forces, were metapersons.

For the greater part of human history and the greater number of societies, human existence, as culturally constituted, has been heteronomous, subject to the governance of metaperson sources of life and livelihood. People are lesser, dependent beings of an enchanted universe. Accordingly, nothing is undertaken without enchantments, the initial invocations of the spirits who potentiate the human social action. These metahuman powers are the decisive agents of an all-around infrastructure of an all-around cultural praxis. Structurally compounded with the people's practices of livelihood, reproduction, social relations, and political authority, they are the prerequisite condition of human endeavors and the arbiters of the outcome, for better or worse. One might even insist again on the "determination by the religious basis"—that is, until religion went from an immanent infrastructure to a transcendent superstructure in the first and second axial ages.

In current academic theory, power ascends from earth to heaven, divinity being a celestial representation of human real-political authority. In immanentist cultures, however, power descends from heaven to earth, human real-political authority being a terrestrial instantiation of divinity. The existence people aspire to control, their own welfare, they will have to gain from its metahuman sources; and those who are able to do so are, by virtue of such powers, elevated among their fellows. Human political power is necessarily and quintessentially hubris, the appropriation of divinity in one form or another—including the human incarnations of immortal ancestral spirits in the Kimberley Desert of Western Australia.

There, the ethnographer Helmut Petri ([1954] 2011) met an old "medicine man" who was widely regarded as the ancient Dreamtime hero, Káluru, the source of the seasonal rains that made the people's foraging existence possible. The old man "regarded himself as immortal and an incarnation of Káluru"; he had always existed and would never die (97). Among a nearby people, Petri's colleague Lommel ([1952] 1997) met similar elders who were in the habit of speaking of the ancestral heroes (*wandjina*) in the first person: "When I came there in primeval times and left my image behind on the stone" (18)—referring to a painted image whose annual renewal brings about the rains. This repainting was the privilege of the oldest living man of the area, the closest to the ancient heroes, whom he personated when doing the work: "I am going now to refresh and invigorate myself, I am now repainting myself so that there will be rain" (18). The African divine kings of Frazerian fame who, by incarnating the god, could exercise control over nature, particularly over rain, had nothing in this regard over the old men endowed with sacred knowledge and ancestral beings who did as much for Australian hunters and gatherers.

One could go on citing other ethnographic verse and text in defense of the realities of the enchanted universe shared by most of humanity, the acknowledgment of which amounts to a call that transcendentalist social science, including my own, adapt itself to, and take seriously, the cultural praxes of others.

BIBLIOGRAPHY

Anderson, Benedict R. O'G. 1990. *Language and Power: Exploring Political Cultures in Indonesia.* Ithaca: Cornell University Press.

Århem, Kaj. 2016a. "Southeast Asian Animism in Context." In *Animism in Southeast Asia,* edited by Kaj Århem and Guido Sprenger, 3–30. London: Routledge.

———. 2016b. "Animism and the Hunter's Dilemma: Hunting, Sacrifice and Asymmetric Exchange among the Katu of Vietnam." In *Animism in Southeast Asia,* edited by Kaj Århem and Guido Sprenger, 91–113. London: Routledge.

Aristotle. 1935. *Metaphysics: Books 10–14.* Translated by Hugh Tredennick and G. Cyril Armstrong. Loeb Classical Library 287. Cambridge: Harvard University Press.

Augustine. 1887. *The Confessions of St. Augustine.* Translated by Rev. E. B. Pusey, DD. London: Walter Smith.

Averbeck, Richard E. 2017. "Enki and the World Order (4.91)." In *The Context of Scripture Online,* edited by W. Hallo. Consulted online January 29, 2021, First published online: 2017.

Bakhtin, Mikhail. 1984. *Rabelais and His World.* Translated by Hélène Iswolsky. Bloomington: Indiana University Press.

Balandier, Georges. 1970. *Political Anthropology.* Translated by A. M. Sheridan Smith. Harmondsworth, UK: Penguin Books.

Balikci, Asen. 1970. *The Netsilik Eskimo.* Garden City, NY: Natural History Press.

Barnes, J. A. 1962. "African Models in the New Guinea Highlands." *Man* 62 (January): 5–9.

Barnes, R. H. 1984. *Two Crows Denies It: A History of Controversy in Omaha Sociology.* Lincoln: University of Nebraska Press.

Barth, Fredrik. 1975. *Ritual and Knowledge among the Baktaman of New Guinea.* New Haven: Yale University Press.

Bauer, Brian S. 2004. *Ancient Cuzco: Heartland of the Inca.* Austin: University of Texas Press.

Bennett, Jessica. 2019. "No Need for a Hunt: Awash with Witches." *New York Times,* October 24, 2019.

Bertman, Stephen. 2003. *Handbook to Life in Ancient Mesopotamia.* Oxford: Oxford University Press.

Best, Elsdon. 1924. *The Maori.* 2 vols. Wellington: Harry H. Tombs.

Black, Jeremy, ed. 2002. *The Electronic Text Corpus of Sumerian Literature.* https://etcsl.orinst.ox .ac.uk/section1/tr113.htm. Oxford: Oxford University Press.

Black, Mary. 1977. "Ojibwa Power-Belief System." In *The Anthropology of Power,* edited by R. D. Fogelson and R. N. Adams, 141–51. New York: Academic Press.

Bloomfield, Leonard. 1934. *Plains Cree Texts.* Edited by Franz Boas. Publications of the American Ethnological Society, vol. 16. New York: G. E. Stechert.

Boas, Franz. (1888) 1964. *The Central Eskimo*. Lincoln: University of Nebraska Press.

———. 1901. "The Eskimo of Baffin Land and Hudson Bay." *Bulletin of the American Museum of Natural History*, vol. 15, pt. 1. New York: Trustees of the Museum.

———. (1908) 1974. "Anthropology." In *A Franz Boas Reader: The Shaping of American Anthropology, 1883–1911*, edited by George W. Stocking Jr., 267–81. Chicago: University of Chicago Press.

———. 1921. *Ethnology of the Kwakiutl*. Bureau of American Ethnology, Thirty-Fifth Annual Report, Pts. 1 and 2 (1913–1914). Washington, DC: Government Printing Office.

———. 1966. *Kwakiutl Ethnography*. Edited by Helen Codere. Chicago: University of Chicago Press.

Bogoras, Waldemar. 1904–9. "The Chukchee." *Memoirs of the American Museum of Natural History*, vol. 11. New York: G. E. Stechert.

Bottéro, Jean. 2001a. *Religion in Ancient Mesopotamia*. Translated by Theresa Lavender Fagan. Chicago: University of Chicago Press.

———. 2001b. *Everyday Life in Ancient Mesopotamia*. Translated by Antonia Nevill. Baltimore: Johns Hopkins University Press.

Brightman, Robert. (1973) 2002. *Grateful Prey: Rock Cree Human-Animal Relationships*. Berkeley: University of California Press.

Brown, George. 1910. *Melanesians and Polynesians*. London: Macmillan & Co.

Brown, Jennifer S. H., and Robert Brightman. 1988. *"The Orders of the Dreamed": George Nelson on Cree and Northern Ojibwa Religion and Myth, 1823*. Winnipeg: University of Manitoba Press.

Brown, Peter. 1975. "Society and the Supernatural: A Medieval Change." *Daedalus* 104, no. 2 (Spring): 133–51.

Brumbaugh, Robert. 1987. "The Rainbow Serpent in the Upper Sepik." *Anthropos* 82, no. 1/3: 25–33.

———. 1990. "Afek Sang: The 'Old Woman' Myth of the Mountain Ok." In *Children of Afek: Tradition and Change among the Mountain Ok of Central New Guinea*, edited by Barry Craig and David Hyndman, 54–87. Oceania Monograph 40. Sydney: University of Sydney.

Cobo, Father Bernabe. [1653] 1990. *Inca Religion and Customs*. Edited and translated by Roland Hamilton. [Selection of Cobo's *Historia del Nuevo Mundo*.] Austin: University of Texas Press.

Codrington, R. H. (1891) 1972. *The Melanesians: Studies in Their Anthropology and Folklore*. New York: Dover.

Confucius. 1869. *Confucius, The Chinese Classics: Translated into English with Preliminary Essays and Explanatory Notes by James Legge. Vol. 1. The Life and Teachings of Confucius*. 2nd ed. London: N. Trübner.

Cunnison, Ian. 1959. *The Luapula Peoples of Northern Rhodesia: Custom and History in Tribal Politics*. Manchester: Manchester University Press.

Danowski, Deborah, and Eduardo Viveiros de Castro. 2017. *The Ends of the World*. Translated by Rodrigo Nunes. Cambridge, UK: Polity.

Danticat, Edwidge. 2020. "Daily Comment: Haiti Faces Difficult Questions Ten Years After a Devastating Earthquake." *New Yorker*, January 11, 2020.

Descartes, René. [1641] 1996. *Meditations on First Philosophy*. Translated and edited by John Cottingham. Cambridge: Cambridge University Press.

Descola, Philippe. 1994. *In the Society of Nature: A Native Ecology in Amazonia*. Translated by Nora Scott. Cambridge: Cambridge University Press.

———. 1996. *The Spears of Twilight: Life and Death in the Amazon Jungle.* Translated by Janet Lloyd. New York: New Press.

———. 2016. "Landscape as Transfiguration: Edward Westermarck Memorial Lecture, October 2015." *Suomen Antropologi* 41, no. 1 (Spring): 3–14.

Dumont, Louis. 1970. *Homo Hierarchicus: The Caste System and Its Implications.* Translated by Mark Sainsbury, Louis Dumont, and Basia Gulati. Chicago: University of Chicago Press.

Durkheim, Émile. (1915) 1965. *The Elementary Forms of Religious Life.* Translated by Joseph Ward Swain. New York: Free Press.

Durkheim, Émile, and Marcel Mauss. 1963. *Primitive Classification.* Translated, with an introduction by Rodney Needham. Chicago: University of Chicago Press.

Eisenstadt, S. N., ed. 1986. *The Origins and Diversity of Axial Age Civilizations.* Albany: State University of New York Press.

Evans-Pritchard, E. E. (1948) 2011. "The Divine Kingship of the Shilluk of the Nilotic Sudan. The Frazer Lecture, 1948." Reprinted in *HAU: The Journal of Ethnographic Theory* 1, no. 1: 407–22.

———. 1956. *Nuer Religion.* Oxford: Oxford University Press.

Fausto, Carlos. 2012. "Too Many Owners: Mastery and Ownership in Amazonia." In *Animism in Rainforest and Tundra: Personhood, Animals, Plants and Things in Contemporary Amazonia and Siberia*, edited by Marc Brightman, Vanessa Elisa Grotti, and Olga Ulturgasheva, 29–47. New York: Berghahn Books.

Firth, Raymond. (1936) 1957. *We, the Tikopia: A Sociological Study of Kinship in Polynesia.* London: George Allen and Unwin.

———. 1950. *Primitive Polynesian Economy.* New York: Humanities Press.

———. 1967. *The Work of the Gods in Tikopia.* New York: Humanities Press.

———. 1970. *Rank and Religion in Tikopia: A Study in Polynesian Paganism and Conversion to Christianity.* Boston: Beacon Press.

———. 1985. *Tikopia-English Dictionary: Taranga Fakatikopia Ma Taranga Fakainglisi.* Oxford: Oxford University Press.

Fletcher, Alice, and Francis La Flesche. (1911) 1992. *The Omaha Tribe.* 2 vols. Lincoln: University of Nebraska Press.

Fortes, Meyer. 1945. *The Dynamics of Clanship among the Tallensi.* Oxford: Oxford University Press.

———. 1956. *Oedipus and Job in West African Religion.* Cambridge: Cambridge University Press.

Fortune, Reo. (1932) 1989. *Sorcerers of Dobu: The Social Anthropology of the Dobu Islanders of the Western Pacific.* Prospect Heights, IL: Waveland Press.

———. (1934) 1965. *Manus Religion: An Ethnological Study of the Manus Natives of the Admiralty Islands.* Lincoln: University of Nebraska Press.

Frankfort, Henri, et al., eds. (1946) 1977. *The Intellectual Adventure of Ancient Man: An Essay on Speculative Thought in the Ancient Near East.* Chicago: University of Chicago Press.

Frazer, J. G. (1911) 2012. *The Golden Bough.* 3rd ed. 12 vols. Cambridge Library Collection Reprint. Cambridge: Cambridge University Press.

Fustel de Coulanges, Numa Denis. (1864) 1980. *The Ancient City: A Study on the Religion, Laws, and Institutions of Greece and Rome.* Baltimore: Johns Hopkins University Press.

Gardner, D. S. 1987. "Spirits and Conceptions of Agency among the Mianmin of Papua New Guinea." *Oceania* 57, no. 3 (March): 161–77.

Gell, Alfred. 1998. *Art and Agency: An Anthropological Theory.* Oxford: Oxford University Press.

Gibson, T. 1986. *Sacrifice and Sharing in the Philippine Highlands: Religion and Society among the Buid of Mindoro.* London: Athlone.

Goldman, Irving. 1975. *The Mouth of Heaven: An Introduction to Kwakiutl Religious Thought.* New York: John Wiley.

Gose, Peter. 1996. "The Past is a Lower Moiety: Diarchy, History, and Divine Kingship in the Inka Empire." *History and Anthropology* 9, no. 4: 383–414.

Graeber, David, and Marshall Sahlins. 2017. *On Kings.* Chicago: HAU Books.

Gubser, Nicholas J. 1965. *The Nunamiut Eskimos: Hunters of Caribou.* New Haven: Yale University Press.

Gudgeon, Lieut.-Col. [W. E.]. 1905. "Mana Tangata." *Journal of the Polynesian Society* 14: 49–66.

Hallowell, A. I. 1934. "Some Empirical Aspects of Northern Saulteaux Religion." *American Anthropologist* 36, no. 3 (July–September): 389–404.

———. 1960. "Ojibwa Ontology, Behavior, and World View." In *Culture in History: Essays in Honor of Paul Radin,* edited by Stanley Diamond, 17–49. New York: Columbia University Press.

Harrison, Simon J. 1990. *Stealing People's Names: History and Politics in a Sepik River Cosmology.* Cambridge: Cambridge University Press.

Hobbes, Thomas. (1651) 1991. *Leviathan.* Edited by Richard Tuck. Cambridge: Cambridge University Press.

Hocart, A. M. (1939) 1953. *The Life-Giving Myth and Other Essays.* New York: Grove Press.

———. 1970. *Kings and Councillors: An Essay in the Comparative Anatomy of Human Society.* Chicago: University of Chicago Press.

Howell, Signe. 1989. *Society and Cosmos: Chewong of Peninsular Malaysia.* Chicago: University of Chicago Press.

———. 2012. "Knowledge, Morality, and Causality in a 'Luckless' Society: The Case of the Chewong in the Malaysian Rain Forest." *Social Analysis* 56, no. 1 (Spring): 133–47.

Hume, David. (1757) 1998. *Principal Writings on Religion.* Edited by J. C. A. Gaskin. Oxford: Oxford University Press.

Jacobsen, Thorkild. (1946) 1977. "Mesopotamia: The Cosmos as a State." In *The Intellectual Adventure of Ancient Man: An Essay on Speculative Thought in the Ancient Near East,* edited by H. Frankfort, H. A. Frankfort, John A. Wilson, Thorkild Jacobsen, and William A. Irwin, 125–84. Chicago: University of Chicago Press.

———. 1976. *The Treasures of Darkness: A History of Mesopotamian Religion.* New Haven: Yale University Press.

Jaspers, Karl. 1953. *The Origin and Goal of History.* Translated by Michael Bullock. London: Routledge & Kegan Paul.

Jensen, Erik. 1974. *The Iban and Their Religion.* Oxford: Clarendon Press.

Johansen, J. Prytz. (1954) 2012. *The Māori and His Religion in Its Non-Ritualistic Aspects.* Vol. 1. Chicago: HAU Classics of Ethnographic Series, 2012. First published 1954 by Ejnar Munksgaard: Copenhagen. Available online at https://haubooks.org/the-maori-and-his-religion.

————. 1958. *Studies in Māori Rites and Myths*. Copenhagen: Ejnar Munksgaard.

Jorgensen, Dan. 1980. "What's in a Name: The Meaning of Meaninglessness in Telefolmin." *Ethos* 8, no. 4 (Winter): 349–66.

————. 1998. "Whose Nature? Invading Bush Spirits, Traveling Ancestors, and Mining in Telefolmin." *Social Analysis* 42, no. 3 (November): 100–16.

Junod, Henri A. 1912. *The Life of a South African Tribe: I. The Social Life*. Neuchâtel: Attinger Frères.

————. 1913. *The Life of a South African Tribe: II. The Psychic Life*. Neuchâtel: Attinger Frères.

Karsten, Rafael. 1935. *The Head-Hunters of Western Amazonas: The Life and Culture of the Jibaro Indians of Eastern Ecuador and Peru*. Helsinki: Centraltryckeriet.

Keesing, Roger. 1982. *Kwaio Religion: The Living and the Dead in a Solomon Island Society*. New York: Columbia University Press.

Kepelino. 1932. *Kepelino's Traditions of Hawaii*. Bernice P. Bishop Museum Bulletin No. 95. Edited by Martha Warren Beckwith. Honolulu: Bishop Museum.

Kirsch, Stuart. 2006. *Reverse Anthropology: Indigenous Analysis of Social and Environmental Relations in New Guinea*. Stanford: Stanford University Press.

Kramer, Samuel Noah. (1956) 1981. *History Begins at Sumer: Twenty-Seven "Firsts" in Man's Recorded History*. 3rd rev. ed. Philadelphia: University of Pennsylvania Press.

————. 1963. *The Sumerians: Their History, Culture, and Character*. Chicago: University of Chicago Press.

Lalande, André. 1960. *Vocabulaire technique et critique de la philosophie*. Paris: Presses Universitaires de France.

Lang, Andrew. 1898. *The Making of Religion*. New York: Longmans, Green.

Lantis, Margaret. 1950. "Eskimo Religion." In *Forgotten Religions, Including Some Living Primitive Religions*, edited by Vergilius Ferm, 311–39. New York: Philosophical Library.

Latour, Bruno. 1993. *We Have Never Been Modern*. Translated by Catherine Porter. Cambridge: Harvard University Press.

Laugrand, Frédéric, Jarich Oosten, and François Trudel. 2002. "Hunters, Owners, and Givers of Light: The Tuurngait of South Baffin Island." *Arctic Anthropology* 39 nos. 1–2: 27–50.

————, eds. 2006. *Apostle to the Inuit: The Journals and Ethnographic Notes of Edmund James Peck, The Baffin Years, 1894–1905*. Toronto: University of Toronto Press.

Lawrence, Peter. 1965. "The Ngaing of the Rai Coast." In *Gods, Ghosts and Men in Melanesia: Some Religions of Australian New Guinea and the New Hebrides*, edited by Peter Lawrence and Mervyn J. Meggitt, 198–223. Melbourne: Oxford University Press.

————. 1984. *The Garia: An Ethnography of a Traditional Cosmic System in Papua New Guinea*. Manchester: Manchester University Press.

Leach, Edmund. 1966. *Rethinking Anthropology*. London: Athlone.

————. 1976. *Culture and Communication: The Logic by Which Symbols Are Connected*. Cambridge: Cambridge University Press.

Leenhardt, Maurice. 1930. *Notes d'ethnologie néo-calédonienne*. Travaux et Mémoires de l'Institut d'Ethnologie 8. Paris: Institut d'Ethnologie.

Lévi-Strauss, Claude. 1966. *The Savage Mind*. Chicago: University of Chicago Press.

Lévy-Bruhl, Lucien. 1923. *Primitive Mentality*. Translated by Lilian A. Clare. London: George Allen & Unwin.

Lienhardt, Godfrey. 1961. *Divinity and Experience: The Religion of the Dinka*. Oxford: Oxford University Press.

———. 1997. "'High Gods' among Some Nilotic Peoples." *Journal of the Anthropological Society of Oxford* 28, no. 1: 40–49.

Lommel, Andreas. (1952) 1997. *The Unambal: A Tribe in Northwest Australia*. Carnarvon Gorge, Queensland: Takarakka Nowam Kas Publications.

Lowie, Robert. 1935. *The Crow Indians*. New York: Farrar & Rinehart.

MacGaffey, Wyatt. 1986. *Religion and Society in Central Africa: The BaKongo of Lower Zaire*. Chicago: University of Chicago Press.

Machiavelli, Niccolò. (1532) 1988. *The Prince*. Edited by Quentin Skinner and Russell Price. Cambridge: Cambridge University Press.

Malinowski, Bronislaw. (1935) 1978. *Coral Gardens and Their Magic*. 2 vols. New York: Dover.

———. 1948. *Magic, Science and Religion and Other Essays*. Glencoe, IL: Free Press.

Malthus, Thomas. (1798) 2015. *An Essay on the Principle of Population and Other Writings*. London: Penguin Classics.

Marett, R. R. 1914. *The Threshold of Religion*. New York: Macmillan.

Meek, C. K. 1931. *A Sudanese Kingdom: An Ethnographical Study of the Jukun-Speaking Peoples of Nigeria*. London: Kegan Paul.

Meggitt, M. J. 1962. *The Desert People: A Study of the Walbiri Aborigines of Central Australia*. Chicago: University of Chicago Press.

———. 1965a. *The Lineage System of the Mae-Enga*. Edinburgh: Oliver and Boyd.

———. 1965b. "The Mae Enga of the Western Highlands." In *Gods, Ghosts and Men in Melanesia: Some Religions of Australian New Guinea and the New Hebrides*, edited by Peter Lawrence and Mervyn J. Meggitt, 105–31. Melbourne: Oxford University Press.

Merkur, Daniel. 1991. *Powers Which We Do Not Know: The Gods and Spirits of the Inuit*. Moscow: University of Idaho Press.

Miles, Jack. 2019. *Religion as We Know It: An Origin Story*. New York: Norton.

Monberg, Torben. 1965. *From the Two Canoes: Oral Traditions of Rennell and Bellona*. Copenhagen: The National Museum of Denmark.

———. 1966. *The Religion of Bellona Island*. Copenhagen: The National Museum of Denmark.

Mosko, Mark. 2017. *Ways of Baloma: Rethinking Magic and Kinship from the Trobriands*. Chicago: University of Chicago Press.

Munn, Nancy. 1973. *Walbiri Iconography: Graphic Representation and Cultural Symbolism in a Central Australian Society*. Ithaca: Cornell University Press.

Murphy, Robert F. 1958. *Mundurucú Religion*. Berkeley: University of California Press

Myers, Fred. 1991. *Pintupi Country, Pintupi Self: Sentiment, Place, and Politics among Western Desert Aborigines*. Berkeley: University of California Press.

Nadel, S. F. 1954. *Nupe Religion*. London: Routledge & Kegan Paul.

Nansen, Fridtjof. 1893. *Eskimo Life*. Translated by William Archer. London: Longmans, Green, and Co.

Needham, Rodney. 1963. "Introduction." *Primitive Classification*, by Émile Durkheim and Marcel Mauss, vii–xlviii. Chicago: University of Chicago Press.

Nemet-Nejat, Karen Rhea. 1998. *Daily Life in Ancient Mesopotamia*. Westport, CT: Greenwood Publishing Group.

Newton, Isaac. [1687] 2016. *The Principia: The Authoritative Translation and Guide*. Translated by I. Bernhard Cohen, Anne Whitman, and Julia Budenz. Berkeley: University of California Press.

Oosten, Jarich G. 1976. *The Theoretical Structure of the Religion of the Netsilik and Iglulik*. Meppel, Netherlands: Krips Repro.

Pallis, Svend A. 1926. *The Babylonian Akîtu Festival*. Copenhagen: Høst.

Pedersen, Morten A. 2001. "Totemism, Animism and North Asian Indigenous Ontologies." *Journal of the Royal Anthropological Institute* 7, no. 3 (September.): 411–27.

Perdibon, Anna. 2019. *Mountains and Trees, Rivers and Springs: Animistic Beliefs and Practices in Ancient Mesopotamian Religion*. Wiesbaden: Harrassowitz Verlag.

Petri, Helmut. (1954) 2011. *The Dying World in Northwest Australia*. Translated by S. Bradley. Carlisle, Western Australia: Hesperian Press.

Pizzaro, Pedro. 1921. *Relation of the Discovery and Conquest of the Kingdoms of Peru. Volume 1*. Translated by Philip Ainsworth Means. New York: The Cortes Society.

Porter, Barbara Nevling, ed. 2009a. *What Is a God? Anthropomorphic and Non-Anthropomorphic Aspects of Deity in Ancient Mesopotamia*. Transactions of the Casco Bay Assyriological Institute, vol. 2. Winona Lake, IN: Eisenbrauns.

———. 2009b. "Blessings from a Crown, Offerings to a Drum: Were There Non-Anthropomorphic Deities in Ancient Mesopotamia?" In *What Is a God? Anthropomorphic and Non-Anthropomorphic Aspects of Deity in Ancient Mesopotamia*, edited by Barbara Nevling Porter, 153–94. Transactions of the Casco Bay Assyriological Institute, vol. 2. Winona Lake, IN: Eisenbrauns.

Radcliffe-Brown, A. R. 1952. *Structure and Function in Primitive Society*. London: Cohen and West.

Radin, Paul. 1914. "Religion of the North American Indians." *Journal of American Folklore* 27, no. 106 (Oct.–Dec.): 335–73.

Rasmussen, Knud. (1927) 1999. *Across Arctic America: Narrative of the Fifth Thule Expedition*. Reprint. Originally published by G. P. Putnam's Sons, New York. Fairbanks: University of Alaska Press.

———. 1929. *Intellectual Culture of the Iglulik Eskimos*. Report of the Fifth Thule Expedition, 1921–24, vol. 7, no. 1. Copenhagen: Gyldendalske Boghandel, Nordisk Forlag.

———. 1931. *The Netsilik Eskimos: Social Life and Spiritual Culture*. Report of the Fifth Thule Expedition, 1921–24, vol. 8, nos. 1–2. Copenhagen: Gyldendalske Boghandel, Nordisk Forlag.

Reiner, Erica. (1958) 1970. *Šurpu: A Collection of Sumerian and Akkadian Incantations*. Reprint. Osnabrück: Biblio Verlag.

Ricardo, David. (1817) 2004. *On the Principles of Political Economy and Taxation*. Edited by Piero Sraffa with the Collaboration of M. H. Dobb. Carmel, IN: Liberty Fund.

Rink, Henry. 1875. *Tales and Traditions of the Eskimo*. Edinburgh: William Blackwood.

Rochberg, Francesca. 2009. "'The Stars Their Likenesses': Perspectives on the Relation between Celestial Bodies and Gods in Ancient Mesopotamia." In *What Is a God? Anthropomorphic and Non-Anthropomorphic Aspects of Deity in Ancient Mesopotamia*, edited by Barbara Nevling Porter, 41–91. Transactions of the Casco Bay Assyriological Institute, vol. 2. Winona Lake, IN: Eisenbrauns.

———. 2016. *Before Nature: Cuneiform Knowledge and the History of Science*. Chicago: University of Chicago Press.

Sahlins, Peter. 1994. *Forest Rites: War of the Demoiselles in Nineteenth-Century France.* Cambridge, MA: Harvard University Press.

Sather, Clifford. 1996. "All Threads Are White": Iban Egalitarianism Reconsidered." In *Origins, Ancestry and Alliance: Explorations in Austronesian Ethnography,* edited by James J. Fox and Clifford Sather, 70–110. Canberra: Australian National University.

Schieffelin, Edward L. 2005. *The Sorrow of the Lonely and the Burning of the Dancers.* 2nd ed. New York: Palgrave Macmillan. First published by St. Martin's Press, New York, 1976.

Schmidt, Wilhelm. 1912–55. *Der Ursprung der Gottesidee.* Münster: Aschendorffsche Verlags-buchhandlung.

Schwartz, Benjamin. 1975. "The Age of Transcendence." *Daedalus* 104, no. 2: 1–7.

Sillander, Kenneth. 2016. "Relatedness and Alterity in Bentian Human-Spirit Relations." In *Animism in Southeast Asia,* edited by Kaj Århem and Guido Sprenger, 157–80. London: Routledge.

Smith, Adam. (1776) 1976. *An Inquiry into the Nature and Causes of the Wealth of Nations.* Edited by Edwin Cannan. Chicago: University of Chicago Press.

Smith, Jean. 1974. *Tapu Removal in Māori Religion.* Supplement to the Journal of the Polynesian Society. Memoir no. 40. Wellington: The Polynesian Society.

Southern, R. W. 1953. *The Making of the Middle Ages.* New Haven: Yale University Press.

Speck, Frank G. (1935) 1977. *Naskapi: The Savage Hunters of the Labrador Peninsula.* Norman: University of Oklahoma Press.

Sprenger, Guido. 2016. "Dimensions of Animism in Southeast Asia." In *Animism in Southeast Asia,* edited by Kaj Århem and Guido Sprenger, 31–51. London: Routledge.

Stanner, W. E. H. 1959–63. *On Aboriginal Religion.* Oceania Monograph no. 11. University of Sydney.

Strathern, Alan. 2019. *Unearthly Powers: Religious and Political Change in World History.* Cambridge: Cambridge University Press.

Strauss, Hermann. 1991. *The Mi-Culture of the Mount Hagen People, Papua New Guinea.* Translated by Brian Shields. Edited by Gabriele Stürzenhofecker and Andrew Strathern. Pittsburgh Ethnology Monographs no. 13. Pittsburgh: Department of Anthropology, University of Pittsburgh.

Tambiah, Stanley J. 1985. "The Magical Power of Words." In *Culture, Thought, and Social Action,* 17–59. Cambridge: Harvard University Press.

Taylor, Anne-Christine. 1996. "The Soul's Body and Its States. An Amazonian Perspective on the Nature of Being Human." *Journal of the Royal Anthropological Institute* 2, no. 2 (June): 201–15.

———. 2017. "L'art d'infléchir les âmes: Les chants anent des Jivaro achuar comme techniques d'apparentement." *Terrain* 68 (October): 46–67.

Taylor, Charles. 2012. "What Was the Axial Revolution?" In *The Axial Age and Its Consequences,* edited by Robert N. Bellah and Hans Joas, 30–46. Cambridge, MA: Belknap.

Thalbitzer, W. 1909. *The Heathen Priests of East Greenland (Angakut).* Vienna: A. Hartleben.

Tylor, Edward B. 1871. *Primitive Culture: Researches into the Development of Mythology, Philosophy, Religion, Art, and Custom.* 2 vols. London: John Murray.

Valentine, C. A. 1965. "The Lakalai of New Britain." In *Gods, Ghosts and Men in Melanesia: Some Religions of Australian New Guinea and the New Hebrides,* edited by Peter Lawrence and Mervyn J. Meggitt, 162–97. Melbourne: Oxford University Press.

Valeri, Valerio. 1985. *Kingship and Sacrifice: Ritual and Society in Ancient Hawaii*. Translated by Paula Wissing. Chicago: University of Chicago Press.

Vanstiphout, Herman. 2009. "Die Geschöpfe des Prometheus, Or How and Why Did the Sumerians Create Their Gods?" In *What Is a God? Anthropomorphic and Non Anthropomorphic Aspects of Deity in Ancient Mesopotamia*, edited by Barbara Nevling Porter, 15–40. Transactions of the Casco Bay Assyriological Institute, vol. 2. Winona Lake, IN: Eisenbrauns.

Van Wing, Joseph, S. J. 1959. *Études Bakongo: Sociologie-Religion et Magie*. 2nd ed. Bruges: Desclée de Brouwer.

Vicedom, Georg F., and Herbert Tischner. 1943–48. *Die Mbowamb. Die Kultur der Hagenberg-Stämme in Östlichen Zentral-Neuguinea*. 3 vols. Hamburg: De Gruyter.

Vicedom, Georg F., and Herbert Tischner. (1943–48) *The Mbowamb: The Culture of the Mount Hagen Tribes in East Central New Guinea*. 3 vols. Translated by F. E. Rheinstein and E. Klestadt. Xeroxed manuscript. Canberra: Menzies Library, Australian National University, n.d.

Vico, Giambattista. (1711) 2010. *On the Most Ancient Wisdom of the Italians*. Translated by Jason Taylor. New Haven: Yale University Press.

———. (1744) 1968. *The New Science of Giambattista Vico*. Unabridged translation of the 3rd edition. Translated by Thomas Goddard Bergin and Max Harold Frisch. Ithaca: Cornell University Press.

Viveiros de Castro, Eduardo. 1992. *From the Enemy's Point of View: Humanity and Divinity in an Amazonian Society*. Translated by Catherine V. Howard. Chicago: University of Chicago Press.

———. 1998. "Cosmological Deixis and Amerindian Perspectivism." *Journal of the Royal Anthropological Institute* 4, no. 3 (September): 469–88.

———. 2004a. "Exchanging Perspectives: The Transformation of Objects into Subjects in Amerindian Ontologies." *Common Knowledge* 10, no. 3 (Fall): 463–84.

———. 2004b. "Perspectival Anthropology and the Method of Controlled Equivocation." *Tipití: Journal of the Society for the Anthropology of Lowland South America* 2, no. 1 (June): 3–22.

———. 2015. *The Relative Native: Essays on Indigenous Conceptual Worlds*. Chicago: HAU Books.

Wagley, Charles, and Eduardo Galvão. (1949) 1969. *The Tenetehara Indians of Brazil: A Culture in Transition*. New York: AMS Press. First published 1949 by Columbia University Press (New York).

Walens, Stanley. 1981. *Feasting with Cannibals: An Essay on Kwakiutl Cosmology*. Princeton: Princeton University Press.

Walker, J. R. 1917. "The Sun Dance and Other Ceremonies of the Oglala Division of the Teton Dakota." *Anthropological Papers of the American Museum of Natural History*, vol. 16, pt. 2. New York: Trustees of the Museum.

———. 1980. *Lakota Belief and Ritual*. Edited by Raymond J. DeMallie and Elaine A. Jahner. Lincoln: University of Nebraska Press.

Weyer, Edward Moffat, Jr. 1932. *The Eskimos: Their Environment and Folkways*. New Haven: Yale University Press.

Wheatcroft, Wilson. 1976. "The Legacy of Afekan: Cultural Symbolic Interpretations of Religion among the Tifalmin of New Guinea." PhD dissertation. Department of Anthropology, University of Chicago.

White, Leslie A. 1959. *The Evolution of Culture: The Development of Civilization to the Fall of Rome*. New York: McGraw-Hill.

Wiredu, Kwasi. 1992. "Formulating Modern Thought in African Languages: Some Theoretical Considerations." In *The Surreptitious Speech: Présence Africaine and the Politics of Otherness 1947–1987*, edited by V. Y. Mudimbe, 301–32. Chicago: University of Chicago Press.

Wood, Allen W., ed. 1988. *Marx: Selections*. New York: Macmillan.

Woolley, C. Leonard. 1965. *The Sumerians*. New York: W. W. Norton.

INDEX

Aboriginal Australians: ancestors of, 31–32, 114; elders as incarnated ancestral spirits, 175–76; nature as a social order and, 125. *See also* dreams; Walbiri

Acholi (East Africa), 112

Achuar (Amazonia): communicating with spirits in dreams, 46; cosmic hierarchy and, 129–30, 131; deceased's body parts becoming animals, 43; humanity as ontological ground of phenomenal world, 79; marriages of men with water spirits, 56–57; metahuman masters in culture of, 83; seeing nature's beings as similar to humans, 36, 73–74; spirits' role in gardening success or failure, 17, 19–20

Afek (Mountain Ok high god), 111–12

African thought, 38–39

Akan (West Africa), 38–39

Akkadian civilization, 135, 137, 148, 152–53, 156–57, 159, 160, 171. *See also* Mesopotamian civilization; Sumerian civilization

Algonquian (North America), 82, 83–84, 106, 114, 115–16

An/Anu (high god, Sumerian and Akkadian civilizations), 135–36, 148, 150, 154–59, 164, 165, 171

ancestors, 94–104; acting under direction of supreme deities, 110; always there, while waking or dreaming, 46; ambivalence toward, 100–101; of Australian Aboriginals, 31–32, 114, 175–76; communication practices with, 96; conflictual relationships with, 96–97; culture received from, 32; features in common, 95–96; as form of

metapersons, 73; high gods present in sacrifices to, 111; of kings and ruling chiefs, 101–4; in Kwaio people's everyday life, 37, 41–42, 57–58; of Mae Enga (New Guinea), 28, 51; Manambu yam cultivation and, 20–21; as moral agents, 95, 98, 113; of Mount Hagen peoples, 26; natural/supernatural distinction and, 37; as present and real in African cultures, 38; punishment by, 98; receiving incantations from Dobuan gods, 28; relation to ghosts, 51, 88; returning for annual festivals, 59, 66; and Sokó (Nupe god), 91–92, 109; souls of, 48–50, 52, 53; of Tallensi (West Africa), 29–30; of Thonga (southern Africa), 30–31, 99–100; totemic, 80–81, 95, 117, 121; of Trobriand Islanders (Melanesia), 62–63, 66, 94; as variety of spirits, 95; Walbiri (Australia) *guruwari* (powers) and, 60–61, 122. *See also* dead, the; demons; god(s); spirits

Anderson, Benedict, 8

animism, 73–81; of Augustine, 4–5; cannibalism and, 81, 87; doubled, 79–80, 85–86, 155; in hierarchical system of beings, 85–86; individualism in anthropological treatments of, 144; of Inuit world, 170; of Javanese villages, 8; lacking natural/supernatural distinction, 35–36; in Mesopotamia, 164–66, 170; metapersons and, 73; personhood not universal in, 77–78; as personhood of things, 75; person-qualities of spirits in, 44–45; in Southeast Asian cosmic society, 125–27; as understood by Western observers, 74–75. *See also* spirits

Printed in the USA
CPSIA information can be obtained
at www.ICGtesting.com
JSHW022014151023
50105JS00003B/5